IN SEARCH OF THE GREEKS

Dionysos and the cast of a satyr-play as depicted
on the Pronomos vase, *c.* 400 BCE.

IN SEARCH OF THE
GREEKS

JAMES RENSHAW

Bristol Classical Press

First published in 2008 by
Bristol Classical Press
an imprint of
Gerald Duckworth & Co. Ltd.
90-93 Cowcross Street, London EC1M 6BF
Tel: 020 7490 7300
Fax: 020 7490 0080
inquiries@duckworth-publishers.co.uk
www.ducknet.co.uk

A catalogue record for this book is available
from the British Library

ISBN 978 1 85399 6993

Typeset by Ray Davies
Printed and bound in Great Britain by
MPG Books Ltd, Bodmin, Cornwall

Contents

Preface

This book was born out of teaching notes which I produced for my Classical Civilisation students at St Paul's School. For a long time now there has been a lack of a suitable coursebook on Greek Civilisation for secondary school students, and I hope that this book will go some way to filling that gap. Of course, no coursebook can be exhaustive and this one is supplemented by a companion website containing additional information and further reading: *www.insearchofthegreeks.com*.

I have received tremendous support from a number of people in writing *In Search of the Greeks*. In particular, I would like to thank all of the BCP committee at Duckworth, and especially Roger Rees and John Taylor, for their frequent encouragement and advice. I have also been very fortunate to have had help with the Sparta chapter from Paul Cartledge and Anton Powell; their input has been invaluable. James Morwood has been a superb mentor and has helped me improve many areas of the book immeasurably, while Caroline Gill has played the role of perceptive 'non-specialist' reader *par excellence*. Of course, any errors which remain are entirely my responsibility!

Above all, it is the students I teach at Colet Court and St Paul's who bring fresh eyes and enthusiasm to this wonderful subject. They have been among the project's keenest supporters and critics – and it is to them that I dedicate this book.

Notes on the Text

1. Greek words have been given their Greek plural forms. The following rules apply:

singular	e.g.	plural	e.g.
-a	kyria	-ai	kyriai
-ês	mystês	-ai	mystai
-ê	stêlê	-ai	stêlai
-os	paidagôgos	-oi	paidagôgoi
-on	syssition	-a	syssitia
-is	mantis	-eis	manteis

Where the letters *e* and *o* have accents (*ê* and *ô*), this indicates that they should be pronounced as long vowels (since the Greek alphabet distinguishes between the long and short pronunciation of these letters).

2. The decision on how to spell Greek words is always a difficult one. In general, I have used the transliteration from Greek (e.g. *paidagôgos*), except where the Latinate spelling is more common in English (e.g. Achilles).

3. All dates are BCE unless stated otherwise. Details of the Greek calendar are given on p. 277.

4. There are review boxes at various stages throughout each chapter, where students are encouraged to reflect on what they have read. Where a question is marked '**R**', it denotes 'Further Reading'; while '**E**' denotes 'Essay'.

Introduction

'We are all Greeks: our laws, our literature, our religion, our arts, have their roots in Greece.'   P.B. Shelley in his preface to 'Hellas', 1820

The legacy of the Greeks is all around us. More than any other ancient people, they have shaped how we in western society think about our world and how we think about ourselves. Indeed, the very idea of 'western civilisation' is itself largely founded upon the philosophy, art, literature and history of the people we call the ancient Greeks. By learning about them, we come to know ourselves more deeply.

This book focuses on six of the most important areas of ancient Greek life. The first chapter examines Greek religion, which permeated every level of society. The next two chapters describe religious festivals – the ancient Olympic Games, which formed the model for the modern Olympic movement, and the City Dionysia at Athens, where plays were performed for the first time in European history. The book then moves on to explore Greek social and political life, focusing first on Athenian society and then on that city's invention of democracy as a political system. Finally, it looks at the unique society which developed in Sparta, Athens' greatest rival.

The six chapters are designed to be independent but inter-related and so there are numerous cross-references between them. They need not be read in sequence, since each investigates one aspect of the same era in Greek history.

Historical outline

In truth, the term 'ancient Greeks' could apply to numerous Greek-speaking peoples who lived in many places around the Mediterranean and Black Seas from the 3rd millennium BCE until the fall of the Roman Empire in the 5th century CE (even then, a Greek-speaking empire – the Byzantine Empire – lived on in the east until its capital, Constantinople, was sacked by the Ottomans in 1453). As a result of this very long passage of time, historians have tended to divide up ancient Greek history into a number of successive 'ages'. These can be summarised as follows:

- **Prehistoric Greece**. There were two important Bronze Age civilisations which flourished in and around Greece during the 3rd and 2nd millennia BCE. The **Minoan** civilisation was centred on the island of Crete between approximately 2700 and 1450, while the **Mycenaean** civilisation developed on the Greek mainland (and particularly in the Peloponnese peninsula), flourishing between approximately 1600 and 1100, eventually taking over the Minoan world too. Later Greeks believed that the Trojan War had taken place during this period.

- **The Dark Age** (11th-9th centuries BCE). Mycenaean civilisation collapsed suddenly during the 12th century (the reasons why remain obscure) and new peoples to the north of Greece, the Dorians, are believed to have migrated south during this period. The defining fact of the 11th to the 9th centuries is that the Greek language largely ceased to be written; as a result, these centuries remain something of a mystery and hence became known as the 'Dark Age' by later historians.

- **The Archaic Age** (8th-6th centuries BCE) was one of dramatic political and social change in the Greek world. The 8th century saw the rebirth of the written Greek language using a new script borrowed from Phoenicia (modern Lebanon); Homer is believed to have composed the *Iliad* and the *Odyssey* at some point during this century. At the same time, a rapidly growing population meant that there was much pressure for land in Greece; as a result, many independent Greeks or Greek cities founded new settlements or colonies around many parts of the Mediterranean and Black Seas (see 'Where?' below). The other key development in this period was the emergence of 'city-states', such as Athens, Sparta, Corinth and Thebes, as independent political units.

- **The Classical Age** (510-323 BCE) is usually considered to be the high point of Greek civilisation. The early years of the 5th century were marked by the Persian Wars, when various Greek city-states joined together and heroically repelled two invasions by the gigantic Persian Empire to the east. However, in the aftermath of the victory in 479, Athens and Sparta soon became rivals for power in the Greek world and this led to the devastating Peloponnesian War (431-404), which ended with Athens' defeat. However, Sparta's rule of the Greek world was short-lived and by the middle of the 4th century the Macedonians in the north of Greece under the rule of Philip II (359-336) were becoming the most powerful group. By the time he was assassinated, Philip had created a single empire of all the peoples of mainland Greece. He was succeeded by his son, Alexander (the Great), who led his men on an extraordinary conquest of the entire Persian Empire and Egypt.

- **The Hellenistic Age** (323-30 BCE). After Alexander's death in 323, his generals fought for control of his new empire. Much land conquered in the former Persian Empire was soon lost and by 281 the Greek Empire had been divided into four roughly equal regions: mainland Greece, Anatolia (modern Turkey), Syria and Mesopotamia (modern Iraq), and Egypt. Greek culture was thus dominant throughout the eastern Mediterranean; indeed, the two greatest cities of Greek civilisation during these centuries were Antioch and Alexandria, the capitals of Syria and Egypt respectively. Alexandria was a centre of great learning and contained the largest library in the ancient world.

  The growing power of the Roman Empire in the western Mediterranean began to encroach further east during the 2nd century. In 146, mainland Greece was conquered by Rome and with the death of Queen Cleopatra of Egypt in 30 BCE the entire Hellenistic world was brought under Roman governance.

- **The Roman Empire** (30 BCE-410 CE). Throughout the subsequent centuries of Roman rule, the eastern Mediterranean remained very Greek in its culture and language; for example, the entire New Testament was written in Greek. Moreover, the Romans were so fascinated by Greek civilisation that a Roman education involved learning the Greek language and reading Greek literature and philosophy; in the words of the Roman poet Horace, 'captured Greece captivated her wild conqueror'. As a result, Greek thought and culture spread throughout the lands of the Roman Empire.

The topics in this book are primarily concerned with the Classical Age. This was the period in which some of Greece's greatest thinkers and writers emerged – philosophers such as Plato and Aristotle, playwrights such as Sophocles and Aristophanes, historians such as Herodotus and Thucydides, and artists such as Pheidias and Praxiteles. The cultural and intellectual development during these centuries was to define Greek civilisation during the Hellenistic and Roman periods.

Where?

Since Greece did not become a single country with a central government until the second half of the 4th century BCE, it is more apt to talk of the 'Greek world' before this time. This constituted a collection of numerous independent city-states, many of which were very small; for example, a 20-mile stretch of coastline in the north-east of the Peloponnese contained three city-states – Epidauros, Troezen and Methana – each of which had its own traditions, laws, constitution and army. In Mycenaean times some Greeks had also moved beyond the mainland to establish communities on the islands of the Aegean Sea and along the west coast of Asia Minor (see map 2).

However, the period of greatest emigration was between 750 and 600 BCE, when many Greek cities founded new settlements all over the Mediterranean and Black Seas. People moved to these 'colonies', which often retained close ties to their 'mother-cities', in search of more prosperous lives. In particular, Sicily and Southern Italy became Greek strongholds, so much so that the region became known as 'Magna Graecia' – 'Great(er) Greece'. During this period cities were founded in places as far apart as the modern countries of Spain and Russia (see map 1); some of these cities, such as Istanbul (known as Byzantium in ancient times), Marseilles and Naples grew into important centres of civilisation.

The Greek identity

By the 4th century, Plato's Socrates was able to speak of the Greek peoples spread out around the two seas 'like frogs around a pond'. The idea of Greekness, therefore, was one of cultural identity rather than of geographical location – one did not have to come from Greece to be a Greek; for example, one of the most famous of all ancient Greeks was the brilliant scientist Archimedes (*c.* 287-*c.* 212), who came from the Sicilian city of Syracuse.

There were three key elements which united all Greeks in their shared identity – language, literature and religion (thus in some ways the concept of the 'Greek world' could be compared to the 'Hispanic world' today). All Greeks spoke the same language, albeit with a variety of dialects, and from this language had arisen superb literature; in particular, Homer was revered by all Greeks as the first and greatest poet in their language. Greek identity was further defined by the worship of common gods and goddesses. This religion had also given rise to the numerous stories of Greek mythology, which were as popular then as they remain today.

Their common identity did not necessarily mean that the Greek cities always had good relations with one another. In fact, they were often at war with one another and sometimes it took a great threat from a foreign power, such as the menace of the Persian Empire in the 5th century, to remind them of their shared values. They knew these foreigners as *barbaroi* (barbarians), a word which applied to any non-Greek speaking people. The term was often used contemptuously – many Greeks would surely have agreed with Aristotle, who argued that barbarians were more naturally suited to slavery than Greeks.

What's in a name?

The Greeks never called themselves by that name. It was the Romans who called their eastern neighbours *Graeci*, a term perhaps originating from the small town of Graia on the border between Boeotia and Attica.

In fact, it took time for the Greeks to settle on one name to describe their civilisation. However, by the 5th century BCE, the many peoples who shared the Greek language knew themselves collectively as *Hellenes*, while they called their Greek-speaking world *Hellas* – the name by which modern Greeks still call their country today.

Contemporary relevance

The ancient Greeks continue to fascinate us today. In spite of the great differences between their world and ours, they resonate with us because we can see our own reflections in them. It is easy to recognise a society where sporting champions are hero-worshipped, where plays mercilessly satirise political leaders and where people enshrine the right to freedom of speech.

While writing this book, I have been startled to see how many ancient issues are reflected in our world today. These pages raise issues such as forced marriage, theory of education, slavery, and the role and responsibilities of citizens in a democracy. On this latter issue, it is particularly remarkable that, in 415, Athens embarked upon a controversial (and ultimately disastrous) foreign campaign in Sicily, when some citizens felt that their leaders had overplayed the case for war. On issues such as this, it is fascinating to compare and contrast ancient and modern approaches.

If there is one quality that marks out the Greeks it is their willingness to engage so deeply with life and to explore its complexity. Their civilisation encouraged people to go beyond easy or traditional answers to life's deepest questions; as a result, they have left us with art, literature, history and philosophy which is profound, entertaining and provocative, and which has defined modern society. In this sense, we are indeed all Greeks.

1

Greek Religion

I. THE CHARACTER OF GREEK RELIGION

'The paradox is that, although Greek religion seems to lack so many of the things which characterise modern religions and which require degrees of personal commitment and faith from their followers, Greeks were involved with religion to a degree which is very hard nowadays to understand.'

J.V. Muir, *Greek Religion and Society,* p. 194

1. Ancient and modern

In many ways, Greek religion was very different from what we might call 'religion' today: it had no centralised religious authority, no scripture, no formal moral code; it offered little hope of a blissful life after death, nor was there any concept of conversion – there did not need to be, since Greek society did not have competing religions, as ours does today. This is probably why there was actually no word for 'religion'; instead, Greeks simply referred to *hiera*, or 'holy affairs'.

Worshipping the same gods was one of the fundamental ways in which Greeks were united in a common identity, an idea famously expressed in a passage from Herodotus' *Histories*. At the culmination of the Persian Wars in 480/79, the Spartans feared that the Athenians were about to go over to the Persian side; in their turn, the Athenians protested that there were many reasons why they could not contemplate such a move:

'The first and chief of these is the burning and destruction of our temples and the images of our gods ... there is our common brotherhood with the Greeks: our common language, the altars and the sacrifices in which we all take part, the common character which we all share.'

Herodotus, *Histories* 8.144

According to this passage, Greekness entailed both speaking the same language and worshipping the same gods. The idea of changing one's religion would have seemed as odd to a Greek as the idea of 'changing one's language' would to us today.

However, this is not to say that there were no similarities between the religion of ancient Greece and those of the modern world. As today, Greek religion tried to help its adherents make sense of the present life, a principle reflected in the following practices:

1

- **Rites of passage**. Moments such as birth, marriage and death were elevated to a sacred status (the way these rituals were marked in Athens and Sparta are described in Chapters 4 and 6 respectively).
- **Festivals** were fundamental to the Greek way of life. Some were local, some regional and some panhellenic (i.e. they were open to the whole Greek-speaking world). Chapters 2 and 3 each describe a religious festival in detail.
- **Pilgrimage**. Pilgrims journeyed to numerous shrines around the Greek world, two of which, Delphi and Eleusis, are described in this chapter. Pilgrims were often given protected status on their travels, most notably those who travelled to the Olympic Games (see p. 77).

All these practices are recognisable to us today. Even in western society, where institutional religion has declined sharply in popularity over the last 50 years or so, most weddings and funerals are still conducted with religious rites. Festivals, such as Christmas, Diwali, or Eid, still mark the passage of the year, while pilgrimage remains central to many faiths, most notably Islam, which requires its followers to visit Mecca at least once in their lives.

Lack of dogma

Where Greek religion was most different from its modern equivalents was in its lack of any formal scripture. As a result of this, there was no dogma and no set of beliefs to which everyone had to subscribe (*dogma* is actually a Greek word which simply meant 'viewpoint'). There was also nothing like a central religious hierarchy, which trained priests and decided on points of religious law, as for example the Vatican does in Catholicism today.

This may actually have been one of Greek religion's great advantages. In the history of most religions, the class of priests has been more educated than the vast majority and so able to wield great power. For they were trained to explain scripture to the masses and so claimed to speak for God; as a result, they exercised great control over the minds of the faithful.

Some believe that the lack of hierarchy and dogma in Greek religion allowed the Greek world to have its 'intellectual revolution' in the 6th and 5th centuries. This was a time of deep philosophical and scientific speculation, when all sorts of commonly held beliefs were openly questioned. Perhaps great thinkers emerged at this time because their religion did not prevent them from asking questions and challenging traditional viewpoints. However, even the Greeks had their limitations in this area; some, such as Socrates and Anaxagoras (who are both mentioned in this chapter), put forward views so radical that they caused outrage.

---

2. The relationship between gods and men

The Greeks were not expected to 'love' their gods but to 'honour' them. Jon Mikalson has described this honour as the sort which 'a subject owes to a king' and, moreover, which 'a good subject owes to a good king'. Greeks recognised that their gods were far more powerful than they were and so needed to be treated with reverence and respect. If humans did this, then they hoped in return to find favour with them and receive good treatment. This attitude is reflected in the following advice given to farmers by the poet Hesiod:

> 'Satisfy the immortal gods with libations and sacrifices, when you go to bed and when the pleasant light returns, so that they may have a kindly heart and spirit towards you, and you may buy other people's land and not have someone else buy yours.'   Hesiod, *Works and Days* 338-41

As Hesiod suggests here, Greeks honoured their gods by presenting them with gifts: animals, libations, prayers and votive gifts were all offered in sacrifice on a regular basis (you can read about all four of these on pp. 23-8); such offerings often took place at temples which, in turn, had been built to honour the gods. In return, Greeks hoped that their gods would help them in every aspect of their lives, be it health, marriage, work, or even warfare.

As a result, moments of good and bad fortune were often attributed to the gods. For example, the following passage relates the rousing speech an Athenian leader delivered to his troops before a battle in 404 (which they went on to win), arguing that the gods were on their side:

> 'The gods are obviously now our allies. In clear weather they create a storm when it is to our advantage ... and now the gods have brought us to a place where the enemy cannot throw their spears and javelins over the heads of the front ranks because their spears and javelins must fly uphill, but we, throwing our spears, javelins and rocks downhill, will reach them and wound many.'   Xenophon, *Hellenika* 2.4.14-15

3. The afterlife

At the heart of most major world religions today are beliefs about an afterlife. For example, both Christianity and Islam promise paradise in reward for a faithful life; alternatively, Hindus and Buddhists believe in a cycle of reincarnation, whose ultimate goal is release into nirvana. What unites all these religions is the belief that ethical behaviour in this life will be rewarded in the next (and, conversely, that unethical behaviour will be punished).

However, traditional Greek religion offered a very different view of the afterlife. After death, a person went down to join the 'shades below' in the Underworld, ruled over by Hades. In Book 11 of the *Odyssey*, Odysseus is allowed to travel there while still alive. Although those who had lived very wicked lives (such as Sisyphus and Tantalus) live in endless torment, the vast majority of souls reside in a place of gloomy shade, pale shadows of their former selves. Perhaps many would have echoed the dead Achilles' famous words to Odysseus:

> 'Do not make light of death, illustrious Odysseus. I would rather work the soil as a serf on hire to some landless, impoverished peasant than be a king of all these lifeless dead.'
>
> Homer, Odyssey 11.489-91

The point about this view was that it was this present life that mattered. For those who wanted a more hopeful view of death, there were outlets such as the mystery religions, the most famous of which was centred on Eleusis in Attica (see p. 43ff.). However, traditional Greek religion was about helping people to live this life as effectively as possible.

4. Ethics

Greek religion contained no moral code for its adherents to follow, probably because it had no formal scripture and little emphasis on judgement after death. This is in major contrast to many contemporary religions; for example, both Jews and Christians believe that God gave Moses the Ten Commandments as a moral code for his people to live by. The Greeks, by contrast, looked elsewhere for ethical guidance: to their law-codes, to their philosophers and to their literature. Aesop's Fables are just one set of famous stories which offer important moral lessons.

Even though their religion offered no moral code, the Greeks often used the gods to strengthen their pre-existing laws – there are various examples of behaviour that was deemed pleasing or abhorrent to the gods. Murderers and traitors, who were believed to be not only legally guilty but also ritually polluted (see p. 16), were banned from all religious shrines and rituals; strangers, guests and foreigners all came under the protection of Zeus (as evidenced in Homer's *Odyssey*). Particularly important were the oaths used in many areas of Greek life, whether commercial transactions, legal proceedings or family relationships. Gods were called upon as witnesses to oaths, which made them even more binding, as these lines from Sophocles illustrate:

> 'When an oath has been added, a man is more
> Careful, for he guards against two things,
> The criticism of his friends and committing a transgression
> Against the gods.'
>
> Sophocles, fr. 472

Review 1

1. How would you define the word 'religion'?
2. Draw up a table listing the similarities and differences between Greek religion and a modern religion of your choice.
3. How does the relationship between the Greek gods and mortals compare with the relationship of a modern religious believer to a divinity?
4. How central to modern religions with which you are familiar are the following: (i) a moral code; (ii) the afterlife; (iii) pilgrimage; (iv) a central religious hierarchy; (v) oaths?
5. How often (if at all) do politicians use religion to justify their behaviour today? Do you think they ought to?
6. How different do you think it would be to live in a society where everyone followed the same religion?
E. What do you find to admire and what do you find to criticise in the character of Greek religion?

II. THE GREEK GODS

Greek religion was **polytheistic**, in other words it had many gods (in Greek, *poly:* many, *theos:* god). The most important gods were the twelve Olympians, but there were hundreds of others besides, some particular to just one village or region. An advantage of this system was that there were gods for every area of life, as each god had different responsibilities. Therefore, a Greek could pray to Demeter for a good harvest, to Zeus for rain, to Ares or Athena for help in war, to Poseidon for a safe sea voyage and to Apollo for success in a musical contest. An individual might feel a close personal link to a god who played an important role in his or her life (for example, a sailor might feel an affinity with Poseidon).

Another feature of Greek religion was that the gods were **anthropomorphic**. In other words, they were represented in human form (in Greek, *anthrôpos:* human being, *morphê:* shape). There were countless statues of the gods, all of them represented with human bodies. In fact, the gods were 'human' in more than their appearance. Greek gods had the faults and imperfections of human beings, a far remove from the modern idea of a God who is wholly good and perfect. Greek gods could be cruel or kind, helpful or vindictive, and all had their favourites. Some Greeks were troubled by the presentation of their gods with moral flaws: Plato wanted to ban from his ideal city all poets who portrayed the gods with human weaknesses.

1. The Olympian family

The Olympians took their name from the mountain they were believed to live on, Mt Olympos in the north of Greece (see map 4). However,

---

Divine epithets – the many faces of the gods

Each god was actually responsible for many different areas of life and was given an adjective, known as an epithet, to describe each one. For example, a farmer might have prayed to *Zeus Ombrios* (the rain-giver) for rain, an Olympic athlete had to take an oath to *Zeus Horkios* (the protector of oaths), while in the *Odyssey* Odysseus appeals to *Zeus Xenios* (the protector of travellers). Meanwhile Athena could be invoked as *Polias* (the protector of the city), *Ergane* (overseer of handicrafts), *Promachos* (enjoiner of battle) and *Nike* (victory). Temples were often dedicated to one specific version of the god. For example, the Acropolis of Athens had temples dedicated to three different aspects of Athena: Parthenos, Polias, and Nike.

Olympos was also perceived to be a fictional place in the sky, much in the way that some people today talk about heaven.

To the Greeks, their gods were both immortal and ageless, meaning that, after their childhoods, they were always imagined to be frozen at the same age; so Zeus was always a fatherly figure in healthy middle-age, while Apollo was ever in youthful manhood. There were twelve Olympians, six gods and six goddesses, all of whom belonged to one family. There is much inter-marriage within the family (for example, Zeus is married to his sister Hera), a common feature of polytheistic systems.

In the short descriptions that follow, the characters and roles of each god and goddess are briefly outlined. However, it is impossible to do justice to such a huge topic in just a few words. Therefore many passages from Homer (and the *Homeric Hymns*) are cited; reading them will shed more light on the character of each god or goddess.

Homer and Hesiod

In the absence of any formal religious scripture, the Greeks looked to their two earliest poets, Homer and Hesiod, for stories and lessons about the gods. Hesiod, who lived in Boeotia in about 700, wrote a poem called *Theogony*, which was a history and genealogy of the gods. As such, it is a major source of our knowledge of Greek mythology.

Homer, the father of western literature (who probably lived in the 8th century), gave important insights into the Greek view of the gods in both his *Iliad* and his *Odyssey*. Homer's gods are vain, selfish and vindictive, as well as powerful and passionate. A common adjective for the Homeric gods is 'easy-living' and this is where they are most distinct from mortals. Homer's gods live easy lives, without the worries of suffering and death.

A further important source of information about the gods are the *Homeric Hymns*. They were probably written in the 7th century and, although they are not the work of Homer, they are similar in style and language. Each of the Olympian gods and goddesses was the subject of a *Homeric Hymn*, which was essentially a poetic biography.

---

1. Greek Religion

The six gods and Dionysos

Zeus was commonly portrayed sitting on a throne holding a sceptre, as he is most famously in the giant cult statue in his temple at Olympia (see p. 61), where the games were held in his honour. An episode in the *Iliad* illustrates his role as a god who upholds fate: he weighs the lives of Achilles and Hector in the balance of his golden scales (22.209-13). In the *Odyssey*, Zeus comes to the fore in his role as *Xenios*, the protector of strangers, guests and foreigners. In both this poem and Hesiod's *Theogony*, he is particularly associated with justice. His personal life was complicated: although he was married to Hera, he had numerous affairs which meant that he had a very turbulent marriage!

As the god of the sea, **Poseidon** was particularly important to sailors and fishermen. Thus he was the patron god of Corinth (where the Isthmian games were celebrated in his honour), a city which made its

Athena, wearing her aegis, converses with Poseidon, who holds his trident in his right hand.

7

fortune through sea-faring and trade. He was also believed to be the god of earthquakes, from which he took his common epithet 'earth-shaker'. A famous passage in the *Iliad* (13.17-31) describes the god's progress across the seas in majestic terms. In the *Odyssey*, Poseidon pursues Odysseus viciously after the mortal hero has blinded his son, the Cyclops Polyphemus; there is an extended description of Poseidon's persecution at 5.282-381.

Hephaistos gives new armour to Thetis for her son Achilles.

Hephaistos was the god of fire and metal-working, who could turn rock into bronze weapons or fine jewellery. Legend said that he lived in volcanoes and he was a god worshipped particularly by smiths. He is involved in two important episodes in the *Iliad*: he calms the quarrel amongst the gods by relating the origin of his lameness (1.571-600) and he makes new armour for Achilles (18.369-617). In the *Odyssey*, his craftiness catches out his adulterous wife Aphrodite (8.266-366).

There were few myths about **Ares**, the god of war, as the Greeks did not like to think about him too much. Indeed, in the *Iliad*, Homer commonly refers to him as 'dread Ares' and he represents unthinking violence and the mindless destruction of warfare. This is perhaps best illustrated in book 5 (5.846-909), where Zeus scolds him with the words: 'always your delight is in strife and war and fighting'. Ares therefore stands in stark contrast to Athena, the goddess of war, who represents the tactical nous and military excellence required to win victory in battle.

God	Responsibilities	Symbols
Zeus	king of the gods; sky and weather, travellers	throne and sceptre; thunderbolt
Poseidon	the sea, earthquakes, horses and bulls	trident and dolphin
Ares	war	armour
Apollo	education, music and the arts, medicine and disease, archery, the sun, prophecy	lyre and bow
Hephaistos	fire, metal-working, artisans	anvil
Hermes	messenger of the gods; travel and trade	winged sandals
Dionysos	drama, wine and revelry	*thyrsos*, vines, ivy, animal skins

Apollo was one of the most important gods for the Greeks, as the range of his responsibilities shows. As god of music, the arts, education, medicine and disease, prophecy, archery and the sun he was often portrayed as a beautiful young man with short, curly hair, who carried a lyre or a quiver full of arrows. His relationship to the sun is reflected in his common epithet *phoebos,* which meant 'shining'. Apollo's sacred tree was the laurel and he was particularly worshipped at Delos (the island of his birth) and Delphi (see p. 35ff.). In the opening book of the *Iliad*, it is Apollo who sends the plague upon the Greeks (1.43-52) which causes the argument between Achilles and Agamemnon.

Hermes was the messenger of the gods who travelled vast distances. As a result he was believed to protect the travellers and traders who crossed the ancient world. The *Hymn to Hermes* (1.20ff.) tells of the

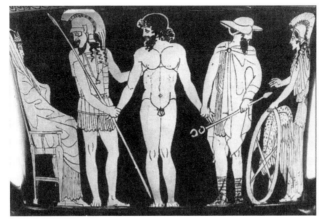

Ares and Hermes present the captured mortal Ixion to Hera, while Athena holds the wheel to which he will be bound.

Hermes, Apollo and Artemis. Which symbols of these gods can you recognise from the painting?

eventful first day of his life, when he invented the lyre and stole the cattle of Apollo. Hermes also had a special role in escorting the souls of the dead down to the Underworld. In this guise he was worshipped as *Psychopompos* (the escorter of souls). In Homer, he gives help both to Odysseus in the *Odyssey* (10.275-308) and to Priam in the *Iliad* (24.334-470).

In addition to these six was **Dionysos**, the god of many areas, including drama, wine and fertility. His worship was traditionally believed to have come late to Greece, which is why he was not one of the original Olympians. He was conceived after Zeus impregnated Semele, a mortal woman from Thebes. However, she fell foul of the jealousy of Hera, who engineered her death while she was still pregnant. Nonetheless, Zeus rescued the foetal Dionysos from Semele's womb and sewed him into his thigh, from where he was born a few months later.

Dionysos is often depicted with vines and ivy, the former associated with wine, the latter with growth and vitality. The god and his two groups of companions, the **maenads** and **satyrs**, are described extensively on pp. 91-6.

The six goddesses

As queen of the gods **Hera** was particularly important to women and was the goddess of marriage. However, her own marriage was not a happy one; she suffered the philandering of her husband and frequently sought vengeance on Zeus' lovers. In a famous episode of the *Iliad* (14.153-353), she seduces her husband in order to distract him from

Dionysos at sea. Vines trail around the mast of his ship, while bunches of grapes are suspended above the sail.

overseeing the Trojan War; this allows the Greeks, whom she supports, to gain the upper hand while Zeus' mind is on other things. Hera is usually portrayed as solemn and majestic, often enthroned and crowned with the *polos*, a high cylindrical crown. Her two main cult centres were the city of Argos and the island of Samos, but she was worshipped far and wide in the Greek world.

Demeter was a vital goddess for the Greeks, as she was responsible for the crops and harvest. The most famous story about her concerns the abduction of her daughter **Persephone**, who is also known as **Kore** (meaning 'the Girl'). According to the *Hymn to Demeter* (l.1ff.) Persephone was picking flowers in a field when Hades, on a visit to the earth from the Underworld, fell in love with her and carried her off to his kingdom below. The distraught Demeter searched all over the earth

Goddess	Responsibilities	Symbols
Hera	queen of the gods; women and marriage	*polos*
Demeter	agriculture and the harvest	flowers, fruit and grain
Hestia	the hearth	fire
Artemis	hunting, the moon, childbirth	moon, bow and arrows
Athena	wisdom, weaving and crafts, war	owl, an aegis
Aphrodite	love and beauty	sea shell

for her lost daughter and fasted in grief. As a result the crops of the earth stopped growing and there was a famine. Zeus intervened to save the world from the famine and persuaded Hades to return Persephone. However, as Persephone had eaten food in the Underworld – a few seeds of a pomegranate fruit – she was forced to spend a few months of every year with Hades. Demeter fasted during these months and the crops stopped growing; thus people came to call this season 'winter'. This myth formed the basis of the Mysteries conducted at Eleusis.

The name **Aphrodite** meant 'born from the foam', since she was born from the foam created by the semen from the castrated Ouranos, Zeus' grandfather. Her birth is often recalled in art and she is frequently depicted alongside a seashell emerging from the sea at Cyprus, an island sacred to her. As the goddess of love, Aphrodite had a powerful hold over human hearts; it was she who helped cause the Trojan War by promising Helen of Sparta to the Trojan Paris. A short episode early in the *Iliad* (3.380-417) describes her beauty as she appears to Helen inside the city of Troy.

Athena was most strongly worshipped at Athens, the city she founded and to which she gave her name. There is a curious story about her birth. After Zeus had impregnated Metis (which literally meant 'Cunning'), he swallowed her, fearing that their child would grow up to overthrow him. However, the baby continued to grow, giving Zeus a great headache. Hephaistos was ordered to split open Zeus' skull, and out popped the fully grown Athena wearing her armour!

One of Athena's most important roles was as goddess of wisdom. As such, her sacred bird was the owl, a symbol of wisdom then as it is today. We have seen that, as goddess of war, she was worshipped for her military intelligence, and she was also often portrayed alongside **Nike**, the winged goddess of victory. One of her military symbols was the *aegis*, a goat-skin cape imprinted with the image of a gorgon's head and fringed with snakes; in battle, Athena displays this to cause panic (cf. *Odyssey* 22.297ff.). She was also responsible for women working in the Greek household in her role as goddess of weaving and handicrafts. Throughout the *Odyssey* she is particularly important as Odysseus' patron goddess.

> **The foundation of Athens**
> Athenian legend told of how Athena entered a competition with Poseidon for the right to be the patron deity of the people of Attica. Poseidon offered them a spring of salty water, while Athena offered the olive tree. Because the water was not drinkable the people preferred the olive tree, so they chose Athena as their patron goddess and founded the new city, which took her name. Athenians believed that an olive tree on the Acropolis was the very tree that Athena had planted to win the contest.

Artemis was the twin sister of Apollo; as such, she was goddess of the moon, and she was also commonly known as *Phoebe* (the feminine form of *phoebos*). She was also particularly important to the Greeks as the goddess of childhood and childbirth (see p. 158). In Attica, there was a celebrated cult of Artemis at Brauron, a little over 20 miles east of Athens. A few young girls from Attica were sent here to serve as 'Bears' for the goddess (see p. 151); even those who did not go had to 'play the bear' at some point in their youth; this was probably a form of initiation ceremony for girls before the onset of puberty.

Hestia was the goddess of the hearth, which was vital to every home as a source of light, heat and cooking (see p. 134). She was therefore a very important household goddess, who oversaw the family and domestic duties, and she received the first offering at every household sacrifice. In public, Greek cities kept a fire burning for the goddess in important government buildings to symbolise the hearth of the state. Hestia was originally one of the Twelve Olympians, but she later gave up her place to Dionysos in order to tend to the sacred fire on Mt Olympos.

2. Chthonic deities

The Greeks also worshipped a set of gods who were in many ways the opposite of the Olympians. These were the chthonic gods, who were associated with the earth (in Greek, *chthôn* meant 'earth'). These gods were generally linked to the Underworld; their most common symbol was the snake, which was believed to be born of the earth. Although some chthonic gods are associated with dark and destructive forces, others are linked with fertility and abundance, since the earth provides food and vegetation. Some gods could be worshipped either as Olympians or as chthonians; for example, while Hermes was generally worshipped as an Olympian, in his role as *Psychopompos*, he was worshipped as a chthonic god.

Hades was the most powerful chthonic god. As ruler of the Underworld, he had full power over all the dead. He was believed to emerge only rarely from his lower kingdom but, as we have seen, on one of the rare occasions when he did, he snatched away Persephone to be

Hades, holding a cornucopia, lies on a couch next to his queen, Persephone.

his wife. He is seldom pictured in art, but his symbol was often the pomegranate, the fruit eaten by Persephone in the Underworld. Other chthonic deities include the **Furies**, female spirits of vengeance with snakes for hair. In Aeschylus' play *Eumenides* they are famously summoned by the ghost of Clytaemnestra to pursue her son Orestes after he has murdered her. **Hecate** was another formidable goddess, who was responsible for sorcery and appeared only at night. The souls of the dead were also worshipped as chthonic beings.

Chthonic worship was different from Olympian worship in many ways. Olympians were worshipped in a spirit of festivity and rejoicing, but chthonic worship was much more fearful and gloomy. One illustration of this is that temples were not built for chthonic gods, even though they were worshipped with sacrifices in their own sanctuaries, just as the Olympians were.

3. Heroes

A further key element in Greek religion was the worship of heroic figures from the past (some legendary, some mythological) who had played an important role in defining Greek society. Sometimes these heroes were important to a specific place; for example, Pelops was worshipped as a founder of the games at Olympia (see pp. 55-6), while the Athenian tribes were named after ten heroes from the early history of the city (see p. 190). Since such heroes were typically worshipped at their tombs, the ritual surrounding them was usually most similar to that of chthonic deities.

In exceptional cases, Greeks believed that such heroes became gods after their deaths. Perhaps the most famous example of this is the mythological **Heracles**, the greatest of the Greek heroes, who was born of Zeus and a mortal mother, Alcmene; he is most famous for completing twelve labours to atone for the murder of his own wife and children. After his death, Zeus raised him to Mt Olympos as a god; he was particularly worshipped by the Spartans, whose kings traced their ancestry back to him (see p. 261).

Another mythological mortal who became a god was **Asklepios**, the overseer of healing, health and medicine, who was born to Apollo and a mortal mother, Coronis. Many pilgrims would travel to his healing sanctuary at Epidauros (see map 4) in the hope of finding a cure for their ills. Asklepios was particularly associated with snakes since the Greeks, in common with many ancient cultures, believed that snakes had special powers of healing and rebirth. The god's symbol was therefore a snake entwined around a staff; today this symbol is used as a logo by many medical organisations, most notably the World Health Organisation.

Logo of the World Health Organisation.

Review 2

1. Explain the meaning and usage of the following words: *aegis, Aphrodite, chthonic, Kore, Olympian, phoebos, polos*.

2. Find out about the family relationships of all the major Greek gods and draw up a family tree showing their links and lineage.

3. Design a web profile for each god and goddess. How would they describe themselves? What other information would they put on their webpage?

R. (i) Read each of the passages cited in the section above. What do we learn about each god and goddess from them?

R. (ii) Read lines 47-59 of Aeschylus' *Eumenides*. How are the Furies described in this passage?

E. Which gods and goddesses would you have felt closest to and why?

III. SANCTUARIES

A god or goddess was usually worshipped at a holy sanctuary, an area of land set apart as sacred to that deity (in fact, sanctuaries were sometimes dedicated to more than one god; for example, the Erechtheion in Athens, which is described on pp. 271-2, served both Athena and Poseidon). The Greek word for 'sanctuary', **temenos**, originated from the verb *temnein*, meaning 'to cut'; thus a *temenos* was literally a patch of land cut off for worship of a god ('temple' is derived from the same root). The *temenos* had to be large enough to contain the temple, an altar outside and all the worshippers present at a sacrifice. A basin of water was also found at the entrance to many sanctuaries, allowing worshippers to cleanse themselves before entering. The *temenos* was marked off either by a surrounding wall or by marker stones.

What caused the Greeks to choose certain places to worship specific gods? In many cases, sanctuaries were found at especially beautiful or bounteous places: for example, it made sense for Athenians to worship Athena, the protector of their city, on the fortified Acropolis at the centre

---

Pollution

The concept of religious pollution, or *miasma*, was very important to the Greeks, who believed that some actions made people impure in the eyes of the gods. Such 'polluted' people were forbidden from entering a sanctuary until they had undergone appropriate purification. If a polluted person did enter a sanctuary, then it was believed that the divinity would refuse to appear.

There were various ways in which a person might become polluted, many of which had nothing to do with a person's moral conduct. For example, anyone who had come into contact with a newborn child or a dead body was automatically polluted for a stipulated number of days. Even the act of sexual intercourse required a person to bathe before entering a sanctuary. Some criminal actions also made a person unclean, most notably all acts of homicide outside warfare, whether voluntary or involuntary.

A polluted person had to follow certain rules of purification: in some cases, a thorough wash was enough; others required the offender to remain outside sanctuaries for a certain amount of time, after which the pollution was thought to have passed; for the most severe cases a series of elaborate rituals or actions was required. At the beginning of Sophocles' *King Oedipus*, the king is waiting to hear from the oracle at Delphi about how to relieve Thebes of its appalling plague. The answer – that he should remove the source of pollution from the city – leads him to discover that he himself is the polluted man and cause of the horror. He therefore removes himself from his city in order to save his people.

16

of Athens; likewise, a sanctuary for Poseidon was located on the headland at Cape Sounion (see map 5), which looked out over the sea lanes of the Aegean. Springs and other water sources were frequently marked out as holy because of their natural benefits; more functionally, the sanctuary of Hephaistos and Athena in Athens was located in the blacksmiths' quarter of the city.

The temple

The centrepiece of the *temenos* was the temple. Temples were very important to the Greeks; their private houses were generally modest, and so they looked to their civic buildings for an inspiring display of architecture. Such grandeur had the double benefit of honouring the gods and flaunting the city's wealth and culture. The most famous example of this today is the Parthenon, the temple to Athena on the Acropolis in Athens.

Greek temples served a fundamentally different purpose from modern places of worship. In fact, temples were not strictly places of worship at all, since all the religious ritual took place on the open ground outside the temple. The sanctuary's altar, where a sacrifice took place, was located in front of the temple steps. This was a practical necessity since the pools of blood from a sacrificed animal could drain away more easily out of doors. It would have been a major health hazard if the rooms of the temple were constantly filled with blood!

The temple itself acted as a home for the god. Most temples were laid out on an east-west axis and supported by an elevated base, giving a sense of grandeur as worshippers walked up into the entrance. The building itself was surrounded by columns and consisted of three main rooms:

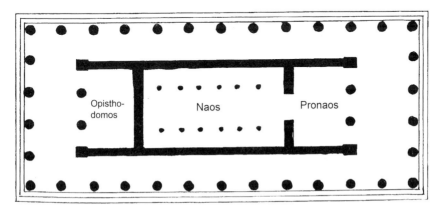

Plan of a typical Greek temple.

- The **naos** ('dwelling-place') was the main room of the temple and housed the cult image (see below).
- The **pronaos** was the entry porch into the *naos*, which housed the temple's most valuable offerings, such as booty from warfare.
- The **opisthodomos** ('behind the house') was at the back of the *naos* and housed the rest of the temple's dedications, such as the treasure accumulated from the sale of skins from sacrificed animals or the profit from any loans offered by the temple.

Greeks entered the *naos* only infrequently, to admire the statue or leave offerings. Only the priest and his assistants used the *naos* on a regular basis. Entrance into the *naos* was usually by grand double doors and led into the focal point of the temple, the cult statue of the deity. The Greek word for this cult-image, *agalma*, meant 'thing of delight', and the image was believed to delight both the god and the worshippers. Some cult statues were huge, most famously the two chryselephantine (gold and ivory) works sculpted by Pheidias – the statue of Zeus at Olympia (see p. 61) and the statue of Athena in the Parthenon. The *naos* had no windows, so the only light would have come through the front doors or from oil lamps. Such a darkened atmosphere must have added to the sense of awe created by the statue.

The altar
Altars came in many shapes and sizes. Some were very simple, just a mound of turf, a slab of natural rock with a flattened surface or even the

A typical stone altar discovered in Athens.

heaped up ashes of sacrifices over many years (see p. 60). However, more elaborate altars were sometimes carved from marble or constructed of bricks and whitewashed with lime. On top of the altar was a metal tablet on which a fire was burnt during sacrifices. An important temple would need an altar large enough for the burning of a hecatomb, the sacrifice of one hundred oxen.

Like the temple, the altar was laid out on an east/west axis. When a sacrifice was made, the sacrificer always faced east. Since sacrifices were normally offered early in the morning, this meant that he faced the rising sun, symbolic of an offering to the heavens.

Sanctuary and asylum

The word 'sanctuary', which originally described a holy place, has come to mean a place of safety in modern English. There is a good reason for this: it was a source of religious pollution to remove or attack a person seeking safety in a sanctuary. The word 'asylum' is also linked to the same practice: *sulon* in Greek meant 'the right of arrest' and so someone who was *a-sulos* could not be arrested (*a-* at the beginning of a Greek word negated its meaning). Even slaves were given safety in sanctuaries (see p. 167).

IV. PRIESTS

Hiereus and hiereia

Each *temenos* had its own priest (**hiereus**) or priestess (**hiereia**). As a general rule, gods were served by priests and goddesses by priestesses (this was one area in which women could have influence in society). There were exceptions to this, most notably at Delphi, where the temple of Apollo was served both by priests and by a priestess known as the Pythia (see p. 40). Priests were not licensed to officiate at different temples. Rather, a priesthood belonged to a specific temple and the priest would be titled accordingly (e.g. the priest of Apollo Pythias, the priestess of Athena Polias, etc.).

The role of a Greek priest was very different from that of a modern religious leader. There was no sense in which a priest had a pastoral role, as might be expected today. A priesthood was not a full time occupation and required no special training. The person simply had to learn the rituals and duties required of the post. Some of the main duties were as follows:

- **Presiding** at sacrifices (although even then it was not necessary for the priest to kill the sacrificial animal himself).
- **Supervising** the ceremonial washing and robing of the cult statue.
- **Looking after** the temple building and *temenos* with the help of attendants.

The following inscription, which refers to the priest of Amphiaraos in Attica, gives a feel for the priest's role:

'Gods! From the onset of winter until spring-ploughing the priest of Amphiaraos is to go to the sanctuary ... with no greater interval than three days between visits. He is to be in residence no less than ten days in each month. He is to require the temple assistant to look after the sanctuary in accordance with the law and also to look after those who look after the sanctuary. If anyone commits a crime in the sanctuary, whether he is a foreigner or a member of the deme, the priest has authority to fine him up to five drachmas [see p. 275 for information about Greek currency values].'

Greek Inscriptions VII.235

Some priests were elected to their position, while others were chosen by lot. We even hear of some people who paid to become priests. In addition, there were some priesthoods which always remained in one particular family. The priest was supervised in his role by the temple commissioners, a small board of citizens appointed by the state to look after the revenues of the temple and oversee the maintenance of the buildings.

There were some restrictions on who could become a priest. For example, candidates had to be free from any physical defects; and if their child died during their term of office then they had to resign immediately, since it was seen to be a bad omen. Some priesthoods were only open to certain groups, such as unmarried young women. Priesthoods could last for a year, a festival cycle or in some instances for life.

The honour of a priesthood

In the *Iliad*, the priest Laogonos is described as 'honoured like a god by his people' (16.605), and many priests certainly held honoured positions in society. They often had prominent places in religious processions or special seats at festivals; for example, the priest of Dionysus sat on a throne in the middle of the front row of seats in the theatre during the City Dionysia (see p. 99). Priests could also make money from their role since they were permitted to take some of the profit from the sale of skins of sacrificial animals, or of other offerings such as fruit, honey and oil.

The mantis

Greeks believed that they could ascertain the will of their gods and foretell the future by divination (the ability to interpret signs and omens). Even today, areas such as astrology, tarot, or palmistry arouse great interest. The Roman orator Cicero, discussing divination in Greek religion, made the following observation:

1. Greek Religion

'It is unarguable that there is no nation, whether the most learned and enlightened or the most grossly barbarous, that does not believe that the future can be revealed and does not recognise in certain people the power of foretelling it.'
                                                    Cicero, *On Divination* 1.2

Some Greeks were happy to interpret signs themselves, but others tried to obtain clearer answers by employing professional soothsayers, known as *manteis* (singular: *mantis*). In fact, the *manteis* were the only full-time religious professionals in ancient Greece. Although anyone could claim to have prophetic powers, some obviously built up a great reputation by achieving a good success rate in their predictions and advice.

The power of a mantis

A respected *mantis* could hold enormous power in the Greek world. In the 5th century, a Greek army always took a mantis on campaign to read the omens; thus he might have a great influence on military tactics. The Athenian general Nikias famously made a disastrous military blunder (Plutarch, *Nikias* 23-5) based on the advice of his *manteis*.

The reliance on seers is not just a characteristic of the ancient world. For example, Nancy Reagan, whose husband Ronald was US President between 1981 and 1989, admitted to consulting astrologers before finalising his diary commitments to try to ensure that he came to no harm.

The most common way to read omens was to inspect the entrails of a sacrificed animal: if these innards showed any sign of blemish or imperfection, then danger was predicted. Greeks often also interpreted omens in the flight of birds, a skill known as **augury**. In the following lines from Sophocles' *Antigone*, the blind prophet Teiresias uses augury to warn King Creon that his crimes will soon be punished:

> 'As I sat on the ancient seat of augury,
> in the sanctuary where every bird I know
> will hover at my hands – suddenly I heard it,
> a strange voice in the wingbeats, unintelligible,
> barbaric, a mad scream! Talons flashing, ripping,
> they were killing each other – that much I knew –
> the murderous fury whirring in those wings
> made that much clear!'
>   Sophocles, *Antigone* 999-1004

In fact, Greeks could see omens (good or ill) in many different events and a *mantis* might also be called on to interpret any of these. Dreams were a particularly common source of prediction, most notably in healing cults such as the sanctuary of Asklepios at Epidauros, where pilgrims would spend the night in a holy building, hoping that the god would appear to them in a dream. Temple attendants were then on hand to interpret their dreams and pronounce a cure.

A young boy presents the liver of a sacrificial victim to a hoplite
who examines it to see if the signs are favourable. The old man
at the left points out the ritual spot for reading the signs.

Review 3

1. Define the following words: *agalma, augury, mantis, naos, pronaos,
   opisthodomos, temenos*.
2. Read the description of the sanctuary and temple of Zeus at Olympia on
   pp. 57-63. What typical features of a sanctuary can you find?
3. What similarities and differences can you find between a Greek temple
   and a modern place of worship?
4. To what extent does the concept of 'holy ground' still exist today? Why are
   some places given a sacred status in the modern world?
5. List the duties a Greek priest may have carried out. How do the roles of an
   ancient priest compare to those of a modern religious leader?
6. Are there any modern equivalents of the *mantis* today? To what extent do
   you think people still rely on interpreting omens to predict the future?

V. SACRIFICE

Sacrifice was part of life in ancient Greece. It always accompanied events such as festivals, oracular consultations, rites of passage and divination. The principle behind a sacrifice was that a person honoured the gods by giving up something valuable for them. Although animal sacrifice is very uncommon in the modern world, the principle of giving up something valuable still remains. For example, Jews and Muslims fast on Yom Kippur and during Ramadan respectively, while there is a Christian tradition of forgoing something pleasurable during Lent.

1. Animal sacrifice

The most important type of sacrifice was a blood sacrifice (the killing of an animal), known as *thysia*. However, we would be mistaken to think that a sacrifice was the mere act of killing of an animal. It was really a ceremonial process by which an animal was offered to a god. This process began with the selection of an appropriate animal and then followed a carefully formulated set of rituals. A comparison might be made with the way in which people today take care over the wrapping and presentation of gifts.

Domestic animals were normally offered, although wild animals were sometimes dedicated to Artemis. If the sacrificer owned livestock then he would probably choose from his own flock; otherwise he would purchase a suitable animal from the local market, trying to find an animal free of any blemishes in order to please the god. Different animals varied in price: a piglet cost about 3 drachmas, a sheep or goat 12, a pig more than 20 while a cow might cost as much as 80. The importance of the occasion determined the expense. Typically at grand religious festivals a hecatomb, the sacrifice of a hundred oxen (or even more), was offered.

The preparation

The animal was adorned with ribbons and, if it had horns, they were gilded (given a thin covering of gold). Before the sacrifice, all the people involved washed themselves thoroughly, put on their smartest clothes and crowned themselves with garlands of twigs. They all then escorted the animal to the altar, with a maiden carrying a sacrificial basket filled with barley grains or cakes. The sacrificial knife was hidden inside this basket. A ewer of water and an incense burner were carried by other participants, while a flute player often accompanied the procession. It was considered a good omen if the animal moved willingly to the temple.

Once the sacrificial party arrived at the sanctuary, the participants gathered into a circle by the altar, upon which a fire was lit. They

A victim being led to the altar for sacrifice.

purified themselves by rinsing their hands in holy water and took some barley grain from the basket. The main sacrificer (who did not have to be the priest) next poured water on the animal's head, causing it to nod its head forward. This nod was interpreted as the animal's consent to be sacrificed, since Greeks believed that all involved in the sacrifice (god, victim and mortals) had to be in favour of the action. The priest then said the prayer of offering to the god, after which all present would throw forward their barley grains to symbolise the fact that they were all taking part in the sacrifice.

The kill
The sacrificer then took the knife from the basket and concealed it as he approached the victim. Producing it suddenly, he first cut a few hairs from the victim's head and threw them on the fire. If the animal was large, it was then stunned and its throat cut. The blood was collected in a bowl and poured over the top and sides of the altar. A smaller victim was simply lifted above the altar to be killed, whereupon its blood automatically spattered the altar. In either case, it was important to 'bloody the altar'. As all this was happening, if there were women present they would utter a high-pitched cry, the *ololygê*, which marked the passage from life to death.

The treatment of the meat
Following the sacrifice, the animal was cut up and the meat divided in three ways. First the thighbones were removed, wrapped in fat and burnt on the altar fire. This was the portion for the gods, and the smoke

24

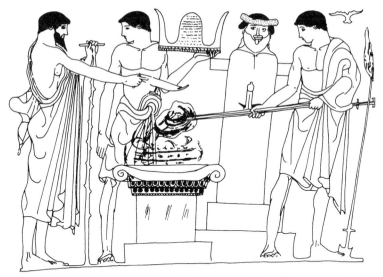

The roasting of meat on an altar after a sacrifice. The man on the left is pouring a libation. To the right of centre is a Herm (see p. 134).

was 'read' for omens as it drifted up to the heavens. Wine was poured into the fire as it burnt.

Secondly, the entrails, particularly the liver, were examined for omens. These were then roasted on skewers and shared out amongst the celebrants. Finally, the rest of the meat was boiled in cauldrons and distributed to the community at large. Thus the ceremony became a feast for gods and men alike. Meat was not common to the Greek diet, and a sacrifice was usually the one special occasion when the Greeks could eat it. At large state festivals, the sacrifice of a hecatomb provided food for the entire population of the city. At the end of the feast, the skin of the victim would be given to the sanctuary or its priest.

Prometheus' trick

The Greeks themselves were unsure why the gods were offered the thighbones, the least nutritious parts of the animal. They used a myth, recounted by Hesiod in his *Theogony* (535-57), to explain the anomaly. The story went that Prometheus, who brought fire to mankind, tricked Zeus into choosing between two parts of a sacrificed ox: the thighbones 'wrapped in shining fat' and the flesh hidden in the ox's stomach. Although Zeus saw through the trick, he played along with it and thereafter thighbones were offered to the gods at a sacrifice.

In practice, this division of meat must have had a more pragmatic origin. Greece could not support a large number of livestock, so people ate meat only infrequently, usually at sacrifices. It was therefore logical that the most nutritious parts of the animal were eaten by the human worshippers.

Olympian and chthonic ritual

The ritual described above was typical of sacrifices to Olympian gods. Since they were believed to inhabit the sky and upper world, the motifs for such offerings were air, the daylight and the colour white. Thus an Olympian sacrifice usually took place during the daytime (early in the morning in particular), the priest wore a white woollen band around his head, and a white victim was usually offered. Upon uttering the prayer, the priest would raise his hands to the sky. Once the victim's throat had been cut, its head would also be lifted up to the sky.

By contrast, a sacrifice to a chthonic deity or to the dead involved a different set of rituals. Since chthonic worship was focused on the earth, the colour associated with it was black: the priest wore a black woollen band around his head and a black animal was usually sacrificed after sunset over a pit rather than an altar. Upon uttering the prayer, the priest would point his hands to the ground and lower the head of the victim once its throat had been cut. The animal would then be burnt entirely and no part of it would be eaten.

However, it is likely that the distinction between Olympian and chthonic worship was not always observed. In particular, scholars now believe that many heroes received the same kind of sacrifice as the Olympian gods, including a feast.

2. Food and drink

Any symbol of life could be offered for sacrifice. Therefore, sacrificial cakes made from grain and fruit were often left for gods on altars, perhaps to thank them for a bountiful harvest or the food on the table. The food was left to decompose or be eaten by animals. Another common form of sacrifice was the **libation**, an offering of liquid. There were two

A hoplite warrior preparing to depart. On the right a woman performs a libation.

types: a *choê* and a *spondê*. A *spondê*, which was poured to the Olympian gods, was an offering of wine, water, milk, oil or even honey. The liquid was poured carefully onto the ground and the help of the gods was requested. By contrast, a *choê* was offered to chthonic beings and the liquid was tipped into the earth in one go.

Libations were a part of everyday life. For example, at the beginning of a symposium (see p. 146), a *spondê* was offered to the gods to try to ensure that the behaviour didn't become too wild. *Spondai* were often poured for sailors embarking upon a voyage or for soldiers setting out to battle. Whenever two peoples made truces with one another, they poured libations; as a result, the Greek word for 'truce' was simply *spondai*. In a famous literary example of a libation, Achilles pours a *spondê* in the *Iliad* (16.225-32) before praying (unsuccessfully) for Patroclus' safe return from the battlefield.

3. Votive offerings

Another way of trying to win favour from the gods was by leaving them votive offerings – gifts, which came in many shapes and sizes. Often they were trophies of war, which soldiers and armies dedicated in order to ask for support or to give thanks for help received. For example, after Odysseus kills Dolon at Troy, he hands over his victim's marten-skin cap, wolf-skin, bow and spear to Athena out of gratitude (*Iliad* 10.458-64; 570ff.). When victorious armies sold prisoners of war, they often donated part of the revenue to a temple.

Other dedications could be more personal. Healing sanctuaries were full of gifts from patients who had been cured; these were often clay images of the affected part of the body. In retirement, a man often donated the tools of his trade to a god: a fisherman might dedicate his net or a huntsman his spear, and so forth. Votive offerings were also left at important moments in one's life: the night before her wedding a young bride would dedicate a lock of her hair and her childhood toys to Artemis (see p. 154).

This bronze Spartan shield was taken as one of the spoils after the Athenian victory over the Spartans at Pylos in 425/4. It was dedicated as a trophy in Athens and inscribed with 'The Athenians from the Spartans of Pylos'.

Such offerings were made not just by individuals but also by cities. At the two most important panhellenic sites in Greece, Olympia (see p. 62) and Delphi, many states set up treasuries. These were small buildings where they could leave offerings and treasures for the gods worshipped at the site. These treasuries came to be among the most important buildings in both centres.

4. Prayer

Any sacrifice or offering would be accompanied by a prayer, in which Greeks would pray for divine repayment in return for their sacrificial offering. Prayers were usually formal and had three main stages. First would come the *invocation*, in which the god or goddess was addressed by name, and sometimes also by habitual residence, functions or qualities. This part of the prayer served to identify and glorify the god(dess). Next came the *argument*, where the praying person tried to persuade the god to help. Typically, any past favours or sacrifices offered for the god were mentioned at this point to remind the god of previous loyalty shown. Finally came the *petition*, when the request was made.

An excellent example of a prayer comes early in the *Iliad*, when the priest Chryses prays to Apollo for punishment to be inflicted on the Greeks, because they had refused to return his captive daughter:

'Hear me, Lord of the Silver Bow, who protects Chryse and holy Killa, and rules powerfully over Tenedos, O Sminthian one. If ever I have built you a pleasing temple, or if ever I burnt fat thigh pieces of bulls and goats, bring this prayer to fulfilment. Make the Greeks pay for my tears with your arrows.'
Homer, *Iliad* 1.37-42

Review 4

1. Define the following words: *choê, ololygê, spondê, spondai, thysia*.
2. Draw up a table listing the events that took place at each stage of an animal sacrifice.
3. Do any modern religions have equivalents to libations or votive offerings?
4. How does the prayer of Chryses quoted above compare to typical prayers of religions with which you are familiar?
5. Do you think that the way of sacrificing an animal in ancient Greece was more humane than the methods used to kill animals for food today?
R. Read two accounts of different sacrifices at *Odyssey* 3.430-63 and 11.22-48. Which is Olympian and which chthonic? How can you tell?
E. 'A blood sacrifice was much more than the mere killing of an animal'. Do you agree? Explain your answer.

VI. A FESTIVAL FOR ATHENA

The Greeks did not have a five-day working week followed by a weekend as we do today. Rather, they found their days of rest in numerous festivals; in classical Athens, there were at least 120 festival days in the year. On these days, work ceased and the government met only in an emergency. Thus, a life without festivals would have been, as the philosopher Democritus put it, 'a long road without an inn'.

The character of each festival generally reflected the cycle of the seasons. Therefore the City Dionysia, which celebrated fertility and new life, was held in Spring. Conversely, the Genesia, when the city remembered its dead, was held in September just as the campaigning season for soldiers was drawing to a close. Some festivals lasted for several days, and many involved the whole population of a city, including resident foreigners, women and sometimes even slaves. Plato explained the importance of festivals as follows:

> 'The gods ... took pity on the human race, born to suffer as it was, and gave
> it relief in the form of religious festivals to serve as periods of rest from its
> labours. They gave us the Muses, with Apollo as their leader, and Dionysos;
> by having these gods to share their holidays, people were to be made whole
> again and, thanks to them, we find refreshment in the celebration of these
> festivals.'   Plato, *Laws* 2.653D

The most important festival of the Athenian year was the **Panathenaia**, which celebrated Athena's birthday on 28th *Hekatombeiôn* (in the middle of July – see p. 277 for an explanation of the Greek months). *Panathenaia* meant 'all-Athenian', and the festival was indeed a chance for all Athenians to come together and worship Athena Polias, the protector of their city. Although it is hard to make precise comparisons with the modern world, similarities could be drawn with the way in which Irish people today celebrate St Patrick's Day as a festival of their culture, beliefs and history.

In fact, every four years there was a much larger celebration of Athena's birthday. Introduced in 566 and known as the **Great Panathenaia**, it included a wider range of activities, such as athletic, choral, poetic and naval competitions, which took place in the days around the 28th. This day still contained the focal-point of the festival, when a grand procession culminated in the sacrifice of many animals and the presentation of a new robe, the **peplos**, to the cult-statue of Athena Polias in the Erechtheion.

The peplos

The *peplos*, which was about 2 by 1.5 metres in size, was the central icon of the festival. The process of weaving it began nine months beforehand during another festival, the Chalkeia, which celebrated Athena Ergane, goddess of arts and crafts. The loom was set up then by the priestesses of Athena and the *Arrêphoroi*, four young aristocratic girls chosen to serve the goddess. Thereafter the *peplos* was woven by a team of young women, the *Ergastinai* (women thus played a vital role in their city's grandest festival). Into the saffron-yellow and purple cloth they wove scenes depicting the myth of the Olympians' victory over the Giants, with Zeus and Athena at the forefront.

In fact, a second *peplos* may have been made for the Great Panathenaia: records from the 4th century indicate that a much larger *peplos* was attached to a ship-cart and wheeled along as part of its procession. If this were the case, then it is tempting to think that the larger version was introduced in the late 5th century for Pheidias' enormous gold and ivory statue of Athena, which was installed in the Parthenon in 437; because of this statue's height (about 12 metres), the second *peplos* is likely to have been made by professional weavers in Athens.

The programme

Although the evidence is not totally clear, one view is that the Great Panathenaia lasted for eight days, starting on 23rd *Hekatombeiôn*. According to this version, the programme ran as follows:

Day	Date	Contest
1	23rd	rhapsodic and musical contests
2	24th	boys' and youths' athletics
3	25th	men's athletics
4	26th	equestrian events
5	27th	tribal contests
6	28th	torch race and *pannychis* processing and sacrifice
7	29th	*apobatês* boat race
8	30th	prize-giving

1. Rhapsodic and musical contests

In the late 6th century, Hipparchos, the son of the tyrant Peisistratos (see p. 184), added to the elaborate nature of the Great Panathenaia by introducing a poetry competition. The competitors were rhapsodes (reciters of epic poetry) and the prize was awarded to the rhapsode who best recounted passages from the *Iliad* and the *Odyssey*.

Other musical competitions were also integral to the festival. Indeed, Pericles commissioned the construction of the Odeion (see p. 98) in the 440s specifically so it could act as a concert hall for the Panathenaic

---

Preserving Homer

The recitals of Homer at the Panathenaic festival may well have ensured the preservation of the *Iliad* and the *Odyssey* for us today. Since both poems had evolved in an oral culture, there was little tradition of writing down definitive versions. The recitals at Athens probably caused both poems to be recorded in single, authoritative versions, which have survived to the present day.

---

music contests. There were four main categories of competitor: singers to the *kithara*, soloists on the *kithara*, singers to the *aulos* and soloists on the *aulos* (see pp. 278-9 to read about Greek musical instruments).

An inscription from the 4th century gives some details about the prizes awarded: the victorious singer to the *kithara* won a golden crown worth 1,000 drachmas and 500 silver drachmas in cash; second prize was 1,200 drachmas. There were even prizes for third, fourth and fifth place (600, 400 and 300 drachmas respectively). Since one drachma was the equivalent of a day's wage for a skilled worker, the competition was clearly very prestigious and lucrative.

2. Sporting events

As part of the new festival of the Great Panathenaia in 566, athletic contests were introduced to rival the four great games in other parts of Greece (see p. 53). However, there was an important difference: in contrast to the other four, the competitors at the Panathenaia were rewarded with valuable prizes. A victorious athlete usually won a large number of amphorae (jars) full of olive oil; each amphora could typically hold about 38 litres. Many Panathenaic amphorae are well preserved today; on one side of an amphora was always an image of Athena with the inscription 'from the games at Athens'; on the other was depicted the event in which the victor had competed.

The Panathenaia hosted all the events contested at the four great games, such as the stadion, pentathlon, combat events and equestrian events (see pp. 67ff. for more details on these). In addition, there was one distinctive chariot race, the *apobatês*, which involved charioteers dismounting from their chariots during the race. Competitors in all events were divided into three classes – boys, beardless youths and men (the great games only had events for boys and men) – and the events were open to all Greeks, not just Athenians.

The same 4th century inscription gives details of the sporting prizes: the most important event was the chariot race, in which the winning charioteer won 140 amphorae of olive oil. We also hear of a winner in the youths' stadion who won 60 amphorae of olive oil; in the same race, even the runner-up was awarded 12 amphorae.

31

Front and back of a
Panathenaic prize amphora.

3. Tribal contests

In order to preserve a distinctively Athenian element to the festival's competitions, four events were contested by teams drawn from the city's ten tribes (see p. 189). One such contest was the torch-race (see below), while the other three are listed in the table below, together with the prizes awarded to the winning tribe in the 4th century:

Event	Description	Prize
Euandrion	trials of strength (*euandrion* means 'fine-manliness')	100 drachmas and an ox
Boat race	regatta at the Piraeus	300 drachmas and 200 free meals
Pyrrhic dance	war dance performed to the *aulos*	100 drachmas and a bull

4. The procession

The build-up to the procession began the previous evening with the *pannychis* ('all-night'), a service in honour of Athena lasting through the night. It took place beside the Parthenon and involved young men singing hymns and maidens singing and dancing in choruses.

The Parthenon frieze

The 160 metre long frieze sculpted on the Parthenon depicted a series of scenes from the Panathenaic procession. This choice of subject matter was remarkable: there is no other example of architectural decoration on a Greek temple which shows, rather than scenes from a myth, a contemporary event. The Parthenon was designed as a monument to Athens' victories over its enemies and the frieze therefore emphasised the spirit of the city and the devotion of its citizens to their patron goddess.

The procession began at sunrise on the 28th at the Dipylon Gate, proceeding through the agora along the Panathenaic Way (its namesake – see map 6) and finally arriving at the foot of the Acropolis. It was the largest parade of the Athenian year, considerably grander than the *pompê* of the City Dionysia (see pp. 106-7); there was another important difference between the two: the Dionysiac festival was far less structured than the Panathenaic, which emphasised the order and hierarchy of Athenian life; where Dionysos encouraged wild abandon, Athena supervised the established order of things.

Allowing for two *peploi*, the order of the parade may have been as follows: (1) the *Arrêphoroi* carrying the smaller *peplos*; (2) priestesses of Athena and other women carrying gifts; (3) sacrificial animals such as cows and sheep (each of Athens' subject allies had to provide a cow for sacrifice, adding to the number of animals); (4) wealthy metics (see pp. 201-2), dressed in purple cloaks, carrying trays of cakes and honeycombs; (5) bearers of holy water, together with musicians playing flutes and lyres; (6) the ship-cart with the larger *peplos* attached to its mast; (7) old men carrying olive branches, charioteers alongside chariots, the *Ergastinai*, infantrymen and cavalrymen, as well as victors in the games; (8) the final, longest section of the procession was made up of ordinary Athenians who were organised by deme (see p. 187).

Once the procession arrived at the Acropolis, preparations were made for the great sacrifice to Athena. At least a hundred animals were slaughtered; even in 410, a time of economic hardship, there is a record of exactly one hundred animals, costing 5,114 drachmas; in more prosperous times many more animals may have been offered. After some of the meat had been offered in the fire to the goddess, the rest was taken to the kerameikos (see p. 274) and shared out amongst the people, who partied well into the evening.

33

The Panathenaic Way looking towards the Acropolis.

The torch race

By the time the procession reached the Acropolis, the fire on the altar beside the Parthenon had already been lit by the winner of a torch-race, which was either run earlier that morning or on the previous evening. It began outside the Dipylon Gate and finished on the Acropolis, a distance of more than 3 km. Each runner had to carry a torch, with the winner the first to the altar with his torch still ablaze. He then lit the fire and was awarded a prize of 30 drachmas and a water jar.

This tradition may have been the inspiration for the torch relay at the modern Olympic Games, since there was no equivalent at the ancient Olympics. However, a rather more irreverent picture of the race is painted by Dionysos in Aristophanes' *Frogs* (1089ff.), when he describes a 'short, fat fellow, plugging along miles behind everyone else' who manages to keep his torch alight by a prolonged bout of flatulence!

Vase painting of a torch race.

Review 5

1. Define the following words: *Arrêphoroi, Ergastinai, pannychis, peplos.*
2. What benefits do you think the people of Athens derived from the Great Panathenaia?
3. Which events would you most like to have competed in at the Great Panathenaia and why?
3. To what extent do you think the Great Panathenaia was a religious occasion?
4. Do you think there are any festivals or events today which could be compared to the Great Panathenaia?
E. Imagine you are part of the Panathenaic procession. Describe everything that you see and hear during the day.

VII. THE ORACLE AT DELPHI

All people arrive at stages in their lives when they are faced with momentous decisions; today, religious believers typically pray for help and guidance at such moments. The same principle applied in ancient Greece, although in a slightly different form. At these pivotal moments, a Greek would consult an oracle.

Greeks believed that an oracle was the mouthpiece of a god: when an oracle spoke, a god spoke. Most commonly (though not exclusively) it was Apollo, the god of prophecy, who was believed to preside over oracular shrines, the most famous of which was his oracle at Delphi on the slopes of Mt Parnassus in central Greece.

1. What did they ask?

Oracular consultations could be divided into two categories: enquiries by private individuals and those by the ambassadors of rulers or cities. Private individuals would visit oracles seeking help with the most important decisions in their lives; Plutarch says that people asked questions such as 'if they shall be victorious, if they shall marry, if it is to their advantage to sail, to farm, to go abroad'. Some questions were framed in religious terms; for example, in 402, before setting out on a military campaign, Xenophon asked the Delphic oracle to which gods he should sacrifice in order to guarantee a safe return. The following enquiries, made to the oracle of Zeus at Dodona, were probably typical:

> Nicocrateia asks to which god she should sacrifice in order to fare better and to stop her disease.

> Lysanias asks Zeus Naios and Dione whether or not the baby with whom Annula is pregnant is from him.

Oracles could also have a profound influence on Greek (and non-Greek) politics. Herodotus, the historian whose work covers the 6th and early 5th centuries, repeatedly tells of rulers and governments consulting oracles in the face of a dilemma. For example, when Lycurgus wanted to reform Sparta, he visited Delphi for guidance (see pp. 230-1); Cleisthenes headed there too when overhauling the tribal system of Athens in 508/7. Other envoys sought advice on matters such as where to establish a new colony, whether to go to war or how to rid a city of a disease (as King Oedipus asked to his own cost).

Delphi, in particular, had a powerful hold over political leaders. The local region, which had only about a thousand inhabitants, was not attached to any city and so the oracle claimed to maintain political independence. Greeks came to Delphi from far and wide and, together with Olympia (which also claimed political independence), it was the pre-eminent panhellenic site in the world. From the 6th century, it was administered by the *Amphictyonic League* ('the league of those living around'), a council of twelve states which met twice a year. The League consisted of local cities as well as Athens and Sparta.

Neutrality?
No fewer than four wars were fought to maintain the independence of the Delphic oracle. In spite of this, some thought it took a pro-Persian stance during the Persian wars, while the Athenians believed that it was biased in favour of the Spartans during the Peloponnesian War.

---

2. The site of Delphi

Delphi was, and remains, a stunning site. Located on the terraced lower slopes of Mt Parnassus (2458m), its breathtaking views into the valley below must have made a traveller feel closer to the gods.

At the heart of the site lay the walled sanctuary of Apollo. The main entrance (there were at least eleven) was by the Sacred Way, which zigzagged up the hill towards the temple of Apollo. Pilgrims entering from this direction immediately saw some of the Treasuries lining the route. The dedications left at the site meant that Delphi was fabulously wealthy; even today visitors can still see the Treasury of the Athenians, probably built out of gratitude for the Athenian victory over the Persians at Marathon in 490.

Outside the temple of Apollo was a remarkable panhellenic gift, the 'tripod of Plataea', which was dedicated by every one of the 31 Greek states who had played a part in the final defeat of the Persians at Plataea in 479. Made of gold and standing at between 7 and 8 metres high, it was inscribed with the names of all 31 cities. Turning next towards the temple, a pilgrim was faced above the entrance by two of the most famous phrases in ancient Greece: *mêden agan,* 'nothing in excess', and *gnôthi seauton,* 'know yourself'.

The Treasury of the Athenians.

General plan of
Delphi: 1. Stadium;
2. Sanctuary of Apollo;
3. Castalian Spring;
4. Gymnasium.

Sanctuary of Apollo
at Delphi: 1. Treasury
of the Athenians;
2. Athenian Portico;
3. Base of the tripod
of Plataea.

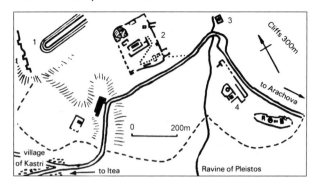

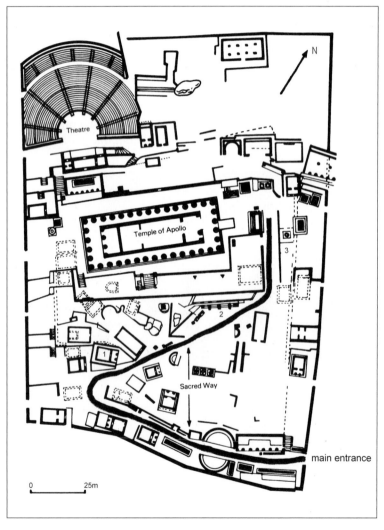

1. Greek Religion

The view of Delphi from higher up Mt Parnassus.

The first major temple building was burnt down in 548 and replaced in the 520s with a grander version. When this was destroyed by an earthquake in 373, it was replaced by another even more magnificent. Throughout its history, the temple was unusual in that it did not simply house the god – oracular consultations took place in its innermost shrine too. The votive offerings inside the temple were every bit as fabulous as those outside; for example, in the *pronaos* a visitor would have passed an enormous silver mixing bowl (*kratêr*), dedicated by Croesos of Lydia in 546, which could hold 21,730 litres of wine!

The mythology of Delphi

The site of Delphi was rich in mythology. The Greeks liked to believe that it marked the centre of the world, and they told a myth to reflect this. In the temple of Apollo was a large stone, the *omphalos* ('navel stone'); in legend, Zeus had sent two eagles out from the ends of the earth to find its centre, and their beaks touched at the *omphalos*.

A second myth explains Apollo's importance to Delphi. The *Hymn to Apollo* recounts the god's first arrival at the site in the shape of a dolphin (the name Delphi is derived from the Greek word for a dolphin). Until then, the site was inhabited by a huge snake, the Python, which Apollo slew. Its body fell into a gap in the earth, from which the fumes of its decomposing body were believed to rise (in Greek, *pythein* meant 'to rot'); these fumes were later said to inspire the priestess in the temple. Apollo assumed the epithet 'Pythian' and ordered a temple to be built for all the Greeks 'to whom I could give unfailing advice through prophetic responses'.

Beyond the temple was a theatre and, further up the hill, an athletics stadium. Every four years these venues played host to the Pythian

Games (see p. 53), which commemorated Apollo's killing of Pytho and included athletic and musical competitions in his honour; the prize for victors was a wreath of laurel, the god's sacred tree. Other significant points outside the sanctuary included the gymnasium, a sanctuary to Athena and the Castalian Spring, the water of which was believed to be sacred; participants had to purify themselves in the spring before an oracular consultation could proceed.

3. The consultation

Consultations at Delphi were held on the 7th of every month, apart from November, December and January when winter conditions prevented pilgrims from making long journeys. Oracles were only ever consulted by men; if a woman had a question, she had to send it by proxy. Enquirers drew lots for their place in the queue, although the delegates from some states had *promanteia* – the right to go to the front. The Delphians normally awarded *promanteia* to states who had given the sanctuary special financial or political support. The sanctuary was served by two full-time priests, who were supported by five *hosioi* ('holy men'); however, the most important religious figure was the Pythia.

The Pythia
The Pythia, who was believed to speak Apollo's words, was the god's priestess at Delphi. According to one ancient writer, she had to be an ordinary peasant woman from the Delphi area, who was over the age of 50 (although she dressed as a young maiden) and who had lived a blameless life.

On the day of a consultation she rose before dawn and purified herself by washing in the Castalian Spring. Together with the priests, she then sacrificed a goat to check the omens. If they were favourable, she would enter the temple, heading into a hidden sacred room, the *adyton* (literally: 'the forbidden place'), which was fumigated by the smoke of barley grain and laurel leaves burning on its hearth. Laurel was a particularly important emblem – the Pythia also wore a garland of it in her hair and held a branch in her hand.

There is much debate about what she did next. The most popular account has traditionally run as follows:

- The Pythia purified herself, munched on a laurel leaf and took her seat on a tripod which was placed over the chasm in the *adyton*.
- The Pythia next became intoxicated by the vapours rising from the chasm. She was now ready to answer questions, and so one of the priests then put an enquiry to her.
- In response, she uttered incoherent sounds which were interpreted by one of the priests and written down in hexameter verse. He then returned the response to the enquirer. Responses were sometimes so confusing and ambivalent that they left the enquirer perplexed.

The Pythia, seated on a tripod and holding a spray of laurel, prophesies to Aegeus, king of Athens. Aegeus, who was enquiring about his lack of children, later fathered Theseus.

However, this description perhaps owes more to later writers who wanted to exaggerate the legend of Delphi. In fact, other evidence suggests that the Pythia actually spoke 'the words of Apollo' directly to the enquirer in understandable Greek. Intriguingly, however, a 1996 geological survey of the site established that ethylene, a gas with anaesthetic properties, does emerge from a fault-line directly under the temple. Maybe the Pythia was intoxicated after all.

The enquirer
After purifying himself by washing in the Castalian Spring, an enquirer was then assigned a place in the queue; he may have needed to wait patiently, since consultations continued from dawn until dusk. When his turn came, he first paid the consultation fee, which had originally been a sacred cake, but by the 5th century was a fixed monetary cost. A record from the early 4th century shows that, for the city of Phaselis in Asia Minor, a state enquiry cost 7 drachmas and 2 obols, and a private enquiry 4 obols.

Before the enquirer could proceed into the temple, he had to sacrifice a goat. It was taken to be a good omen if the goat trembled when its head was sprinkled with water, perhaps as this suggested the trembling of the Pythia as she gave her answer. If the omens of the sacrifice were good, then it was taken that Apollo was allowing the enquiry to proceed. Only when a priest had pronounced favourable omens could the enquirer enter the temple.

Now the consultation began. He was led by one of the priests into the inner sanctuary of the temple, where he waited near the *adyton*. He then put his question to the priest – this could be done either orally or by writing on a lead tablet (many of which have been found). According to the conventional version, the priest then went into the *adyton*, returning some time later with the response.

4. Two famous oracles

In the first book of his *Histories* (1.46-55), Herodotus tells the story of Croesos, king of Lydia (modern western Turkey) in the middle of the 6th century. Wishing to attack the growing Persian empire to the east before it became too powerful, he first tested the world's most famous oracles to establish which could give him the most helpful advice. Judging Amphiaraus and Delphi to be equally good, he lavished gifts on both and asked whether he should invade Persian territory. Both oracles replied that if he did so, he would destroy a great empire. Delighted with this answer, Croesos set out to war at once. His army was soon trounced by the Persians, who went on to conquer Lydia; the king had indeed destroyed a great empire – his own.

Herodotus later recounts Themistocles' inspired interpretation of another cryptic oracle (7.140-3). Faced with the threat of a Persian invasion in 481, the Athenians consulted Delphi for advice. They were told that 'Zeus the all-seeing grants to Athena's prayer that the wooden wall only shall not fall, but help you and your children'. A debate followed in the assembly, where many believed that the wooden wall referred to the wall around the ancient centre of Athens. However, Themistocles, an Athenian general, argued that it properly referred to the Athenian ships; he therefore convinced his compatriots to evacuate the city and prepare to fight at sea. Soon afterwards, the Athenians defeated the Persians in an epic sea battle in the bay of Salamis; in the meantime, however, the Persians had sacked Athens, slaughtering all those who had chosen to stay in the city.

5. The appeal of the oracle

So what was it all about? Today, many people admire the ancient Greeks for their rationalism and yet here, at the heart of their lives, was a system of decision-making based on the mutterings of a supposedly intoxicated priestess. One answer would be simply to say that Greeks believed in the power of the oracle. However strange it might seem to us, many Greeks certainly thought that the oracle communicated the infallible will of the gods; it was thus natural for them to want to listen to its advice.

However, two further points could be made. The first is that consulting an oracle allowed the Greeks to give sacred importance to a momentous decision: if a man visited Delphi to ask whether he should get married, he was acknowledging the life-changing nature of the issue and giving himself time to think about it. The second point follows on from this; for, as we have seen, the oracle could sometimes give confusing or cryptic advice, which the enquirer then had to interpret for himself. The story of Croesos shows what could happen if a man didn't think carefully about an oracle. In this context, the temple's mottoes come sharply into focus: 'nothing in excess' and 'know yourself'.

Review 6

1. Define the following words: *adyton, hosioi, omphalos, promanteia, Pythia.*
2. Why do you think Delphi became one of the most important religious sanctuaries in the Greek world?
3. Is there anything in the modern world that could be compared to the oracle at Delphi?
4. Why do you think that the oracle was so respected by Greeks? Do you think that there was more to it than mere superstition?
R. Read Herodotus 5.62-3 and then 5.91. What does this story indicate about the potential corruptibility of the oracle?
E. Imagine you are a Greek who needs to consult the Delphic oracle over an important matter. Describe your visit to the site and how you interpreted the response to your question.

VIII. MYSTERY RELIGIONS

An interesting development in traditional Greek religion was the growth of various 'mystery' religions. In fact, these were not really alternative religions as we would think of them, since they generally centred on traditional gods such as Dionysos or Demeter; a follower of a mystery religion continued to worship all the gods just as before. Rather, these branches of Greek religion seem to have offered initiates a more personal experience of the divine and, often, the hope of a blissful life after death.

In Greek *mystêrion* meant 'a ceremony or place of initiation' and the basic tenet of a mystery religion was that its followers were initiated into its secret practices. Consequently, our knowledge of these religions is limited. However, we do know that the most important one was centred on Eleusis, a town about 23 km (14 miles) west of Athens on the coast of Attica (see map 5). According to some sources, initiation into this cult gave the individual a profound spiritual experience.

The Eleusinian Mysteries

The celebration of the Mysteries at Eleusis took place every year over a period of nine days in late September. It was held in honour of the goddess Demeter and her daughter Persephone. At its heart was the celebration of Persephone's return from the Underworld each spring, which heralded the return of crops and the fertility of the soil. However, her return from the dead also symbolised the hope that human beings could live on in a blissful life after death. Isocrates captures this hope in the following lines:

> 'When Demeter came to our land ... she gave us two supreme gifts, grain and the holy rite, which brings its initiates more joyful hopes about the end of life and eternity.'
>
> Isocrates 4.28

Demeter and Eleusis

The *Homeric Hymn to Demeter*, which recounts the myth of Persephone's abduction, explains the importance of the town of Eleusis to the story. As Demeter roamed the earth in mourning for her lost child, she disguised herself as an old woman and came to Eleusis. Here King Celeus and Queen Metaneira welcomed her and appointed her as a nurse to their youngest son, Demophoön.

Without revealing her identity, the goddess tried to make the small boy immortal by placing him over a fire every night. However, one night Metaneira saw this happening and screamed out loud. Demeter, greatly angered by the lack of trust shown in her by Metaneira, revealed her divinity to the king and queen. She would no longer allow Demophoön to become immortal but, because the family had treated her well, she still promised them blessings in their mortal lifetimes. She ordered them to build a temple in her honour. In turn, the goddess taught the secrets of fertility to another son, Triptolemos, and instituted the festival of the sacred Mysteries (to be held on an annual basis). As the *Homeric Hymn* (476) explains:

> 'To the Kings of Eleusis Demeter showed the conduct of her rites and taught them her mysteries, awful mysteries which no one can transgress or utter.'

Triptolemos, holding stalks of grain, sits on a wheeled, winged throne. Demeter (left) and Persephone, holding torches, attend his departure to spread knowledge of agriculture among mortals.

1. The participants

Initiation into the Eleusinian Mysteries was open to a wide variety of people. In fact, there were only two conditions for initiation:

- Initiates had to be Greek speakers.
- Murderers who had not purified themselves were banned.

One of the astonishing things here is that the cult ignored the normal hierarchies of Greek society and was equally open to groups who were typically marginalised: women, slaves and non-citizens. All initiates, known as *mystai*, were assigned a spiritual guide (*mystagôgos*), who led them through the process of initiation.

Initiation came in three stages. Initiates first had to undergo a 'lesser initiation' at an earlier festival known as the Lesser Mysteries held at Agrae (less than a mile south-west of Athens) some seven months before the Eleusinian Mysteries. The main initiation then took place at Eleusis in September. Initiates who wished to reach the highest level of initiation could return any subsequent year, after which they were known as *epoptai* (literally: 'those who have seen closer').

The cult had its own chief priest, known as the **Hierophant** ('the revealer of sacred things'). He oversaw the initiation ceremony; he alone was allowed to enter the most sacred room in the sanctuary where the sacred objects, the **hiera**, were kept. His deputy was called the Torch-bearer and he too played an important role, which included lighting the sanctuary. The priests wore elaborate and colourful clothing for the ceremonies.

2. The festival

The festival itself was administered at Athens as a state festival by the king archon (see p. 178). In practice, however, it was led and run by the priests of the sanctuary at Eleusis. On the eve of the festival the *hiera* were boxed up and escorted in procession from Eleusis to the Athenian agora, where they were placed in the *Eleusinion*, a temple to Demeter.

Days 1-4: Athens

The first four days of the festival took place in and around Athens. On the first day all the participants gathered in the agora to hear the Hierophant make a formal invitation to the initiates. At this stage the initiates paid their fees, which were sometimes quite substantial. In the 4th century, evidence suggests that it cost 15 drachmas to enrol. A large slice of the funds must been spent on organising the festival and maintaining the sanctuary.

The second day of the festival was one of purification. The initiates journeyed the five miles down to the old harbour at Phaleron (see p. 270), where they walked into the sea carrying a piglet (the animal most sacred to Demeter). Since sea-water was believed to have purifying powers, this ritual was believed to purify both the initiate and the animal. After this sea-bath, the piglet was sacrificed to the Two Goddesses (Demeter and Persephone) and the initiate sprinkled with its blood. The following day was probably set aside for public sacrifices in Athens, which was followed in turn by a day of remaining indoors for contemplation.

Days 5-9: Eleusis

The grand procession from Athens to Eleusis took place on the fifth day and would have lasted well into the evening. At its head was a statue of a boy god, Iacchos, carrying a torch; it was followed by priestesses carrying the *hiera*. The rest of the crowd was made up of initiates who wore garlands of myrtle as well as carrying *bakchoi*, branches of myrtle tied with wool; they also carried on a stick their provisions, items such as bedding and clothing. This must have been a lively and colourful procession, with participants dancing to the music of flute players and stopping to chant ritual obscenities and shout 'Iacche' in exultation. Upon arrival at Eleusis, the *hiera* were handed back to the Hierophant.

Artist's impression of the sanctuary of the two goddesses Demeter and Persephone at Eleusis as it might have appeared in the 5th century. The *telestêrion* is in the centre. The procession entered by the gate at the top of the picture.

Artist's impression of the inside of the *telestêrion*. Its roof was supported by more than 20 columns. The *anaktoron* is in the centre, with the throne of the Hierophant to the left.

During the hours of daylight on the sixth day the participants rested and fasted, so imitating Demeter's fast after the abduction of Persephone. The main event came that evening: initiation into the Great Mysteries. This took place in the Sanctuary of the Two Goddesses in Eleusis. At the heart of this sanctuary was a large building (51m²) called the *telestêrion* (the hall of initiation), which held thousands of worshippers. In the middle of the *telestêrion* was the holiest room of all, the *anaktoron*, which housed the *hiera*.

The initiates would break their fast by drinking a sacred drink made up of barley, water and pennyroyal mint leaves. Thereafter, little is known of what took place, except that it was divided into three areas: **things said, things done** and **things revealed**. The threefold nature of the Mysteries is captured in the following quotation of Sophocles:

> 'How three times blessed are those who pass to Hades after seeing these Mysteries; for only to them is it given to have life there, but to others all is evil there.'
> Sophocles, fr. 837

Initiates were forbidden to discuss what had taken place, even amongst themselves; those who flouted this rule were liable to prosecution and the death sentence. At the end of the ceremony, an all-night feast took place, accompanied by merriment and dancing.

Thereafter the festival wound down quietly. The seventh day was one of rest, while on the eighth rites were held for the dead, including the pouring of libations. On the ninth and final day of the festival the participants would make their way, no doubt wearily, back to Athens.

3. The evidence

So what did happen in the initiation ceremony? In truth, we shall probably never know; some of the main sources on the topic are written by early Christians who wished to discredit what they saw as 'pagan' festivities. However, some writers do offer hints.

According to Aristotle, no secret doctrine was taught, but at the culmination of the Mysteries there was simply 'an experience' and a 'changing of one's state of mind'. Proclus, writing in the 5th century CE, said that some *mystai* 'experienced panic, being filled with divine awe; others assimilate themselves to the holy symbols, leave their own identity, become at home with the gods, and experience divine possession.' This sense of leaving oneself behind was echoed by another *mystês*: 'I came out of the mystery hall feeling a stranger to myself.'

However, the most intriguing passage belongs to the historian Plutarch, who imagines that the process of dying might be similar to initiation into the Eleusinian Mysteries:

1. *Greek Religion*

'Wandering astray in the beginning, tiresome walking in circles, some frightening paths in darkness that lead to nowhere; then, immediately before the end, all the terrible things – panic and shivering, sweat and amazement. And then some wonderful light comes to meet you, pure regions and meadows are there to greet you, with sounds and dances and solemn, sacred words and holy views.' Plutarch, fr. 168

Two things stand out here. The first is that, in great contrast to conventional Greek beliefs, the view of death is so optimistic. Secondly, the description of the 'wonderful light' and what follows it is strikingly similar to descriptions by those today who, drawn from many different cultural and religious backgrounds, claim to have had 'near-death experiences', something which only adds to the mystery of Eleusis.

Review 7

1. Define the following words: *anaktoron, epoptai, hiera, hierophant, mystagôgos, mystêrion, mystês, telestêrion.*
2. Why do you think the Eleusinian Mysteries held such an appeal for so many people in ancient Greece?
3. Draw up a table listing the similarities and differences between the Eleusinian Mysteries and traditional Greek religion.
4. In what ways might the Eleusinian Mysteries be thought more similar to a modern religion than to traditional Greek religion?
5. What do you think might have happened in the initiation ceremony?
R. Read lines 316-459 of Aristophanes' *Frogs*. What can we learn about the Eleusinian Mysteries from this passage?
E. Imagine you are initiated into the Mysteries. Describe your experience of the entire nine-day festival.

IX. BELIEF AND SCEPTICISM

Historically, all religions have undergone periods when their fundamental beliefs have been questioned and challenged. Such periods often allow a religion to incorporate new and progressive insights into its thinking. One example would be the Catholic Church's eventual acceptance that the earth did rotate around the sun, a view it denounced as heretical when Galileo first put it forward in the 17th century.

Since Greek religion had no scripture and was largely accepted as a part of life, it generally managed to evolve successfully as social customs changed. However, the gods came under increasing scrutiny during Greece's intellectual revolution in the 6th and 5th centuries, a period comparable to the 18th century Enlightenment in Europe and North America.

The Presocratics and the sophists

By the 5th century Greece was witnessing an intellectual revolution the like of which had never been seen before. This had originally developed in the Greek colonies in Ionia (see map 2) and involved men asking profound questions about the world around them. The greatest intellectual figure in this enlightenment was Socrates (*c.* 470-399) and those thinkers who came before him are therefore known as the **Presocratics**.

A leading light in this revolution was Xenophanes of Colophon who lived in the second half of the 6th century. He in particular was unimpressed with the traditional view of the gods. His main complaint was that people made the gods in their own image: 'The Ethiopians say their gods are snub-nosed and black-skinned, the Thracians that they are blue-eyed and red-haired.' From this, he went on to surmise that:

> 'If oxen or horses or lions had hands or could paint a picture and create works of art like men, horses would draw pictures of gods like horses, oxen pictures of gods like oxen, and each species would make the body of its gods in accordance with its own appearance.'
> DK 21 fr. 15

Yet Xenophanes was no atheist. He just believed that the traditional view of the gods was misplaced and short-sighted. Instead, Xenophanes believed in 'one god, one who is greatest among gods and among men who has neither a body nor a mind that resembles that of mortals.'

A development in this revolution came with the arrival of the **sophists** (see p. 142), who set themselves up as professional teachers of the new learning. They too developed important arguments about the nature of the gods. One delightful expression of agnosticism came from the sophist Protagoras (*c.* 485-415), who claimed that:

> 'Concerning the gods I am unable to discover whether they exist or not; there are many obstacles to knowledge: the obscurity of the subject and the brevity of human life.'
> DK 80 fr. B4

As a result, Protagoras famously claimed that 'man is the measure of all things'; in other words, a person should rely on his own experience to make judgements about the world and should not base his values on gods whose existence could not be proved.

Another sophist of the period was Anaxagoras (*c.* 500-428), a close associate of the Athenian politician Pericles (see p. 196). He was successfully prosecuted at Athens for claiming that the sun was not a god but rather a fiery ball of iron. His story seems startlingly similar to the 17th century dispute between the Catholic Church and Galileo.

At the heart of the new learning was the great thinker **Socrates**, whose dialogues have been preserved in the writings of two of his disciples, Plato and Xenophon. Socrates was an active citizen of Athens during the turbulent years of the Peloponnesian War who frequently attracted rage and frustration from the city's leaders for his wish to question everything. Indeed, he once described himself as the 'gadfly' of Athens, who set out to expose the falsehoods of the city.

Socrates' influence at Athens was so great that when the comic playwright Aristophanes wrote a play (*Clouds*) satirising the new learning of the sophists, Socrates was the central character. Socrates claimed that this depiction was unfair since, unlike the sophists, he did not charge any money for his services. However, he was brought to trial for 'corrupting the young' and 'disbelieving in the traditional gods'. Found guilty, he was sentenced to death and forced to drink hemlock.

Yet, upon receiving his sentence, Socrates is described by Plato as calmly addressing the jury which had convicted him, full of hope about the moral order of the universe and the role the gods play in it:

'You too, Gentlemen of the Jury, must look forward to death with confidence, and fix your minds on this one belief, which is certain: that nothing can harm a good man either in life or in death, and his fortunes are not a matter of indifference to the gods.' Plato, *Apology* 41c-d

---

Review 8

1. Why do you think that religions have often had great problems with new and radical ideas?
2. Are there people or movements today who question traditional beliefs in the way the Presocratics and sophists did?
3. Do you agree with Protagoras that we can never find out for sure if a God or gods exist? If so, what are the consequences of this?
4. Do you agree with Xenophanes that people make their gods in their own image?

2

The Ancient Olympic Games

I. THE SACRED GAMES

The single most remarkable fact about the ancient Olympic Games is that they were held as a religious festival. For a Greek male, the journey to Olympia every four years was a pilgrimage which culminated in the worship and celebration of Zeus, the king of the gods. At the heart of Olympia was a holy sanctuary, the Altis, where Zeus had been worshipped long before athletic contests were held. The five day Olympic festival was full of sacrifices and religious symbols, most notably the victor's crown of olive. It is impossible to grasp the meaning of these games without understanding them as a religious event.

In fact, they were just one of four great religious festival games in the Greek world. These were the only major games where prizes were just symbolic wreaths and the competitors fought merely for honour. Religion was central to all four and so collectively they were known as the 'Sacred Games'.

Games	Location	First held	Sacred to	Wreath
Olympic	Olympia	776	Zeus	olive
Pythian	Delphi	586	Apollo	laurel
Isthmian	Corinth	582	Poseidon	pine
Nemean	Nemea	573	Zeus	wild celery

Together these games formed a grand athletic quartet, known as the *Periodos*, or 'Circuit' (similar sporting quartets exist today: tennis has four Grand Slam tournaments, golf the four Majors). However, there is no doubt that the Greeks considered those at Olympia to be the greatest, a belief powerfully expressed by the poet Pindar:

'Just as the sun shines brighter than any other star, so shines Olympia, putting all other games into the shade.'   Pindar, *Olympian* 1.1ff.

It may seem strange to us that sporting competition was so closely linked to religious worship. However, the Greeks believed that winners had divine support, and great athletes were hero-worshipped as if they were gods. Moreover, Greeks thought that their gods existed with perfect human bodies and could perform super-human tasks; the feats of a champion athlete came closest to matching this ideal. Greek mythology is also full of heroes and heroines who display great athletic talent – athletic excellence was a key part of a hero's nature.

A further link between athletics and religion was the practice of funeral games. In book 23 of the *Iliad*, Achilles holds such games to commemorate the life of Patroclus and to give him a suitable send-off to the Underworld. We also hear of funeral games for Oedipus while, as we shall see, some believed that the Olympic festival started with funeral games commemorating Pelops' victory over Oinomaos.

Panhellenic politics

A key feature of the Sacred Games was that they were *panhellenic*. This meant that they were open to any Greek in the known world. Greek colonists from beyond the Greek mainland particularly valued a trip to the Sacred Games; it was a way for them to preserve their Greek identity and to promote the reputation of their colony. Many of the great Olympic victors came from cities spread far and wide around the Mediterranean and Black Seas.

Politics were therefore an important element at the games. In fact, the entire site of Olympia was littered with political memorabilia since cities often chose this panhellenic site to parade their successes. Many monuments were built to thank the gods for military victories, while twelve treasuries to the north of the Altis were symbols of the wealth and success of their respective cities (see p. 62).

Every important city sent a delegation of ambassadors to the games; diplomacy and political discussion must have been ever-present. Indeed, these official delegations often put on splendid shows of wealth, such as hosting banquets for spectators. In 416, Alcibiades led the Athenian delegation and was also the victor in the chariot race. That evening, he laid on such a sumptuous banquet that he was able to feed everyone at the games. Alcibiades later argued in the Athenian assembly that this display of wealth had strengthened the image of Athens in the Greek world.

---

1. The evidence

Throughout this chapter, references are made to some of the most important sources for the Olympic Games. The main evidence is drawn from the following:

- **Pindar** (*c.* 518-438). A winning athlete in the 6th and 5th centuries would often commission a poem to celebrate his victory at one of the Sacred Games. Such poems were called *epinicians* (or 'victory odes') and the genre's most famous poet was Pindar. His poetry often tells us a great deal about individual contests, such as the date and name of the winner, or even the reception given to him upon returning home in glory.

- **Pausanias** lived during the 2nd century CE and wrote a *Guidebook to Greece*, a traveller's guide which contained extensive details about sites such as Olympia. He is our main source for what Olympia looked like in ancient times. However, by his time of writing the games were over eight centuries old, and so we should not assume that he speaks for their whole history.
- **Art**. Works of art often give important details about of an athletic event; for example, two important statues are Myron's 'discus-thrower' and the 'Delphic charioteer'. Moreover, many events were depicted by ancient painters, most notably on Panathenaic amphorae, awarded to victors in the Panathenaic Games in Athens (see pp. 31-2).
- **Archaeology**. The site at Olympia was excavated between 1875 and 1881 by a team of German archaeologists. The foundations of most of the key buildings were brought to light for the first time in fourteen centuries and corresponded closely to the account of Pausanias. Moreover, the many artefacts gave further information about the use of the site.

2. The origins of the games

Although the first recorded games took place at Olympia in 776, it is almost certain that some form of local festival was taking place at the site for years before this date. At some point it developed into a gathering which attracted Greeks from ever further afield.

This expansion is indicated by the list of victors. Between 776 and 696 the winners came almost exclusively from the Peloponnese. Throughout the 7th century Athens and Sparta provided most of the winners, but during the 6th century the net widened considerably to include many athletes from the rest of Greece and particularly the Greek colonies of southern Italy and Sicily. In the later years of the games, the cities of Asia Minor were the most successful.

True to their culture, the Greeks told various legends to explain the origins of the games, and did not seem to mind that they did not always correspond to one another. In particular, the two most important stories – those of Heracles and Pelops – offered alternative versions of who founded the games. As we shall see, both legends were given prominence at the site of Olympia.

Pelops and Hippodamia

The hero Pelops, who gave his name to the Peloponnese (literally: 'the island of Pelops'), was a prince from Asia Minor who wanted to marry Hippodamia, the daughter of King Oinomaos of Pisa (a town near Olympia). Oinomaos had been warned by an oracle that he was fated to die after his daughter's wedding and therefore tried to prevent her marriage. A brilliant charioteer, Oinomaos would challenge each of Hippodamia's suitors to a chariot race, stating that the first to beat him would win her hand. However, the cost of

Pelops and Hippodamia in a four-horse chariot.

defeat for a suitor was death – thirteen had died before Pelops'
challenge.

Pelops devised a clever plan to beat the king. He bribed Oinomaos'
servant Myrtilos to replace the bronze linchpins of the king's chariot
with linchpins made of wax. When Oinomaos was about to pass Pelops
in the race, the wax melted and he was thrown out of the chariot to his
death. Pelops married Hippodamia and instituted the Olympic Games,
perhaps as funeral games in memory of Oinomaos.

Some Greeks were uncomfortable with this image of the founding
hero winning by cheating. Pindar even wrote a version of the myth
in which Pelops won the race with the help of divine horses, the gift
of Poseidon.

Heracles and the Augean Stables

The alternative myth concerns Heracles, the greatest hero in Greek
mythology, whose fifth labour was to clean the stables of King
Augeas of Elis. Heracles promised Augeas that he would clean the
stables for the price of one-tenth of the king's cattle. However, when
he completed the labour successfully, Augeas went back on his word.
In revenge, Heracles sacked the city of Elis and instituted the
Olympic Games in honour of his father, Zeus. He introduced both
athletic events and chariot races and, so the story went, was the
first to measure out the length of the stadium at Olympia, marking
out a distance of six hundred paces. Heracles was also credited with
planting the sacred olive tree which later provided the victory
wreaths for Olympic winners.

Review 1

1. Define the following: *epinician, Panathenaic amphorae, panhellenic, periodos.*
2. Why do you think that both ancient and modern sporting cultures have chosen to create a 'special quartet' of tournaments?
3. To what extent do politics affect modern sports? Ought they to do so?
4. In your opinion, how reliable are each of the main sources for the games?
5. What do the foundation myths of (i) Pelops; (ii) Heracles, suggest about the games? Why do you think these stories were so important to the Greeks?
6. Are there any myths associated with modern sports? What do they suggest about the sports?
R. Read Herodotus, *Histories* 8.26. What does this (Greek) account of a Persian conversation suggest about the Greek attitude to the Sacred Games?

II. THE SITE OF OLYMPIA

The archaeological evidence suggests that Zeus was worshipped at Olympia from the 10th century, long before any significant athletic games were held there. One can easily see why the Greeks associated this place with their greatest god. It was an unusually green and fertile part of Greece, teeming with springs, groves, rivers and vegetation, and must have seemed an oasis of beauty in the harsh Greek landscape – an oasis worthy of Zeus himself.

Zeus and Olympia

The Greeks told a myth to explain the god's presence at Olympia. One day Zeus looked out all over Greece from Mt Olympos (see map 4), trying to find its most beautiful spot. When he saw the grove in what is now the heart of Olympia, he hurled a thunderbolt down to establish it as a sanctuary for his worship. Olympia was therefore named after Zeus Olympios (Zeus who reigns on Mt Olympos). The altar of Zeus in the Altis marked the place where the thunderbolt struck the ground.

Olympia itself was never inhabited as a town or village; it simply remained a sanctuary with religious and sporting buildings where pilgrims flocked every four years. It was located in the north-western Peloponnese at the convergence of two rivers, the Alpheios and the Kladeos (see map 4). The Alpheios was navigable, which meant that the sanctuary could be easily reached from the sea.

For most of its history, the sanctuary was under the control of Elis, the largest city in the region. It was Elis which ran the Olympic festival, maintained the sanctuary, provided all the judges and hosted the competitors for the month leading up to the games. Aside from these responsibilities, Elis was a relatively small and insignificant state in the Greek world. As a result, other cities did not feel threatened by Elis becoming too powerful because of its Olympic duties.

1. The Altis

At the heart of the site was a religious sanctuary known as the Altis (you can read more about religious sanctuaries on p. 16). The site had

An aerial photograph of Olympia today, where the wooded Hill of Kronos still looks down over the site.

originally been a sacred grove and the name Altis was derived from the Greek word for grove, *alsos*. The area was to the south of the cone-like Hill of Kronos (the father of Zeus) and surrounded by a stone wall. There were three entrances into the Altis, two to the west and one to the south.

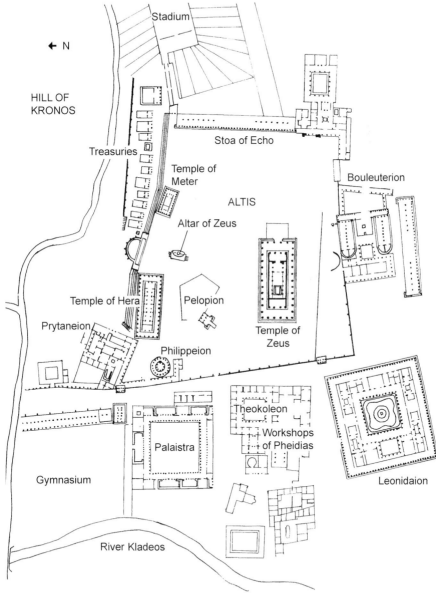

A plan of ancient Olympia.

Only religious buildings were found inside the enclosure itself; various other important buildings lay outside. As well as the temples and shrines, the Altis contained many altars for sacrifices together with hundreds of statues of Olympic victors. The Roman Pliny the Elder, writing in the second half of the 1st century CE, estimated that there were about 3,000 statues in the Altis when he visited!

The Temple of Zeus

The Temple of Zeus was the centrepiece of the Altis. It was considered to be one the finest examples of the Doric order in the Greek world. The temple was designed by Libon, an architect from Elis, and was completed at some point between 470 and 456. It was surrounded by six columns to the front and back and thirteen columns on either side. Its base measured 64.1 by 27.7 metres.

An artist's impression of the Temple of Zeus in the Altis. To the right is the huge altar of Zeus.

The temple was remarkable not just for its size, but also for the artwork adorning it. The east pediment was decorated with a frieze depicting the beginning of the chariot race between Pelops and Oinomaos, with Zeus judging, while on the west pediment was depicted the battle between the Lapiths and the Centaurs. The metopes (the panels which ran above the columns along the sides of the temple) carried reliefs depicting the Twelve Labours of Heracles. A statue of Nike, the winged goddess of victory, crowned the apex of the east pediment. The roof was made of marble tiles, together with water spouts shaped like lion heads.

Inside the temple was one of the seven wonders of the ancient world – an ivory and gold cult statue of Zeus. Although nothing of the statue survives, Pausanias has left us a detailed description:

'The god is seated on his throne. He is made of gold and ivory, and on his head is a wreath representing sprays of olive. In his right hand stands a figure of Victory, also of gold and ivory ... in his left hand is a sceptre, skilfully wrought from a variety of metals. The bird perched on the sceptre is an eagle. The sandals of the god are golden, and so is his robe, which is decorated with animals and lilies.'

Pausanias, *Guidebook to Greece* 5.11.1-2

An artist's impression of the giant cult statue of Zeus. As is suggested in this image, visitors could apparently go up to an upper floor to gain a better view.

The statue, which was about 13 metres high, was created by the famous Athenian sculptor Pheidias in 430. He was given a set of workshops to build his masterpiece and the remains of these can still be seen just outside the Altis to the west.

Other holy sites

Near the Temple of Zeus stood the **sacred olive tree** and the **altar of Zeus**. No trace of the altar survives today – it was simply a huge mound of ash (with an estimated height of between 6 and 7 metres), created by countless sacrifices made over hundreds of years.

The **Temple of Hera** was actually the oldest building in the Altis, and was perhaps originally dedicated to both Zeus and Hera. There was a festival to Hera with games for women at Olympia, and female victors were allowed to add dedication plaques to the columns of the temple (see pp. 86-7). The temple also housed the bronze discus inscribed with the Sacred Truce, and an ivory and gold table where the olive crowns given to the athletic victors were laid out.

The **Pelopion** was a funeral mound at the tomb of Pelops. It was an open air shrine dedicated to the founding hero and was located right next to the Temple of Hera on the south side. It was surrounded by a pentagonal wall with an elaborate gatehouse. Another temple within the Altis was the small **Temple of Meter** which was built in the 4th century and dedicated to the goddess Cybele, who was often worshipped as an eastern version of Rhea, the wife of Kronos and mother of Zeus.

The **Philippeion** was commissioned by Philip II of Macedon to commemorate both his victory over the Greeks at Chaeronea in 338 and his many victories in the Olympic chariot-races. It was a circular building housing gold and ivory statues of all of the Macedonian kings. Philip died in 336 before it was completed, but his son, Alexander the Great, ensured that it was finished after his death.

On the north side of the Altis were the **Treasuries.** These small but ornate buildings were constructed by different Greek cities over the years to house their dedications to the sanctuary, as well as to display and keep safe their treasures. The remains of twelve buildings have been found, ten of which were built by Greek colonies outside the mainland, illustrating the importance of the games to the Greek communities spread far from Greece itself.

In front of the Treasuries could be found the **Zanes**; these were sixteen bronze statues of Zeus funded from the fines of those competitors who had cheated in the games. They depicted Zeus about to hurl his thunderbolt and served as a warning to competitors of the dangers of breaking the Olympic oath!

A model reconstruction of the Altis. The twelve treasuries are clearly visible on the far side of the sanctuary.

2. Outside the Altis

Just outside the north-west corner of the Altis and right next to the Temple of Hera was the **Prytaneion.** This is where the Olympic Council, chosen from the aristocracy of Elis, lived and worked during the games. It also had a special room for the sacred hearth with its eternal flame to Hestia (the goddess of the hearth – see p. 13). In addition, there was a banquet hall where feasts were held for Olympic victors.

To the south side of the Altis was the **Bouleuterion** or Council House. This is where the council would meet to organise the games. The archives of past games were also kept here. It contained an altar to Zeus Horkios (Zeus protector of oaths), where the athletes and judges would come at the beginning of the games to take an oath to obey the rules of the Olympic competition. To the west of the Bouleuterion was the **Leonidaion**, which was the only 'hotel' at Olympia. Named after Leonidas of Naxos, the architect who funded and designed it in the 4th century, it was reserved for distinguished visitors, such as officials of the games or representatives from Greek cities. At its heart was a beautiful inner courtyard.

To the west of the Altis were two buildings which emphasised the importance of religion at Olympia: **Pheidias' workshops** and the **Theokoleon**. The latter was a house for priests to meet and work. Near these buildings could be found bathing facilities and a swimming pool, installed in the 5th century.

The stadium

To the east, the Altis was separated from the stadium by the **Stoa of Echo**. This colonnade took its name from the fact that a voice was said to echo seven times along the walls. It was also called the Painted Colonnade, owing to the fact that it was adorned with paintings in the 4th century. The Stoa contained the 32 metre long entrance tunnel into the stadium, from which the arrival of the athletes must have caused a roar similar to the noise heard when footballers or rugby players enter a modern stadium.

Looking through the entrance tunnel into the stadium.

During the earliest Olympic Games there was no designated stadium; athletes simply used the flat ground to the east of the altar of Zeus. A line was drawn in the sand to denote the starting point for races and spectators would have stood and watched from the Hill of Kronos. The first stadium was built in about 560 to the east of the Altis, and this was updated in about 350 by a superb new edifice, which may have held a crowd of up to 45,000 spectators. The starting line for the races was marked by a stone sill, which can still be seen in place today.

The starting sill in the stadium, with grooves for the runners' toes.

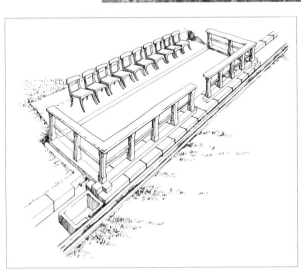

An artist's impression of the stand (*exhedra*) of the judges. The space in front of the seats may have been used in the prize-giving ceremony.

65

The ordinary spectator had to make do with finding a seat on one of the banks around the track. There was one seating area on the south side, the stand (*exhedra*) of the judges. In front of this was a walkway, where palms were probably awarded after the races. On the opposite side of the stadium there was a seat and altar for the priestess of Demeter Chamyne, the only woman allowed to view the games.

The hippodrome

The equestrian events were all held in the hippodrome, which literally meant 'the horse track'. This was located to the south of the stadium, although no evidence for it remains as it was washed away during the Middle Ages by flooding from the river Alpheios. However, Pausanias tells us that the track was about 600 metres long and 200 metres wide. As at the stadium, there was an enclosure for judges, which was located on the north-west side of the arena.

3. Later buildings

During the 3rd century, new buildings appeared to the north-west of the site. The **palaistra** was an exercise area for wrestlers, boxers and jumpers; it contained a central courtyard surrounded by a colonnade, behind which were changing rooms for the athletes. To the north of the palaistra was the **gymnasium**, which was in the shape of a large rectangle (120 x 220 metres). It contained a running track exactly the same length as the stadium, enabling runners to train for their events. It was also used as a space for practising the field events such as the discus or the javelin.

Review 2

1. Define the following: *Altis, exhedra, Olympia, Zanes.*
2. To what extent do you think the buildings at Olympia are concerned with the athletic events?
3. What can we learn about the Greek attitude to the games from the site of Olympia?
4. Design a brochure describing the main buildings at Olympia.
5. Are there any sites in the modern world comparable to Oympia?
R. The statue of Zeus was one of the seven wonders of the ancient world. What were the other six? Who drew up the list of wonders?
E. Imagine you are visiting the games at Olympia for the first time. Write an imaginary letter to your relatives describing what you find there.

III. THE EVENTS

The events contested at Olympia fall naturally into four categories: **track, equestrian, combat** and the **pentathlon**. In addition to the adult events, the games also had competitions for boys: they had to be between the ages of 12 and 18, but as there were no birth certificates, it was left to the judges to decide if a youth was a boy or a man.

Nudity

One notable difference from the modern Olympic Games was the nudity of the competitors. In fact, Greeks were well used to exercising naked, since men trained naked at their local gymnasium. Indeed, the Greek word for naked was *gymnos*, and therefore the word 'gymnasium' can literally be translated as 'the place to go naked'. Similarly, the Greek verb *gymnasdein*, which meant 'to exercise', can be translated as 'to go naked'.

Pausanias relates a legend that the practice of nudity at Olympia had started at the Games of 720, when Orsippos of Megara won the stadion. During the race his loin-cloth apparently fell off, but he carried on to cross the line first. Pausanias actually adds his own suspicion that Orsippos had allowed the loin-cloth to fall in order to help him run faster.

The practice of competing in the nude does seem to make sense. Clothes can be cumbersome in some sports, a fact which modern sprinters try to overcome by using body suits. Moreover, since the Greeks believed that a strong and beautiful body was 'godlike' it was therefore fitting that their greatest athletes proudly showed off their full form.

---

1. Track events

Races were run from one end of the stadium to the other. The track itself was merely a mixture of earth and sand, with a stone kerb round the edge. A key difference from modern track events was that races were all run on the straight, rather than on a curved track. It is believed that each end of the track had a turning post to ensure that the runners completed the correct distance.

Starting lines were built in the 5th century (to replace the earlier practice of drawing a line in the sand) and these can still be clearly seen. Stone blocks run from one side of the track to the other. The blocks have grooves in them for feet (each pair of grooves was 18 cm apart), as well as holes to hold the posts (175 cm apart) which acted to mark out starting lanes. At Olympia, there were 12 starting lanes. The races were started by a loud blast from a trumpeter – and he would blast again if there had been a false start. The four running events are listed below, together with the year in which they were first contested in the Olympic Games:

A Panathenaic amphora
depicting five sprinters.

An armed runner with
helmet and shield.

- **Stadion** (776). This was the only event at the games for the first thirteen Olympiads and was therefore considered the most important Olympic event. Each Olympiad was named after the winner of the stadion, which consisted of a sprint from one end of the stadium to the other, a distance of 192.27 metres.
- **Diaulos** (724). This was double the length of the stadion, racing from one end of the stadium to the other and then back again.
- **Dilochos** (720). This was a long distance race, although the exact length is unclear. It is most likely to have been 20 or 24 lengths of the track. As this was a longer race, it was less spectacular to watch and so was often

the first of the track events, which would build up to the exciting sprint events.

- **Hoplitodromos** (520). This is also known as the 'race-in-armour'. Twenty-five runners raced the length of a diaulos (two stadia) with a helmet, greaves (lower-leg armour), and a round shield. The shields were kept in the Temple of Zeus.

2. Equestrian events

Horse racing today is known as the 'sport of kings' and the same was true in the Greek world. Chariot races were often associated with the noble heroes of Greek myth; as we have seen, many believed that the Olympic Games were instituted after the victory of Pelops in a chariot race, while in Book 23 of the *Iliad* the funeral games for Patroclus feature a chariot race between some of the Greek heroes.

Only the wealthiest could afford the costs associated with the equestrian events (training stables of horses, paying for chariots and equipment, etc). Therefore the winner's crown was not awarded to the jockey or charioteer, but to the owner of the horses. It was very unusual for owners to ride their own horses (for one thing, it was very dangerous and risked death or serious injury) and so they would hire riders and pay them a modest amount. It is rare to hear of a rider who is given credit for a victory.

Two jockeys ride in a horse race.

The equestrian events were therefore the one area of the Olympic Games where a wealthy person could effectively 'buy' himself – or herself – a victory. In 396 Kyniska, a princess from Sparta, was the first woman to be awarded an Olympic wreath after her horses won the four-horse chariot race. She then repeated the feat in the following Olympiad of 392.

The most important chariot race was the **tethrippon** (680), in which four-horse chariots raced over twelve circuits. Charioteers had to be very resilient – there was no suspension on the chariots and so traversing the bumpy track could have thrown them in any direction. The **keles** (648) was the major horse race, during which fully grown horses had to cover six stadia, about 1,200 metres. Ancient jockeys had neither a saddle nor stirrups, although they were allowed to use a whip on the horses.

The equestrian events were obviously particularly popular with the spectators as they had a high 'blood and guts' factor. Races were held at great speed and many accidents occurred as competitors rounded the turning post. At this point they could be thrown from their seats, crushed, or trampled underfoot by oncoming horses. The Greek doctor Galen wrote of riding injuries in the 2nd century CE:

'Strenuous horse-back riding has been known to rupture parts in the region of the kidneys, and has often brought injuries to the chest or sometimes to the spermatic passages – to say nothing of the missteps of the horses, because of which riders have often been pitched from their seat and instantly killed.'   Galen: Kühn 5.902ff.

Further reading

There are two famous passages from Greek literature which describe a chariot race. Read Homer, *Iliad* 23.262-650 and Sophocles, *Electra* lines 680-763. What can we learn about the sport from these passages?

---

3. Combat events

The combat or 'heavy' events were **wrestling** (708), **boxing** (688) and the **pankration** (648). They differed from modern combat events in the fact that there were no weight divisions; therefore heavier athletes usually had a great advantage. These events were all controlled by one of the judges of the games, the *hellanodikai* (see p. 82), who carried a forked stick to separate contestants when necessary. Unlike modern wrestling and boxing bouts, contests were not divided into rounds to give the athletes respite – the event just continued until one man won.

A wrestling bout is watched over by a judge.

Wrestling bouts were held in an area filled with sand. If an athlete's back or shoulders touched the ground, this constituted a 'fall'. The athlete who managed to 'fall' his opponent three times won the fight. However, it was hard for wrestlers to get a grip on one another because they would cover themselves in oil before the fight. Contestants were allowed to trip, but not to bite, gouge, or punch.

Boxing was considered the most dangerous sport of them all. One key difference from modern boxing was that competitors did not wear real 'boxing gloves'. Instead, they wrapped leather thongs – called *himantes* – around their hands, which were designed to protect not the opponent but simply the knuckles of the wearer. Another important difference from modern boxing was the lack of a ring, which meant that there was no opportunity to corner opponents as today. Victory was won either when one contestant was knocked unconscious or when a contestant conceded defeat by holding up a hand with an uplifted finger. It seems that most blows were to the head, and boxers were allowed to use the punch, the slap and the back of the hand. No wrestling or holding was allowed, but competitors were allowed to hit a fallen opponent. Boxers often needed great stamina – if no knock-out blow occurred, bouts could last for hours.

Pankration meant 'total power', and it was almost a fight without rules. Indeed, the only two actions banned in the pankration were biting and the gouging of eyes. All sorts of other tactics seem to have been allowed, including breaking fingers, kicking, strangleholds and throwing. Punching was allowed but, unlike in boxing, the competitors

Two boxers slug it out. Note their *himantes* and the nosebleed!

fought with bare hands. The event was won when one competitor admitted that he could no longer continue (or was knocked unconscious). An ancient writer tells us about the different skills needed in the pankration and in wrestling:

> 'Pankratiasts ... must employ backwards falls which are not safe for the wrestler ... they must have skill in various methods of strangling; they also wrestle with an opponent's ankle and twist his arm, besides hitting and jumping on him, for all these practices belong to the pankration, only biting and gouging being excepted.'   Philostratos, *Pictures in a Gallery* 2.6

4. The pentathlon

The pentathlon (708) was very popular with spectators. It consisted of five events: **discus**, **long jump**, **javelin**, **stadion** and **wrestling**. The first three of these, the field events, were not held separately but only as part of the pentathlon. The whole contest took place in the stadium over the course of one afternoon; the pentathletes would have needed great stamina. Indeed, Aristotle said that 'the pentathletes are the best, because they are naturally endowed with both strength and speed'.

There is some debate about how the winner of the pentathlon was decided. The most popular theory is that the first man to win three events won the whole competition. Therefore the three field events were held first. If one man won all three events, then he was declared the winner and the last two events were not held. If a man had two wins from the first three events, then he would run a stadion race against the other winner. If he lost this, the two would then go on to wrestle for the prize. The first man to get three wins was declared the overall winner.

The **discus** was the first of the five events. It is likely that an ancient athlete made no more than a three-quarter turn, in contrast to the full spin of modern discus throwers. The discuses were made of stone or metal and were often marked with inscriptions.

This bowl illustrates four events from the pentathlon: discus, long jump, javelin and wrestling.

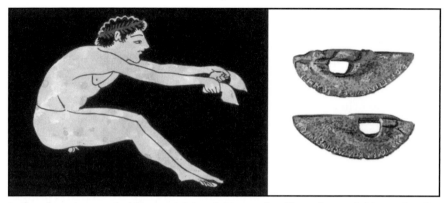

Left: a long-jumper holding weights; right: a pair of jumping weights made of stone.

Pausanias tells us that the ancient Olympic truce (see p. 77) was engraved on a discus and displayed in the Altis. The discuses which have survived range in diameter from 17 to 32 cm, while the weight ranges from 1.3 to 6.6 kg. At Olympia, three official discuses of the same weight were always used, ensuring that the throwers competed on equal terms.

The **long jump** was fundamentally different from its modern equivalent because the jumper carried two metal jumping weights, one in each hand, known as *halteres*, which weighed between 1 and 4.5 kg. The jumpers would have used these to propel themselves forward by swinging their arms back and forward to gain momentum. Experts cannot agree on whether it was a jump from a standing start or with a run-up. Some even believe that it was really more like the modern triple jump. The jumpers leapt into a rectangular sandpit in the stadium which was 15 metres long. It was important for a jumper to get his body into a rhythm for the jump. To enable this, the event was performed to the musical sound of the *aulos* (see p. 278).

The **javelin** event clearly had its origins in military training, although athletic javelins were lighter than military javelins to allow them to fly further. They were made of elder wood, normally standing about the same height as the athlete. The main difference between the ancient and modern javelin throw was the ancient use of a leather thong. This was wrapped around the javelin's shaft by the thrower, who would then hold onto one end of it. When releasing the javelin, he would flick the thong to impart side-spin, allowing the javelin to travel further and maintain a steadier flight.

If needed, the final two events in the pentathlon were the **stadion** and **wrestling**, which were held under exactly the same rules as when they took place as individual events.

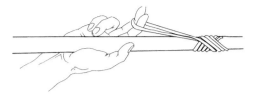

One possible method of using the leather
thong to propel a javelin.

Violence and the games

It is very striking how much violence occurred in the ancient games.
While modern combat sports such as boxing do allow for a degree of
violence, this is closely controlled to ensure that a modern competitor
does not come to any serious harm.

The opposite was true of the ancient games, where the combat and
equestrian events could sometimes result in the death of a competitor.
Two stories illustrate this. One concerns the pankratiast Arrachion of
Phigalia (a city near Olympia) who won his third Olympic title in 564,
although he died in the process! During the bout, Arrachion, while
himself being strangled, managed to dislocate his opponent's ankle. The
opponent rolled away in agony and raised his finger in admission of
defeat. At the same moment Arrachion suffocated and it was left to the
judges to award the olive wreath to his corpse.

A second story describes a boxing bout at the Nemean Games between
Creugas of Epidamnus (in north-west Greece) and Damoxenos of
Syracuse. They fought for many hours and night was falling. Therefore
they agreed to a 'climax' – a practice in which each competitor took an
uncontested blow from the other to see if they could settle the matter
with one punch. Creugas first struck Damoxenos round the head but
was unable to fell him. In reply, Damoxenos supposedly struck Creugas
under the ribs with three fingers outstretched. His sharp nails pierced
Creugas' skin and ripped out his guts, killing him on the spot. However,
the judges disqualified Damoxenos, ruling that he had used three blows
(one for each finger), and awarded the wreath to Creugas.

What are we to make of such violence? In the first place, the Greeks
were far more used to violence and death in their everyday lives. The
mortality rate was far higher, while cities were often at war during the
summer campaigning season. This might explain a second reason why
the games were so violent – many of the events probably had their
origins in the military training of soldiers and were closely linked to
warfare. Finally, it was central to the idea of a Greek hero that he should
die gloriously – by risking his life in combat, an athlete would truly
believe that he was following in the tradition of a hero like Achilles.

Review 3

1. Define the following: *gymnos, halteres, himantes.*
2. Draw up a table outlining the rules for each of the events at the games and comparing each of them to their modern equivalent.
3. Do you think that violence added to the enjoyment for a spectator at the games? To what extent is violence a part of sport today?
4. Draw up a 'match programme' for the events at an Olympic festival.
5. Find out what the following Olympic athletes are famous for: (i) Milo of Croton; (ii) Diagoras of Rhodes; (iii) Leonidas of Rhodes; (iv) Sostratos of Sicyon.
R. Read Homer *Iliad* 23.651-897 and *Odyssey* 8. What can we learn about Greek sporting contests from these passages?
E. To what extent do you think the events at the Olympic Games were associated with military training?

IV. THE OLYMPIC FESTIVAL

The Olympic festival took place every four years. It was timed so that the middle day of the festival was always the second or third full moon after the summer solstice. In practice, this meant that it was always held in mid-August or mid-September. It is perhaps strange that the games were held at the hottest time of year, but the festival may have originated from ancient harvest rites practised in these months, a theory supported by the presence of the priestess of Demeter at the games.

An Olympiad
The word 'Olympiad' was used to describe both the festival itself and the four year period between each festival. It is a measure of the importance which the Greeks attached to the games that they measured their dates by Olympiads. Therefore, the years 776-773 constitute the first Olympiad, and so forth.

Two days before the games were due to begin, there was a grand procession along a road known as the Sacred Way, which spanned the 64 km (40 miles) from Elis to Olympia. The judges led all the competitors, trainers and even the competing horses. The participants made sacrifices at various points along the route, the most important of which was the sacrifice of a pig at the fountain of Piera. They stayed overnight at Lentrinoi, a town two-thirds of the way along the route.

The Sacred Truce

All those travelling to the games were protected by the 'Sacred Truce'. The truce required that all athletes, spectators and officials be afforded safe travel to and from Olympia for a period of one month (which later increased to three). In addition, no armed men were allowed to enter the site. Some time before the games, heralds (wearing olive wreaths and carrying staffs) travelled from Elis to every corner of the Greek world to announce the truce and the date of the games.

Greeks believed that the Sacred Truce was instituted by King Iphitos of Elis, when he re-established the games (from the age of heroes) in the 9th century. He was so fed up with the wars destroying Greece that he consulted the Pythian oracle at Delphi (see p. 35ff.) to try to bring about peace. The prophetess advised him to organise games at Olympia in honour of the gods. He duly did so and made a treaty with Kleomenes of Pisa and Lycurgus of Sparta for the period of these games, the first Sacred Truce. The oracle also instructed Iphitos to award prizes from the olive tree in the heart of Olympia.

The truce was known as 'sacred' because it fell under the protection of the gods. In particular, Greeks believed that Zeus Xenios, the patron of travellers, was the guardian of all visitors to the games. It was scrupulously observed: the ancient Olympic Games were never cancelled due to warfare during their thousand year history. By contrast, war has caused the cancellation of the modern games three times (1916, 1940 and 1944) in little over a century.

The five day programme

From the 5th century, the Olympic festival was held over five days. In earlier times, a shorter period had sufficed. In fact, for the first thirteen Olympiads all the action was over in a day as the stadion was the only event. As can be seen from the table on p. 78, the five days were full of ceremonial and religious events.

Day 1 was predominantly ceremonial. The festival began with a procession to the Bouleuterion. After a boar was sacrificed at the altar of Zeus Horkios, the competitors and the judges swore their oaths. The former swore that they would do nothing to dishonour the Olympic Games and that they had been in training for ten months. The latter swore to judge fairly, take no bribes nor reveal how they had reached their decisions.

Then came the contests for heralds and trumpeters which were held by the Stoa of Echo. The winner of each competition had the honour of being the official herald or trumpeter of the games. Ancient sources tell of one remarkable trumpeter, Herodoros of Megara, who won the competition at ten consecutive Olympiads between 328 and 292. Following this, the boys' events came later in the morning and acted as a prelude to the men's events to come.

Day	Time	Event
Day 1	Morning	Swearing-in ceremony in the Bouleuterion. Contests for heralds and trumpeters. Boys' running, wrestling and boxing contests. Prayers, sacrifices and consultation of oracles.
	Afternoon	Speeches by philosophers. Recitals by poets and historians. Sight-seeing tours of the Altis.
Day 2	Morning	Procession to the hippodrome. Chariot and horse races.
	Afternoon	The pentathlon.
	Evening	Funeral rites in honour of Pelops. Parade of victors around the Altis. Communal singing of victory hymns. Feasting and revelry.
Day 3	Morning	Grand procession around the Altis followed by sacrifice of one hundred oxen to Zeus.
	Afternoon	Foot-races.
	Evening	Public banquet in the Prytaneion.
Day 4	Morning	Wrestling.
	Afternoon	Boxing and pankration. Race in armour.
Day 5	All day	Procession of victors to the Temple of Zeus. Crowning of victors by the judges. *Phyllobolia*. Feasting and celebrations.

Throughout the day, all sorts of sights and sounds were to be witnessed in the Altis. There would be many sacrifices to the gods and consultations of oracles, as people tried to win favour with the gods or glean a prediction for the approaching contests. Sightseeing tours of the Altis were held for spectators – for many it was the first time that they would have seen the magnificent architecture of its buildings. The games also took on the character of an arts festival, with speeches by philosophers and orators, as well as recitals from some of the most celebrated poets and historians of the time.

Day 2 started with a grand procession to the hippodrome, where the equestrian events took place. This was followed in the afternoon by the pentathlon, one of the most important and spectacular events of the games. More ceremonies took place in the evening, with funeral rites to honour Pelops followed by the victors parading around the Altis. Later, celebrations took a less formal turn – the feasting in honour of the victors would be accompanied by communal singing of victory hymns.

Day 3 was the day of the full moon and therefore the most sacred day of the games. In the morning a grand procession of judges, ambassadors and competitors, together with one hundred oxen, would walk to and parade around the Altis, finishing at the altar of Zeus. The oxen were then sacrificed to the god as a gift from the people of Elis – this was the most sacred moment in the entire festival. The running events in the afternoon were followed in the evening by a public banquet for victors and officials in the Prytaneion.

Day 4 was dedicated to the combat events: wrestling, boxing and the pankration. The final event of the games was the hoplitodromos, a clear reminder to everyone that the festival and its sacred truce were nearly over and that warfare might soon be upon them again.

Day 5 was set aside for the prize-giving and closing ceremony. As the victors proceeded to the temple of Zeus they would be showered with leaves and flowers by cheering spectators, an event known as the *phyllobolia*. In front of the temple of Zeus, the *hellanodikai* would read out the names of the victors, as well as their fathers and cities. The victor would then be crowned with a wreath from the sacred olive tree.

As today, this prize-giving would be the highlight of the lives of the athletes and the culmination of years of training. The religious symbols showed just how close the victors had come to the gods on Mt Olympos.

Review 4

1. Define the following: *Olympiad, phyllobolia.*
2. Design a poster advertising the programme for an Olympic festival.
3. How much of the festival was not specifically about sporting events? Do you think that this made it a more interesting and important occasion?
4. Is there anything comparable to the Sacred Truce in sport today? Do you think that it would work if there was?
5. How might the timing of the festival in the heat of the summer have had an influence on the contests, the athletes and the visitors?

V. THE ATHLETES

Winning at all costs

Ancient Greece was a highly competitive, winner-takes-all society. To the victor came extraordinary fame, an idea which is present in Greek thought from the time of Homer. In the *Odyssey*, the Phaeacian noble Laodamas greets Odysseus as follows:

> 'You must be an athlete – since nothing makes a man so famous during his lifetime as what he can achieve with his hands and feet.'
>
> Homer, *Odyssey* 8.146-8

Athletes competed for individual glory, which surely explains why there were no team events at the ancient games. In contrast to the winners, there was no place for losers. The ancient games had no silver or bronze medals, while the concept of a 'good loser' would have seemed contradictory to a Greek. Losing was seen as a disgrace. In a famous ode, Pindar speaks of the return home of defeated wrestlers:

> 'They, when they meet their mothers, have no sweet laughter around them moving delight. In back streets out of their enemies' way they cower; disaster has bitten them.'
> Pindar, *Pythian* 8.85-7

It is perhaps no wonder then that, before a contest, some competitors used to pray for 'the wreath or death'.

Agony

Two English derivations from Greek words emphasise the ruthlessness of sporting competition. The word for a competition, *agôn, gives* us the English word 'agony'. The English word 'athletics' is derived from Greek *athlos,* which meant 'a contest for a prize'. Its adjective, *athlios,* meant both 'winning the prize' and 'struggling' or 'wretched'.

Training

On the first day of the games, athletes had to swear that they had been in training for their event for the previous ten months. This emphasis on training ensured that the standard of competition was as high as possible. For the last of these months, the athletes were required to be in Elis under the supervision of the Olympic judges. At this stage, heats would be organised and the judges would attempt to sift out weak candidates before the games began.

Like modern sportsmen, ancient athletes understood that diet was particularly important for strength and fitness. The standard diet for an athlete would normally be made up of fruit, cheese, vegetables, fish and bread. Meat was not very popular, except with the combat athletes. Boxers, wrestlers and pankratiasts would eat mutton, beef, lamb or even venison to build up their muscle strength. Another key element of training was massage, which was seen as an important method of loosening up the body and treating the muscles.

Rewards

Although the prize of an olive wreath at first sight seems humble, the ultimate rewards were huge. As soon as an athlete won an event, he was given a palm branch and red ribbons were wrapped around his head. The herald then proclaimed him 'the best among the Greeks'. During the games, some winners might hold private feasts with supporters and relatives from their home city. However, the moment of greatest glory at the festival came at the prize-giving on the fifth day.

A vase painting showing an award ceremony. A bearded official ties a red ribbon round the head of a young man who wears long woollen ties round his left arm and holds a sprig of olive.

Even after the games were completed, the winners left their mark on the site. Olympic victors were allowed to erect a statue in the Altis. On the base of the statue were the names of the athlete, his father and his city, as well as the event in which he had triumphed. If a man won three Olympic victories, he could commission a statue of himself to be carved. All the winners were also entered into the official archives at the site, while, as we have seen, the winner of the stadion gave his name to the Olympiad of that year.

Perhaps the greatest moment remained for the athlete when he returned to his home city. A victorious athlete brought great glory to his city and his return would be greeted with wild excitement. Pindar talks of such fame as 'the supreme prize, the splendour of speech from citizen or stranger'. The winner was usually granted a civic reception, including a triumphant tour on a chariot through the city. There is the remarkable story of Exainetos of Akragas in Sicily, who retained his Olympic stadion title in 412. On returning home, he was escorted into Akragas by 300 chariots pulled by white horses. Many cities gave great financial rewards to winners – in Athens, they could dine at the public expense for the rest of their lives. Of course, if the victor was named in an *epinician*, he could expect his name to be remembered for years – perhaps even to the present day.

Punishments

The *hellanodikai* held great power both before and during the games. Any athlete or trainer who did not obey their instructions was liable to be whipped by the whip-bearers (*mastigophoroi*). This too was the fate which befell any runner who made a false start – he was hauled off to the side of the track and beaten there and then. The *hellanodikai* also had the power to issue fines for any breach of the rules, in particular for bribery. The Zanes on the north side of the Altis served as a powerful reminder to athletes not to break their oath to Zeus.

Review 5

1. Define the following: *agôn, athlios, magistophoroi*.
2. How does the Greek attitude to winning and losing compare to our attitude today?
3. How does the diet and training of ancient athletes compare to those of modern day athletes?
4. Why do you think that ancient winners were treated with such awe?
5. How do the possible rewards and punishments for an ancient athlete compare to those of a competitor at a major sporting event today?
6. Is there anything comparable to an *epinician* today?

VI. THE JUDGES

One very important group of people at the Olympic Games were the judges. They were known as *hellanodikai*, which literally meant 'judges of the Greeks' and always came from the city of Elis. Here we can read the story of an imaginary judge, Hippomenes of Elis, who might have judged a games at the start of the 5th century:

* * *

'My name is Hippomenes of Elis, and last year I was honoured to have been a *hellanodikês* for the 71st Olympiad [496]. Every four years, ten citizens of Elis are chosen by lot to take on this crucial task. We Eleans are very proud of the role our city plays in running the Olympic Games

– the greatest of athletic festivals. We have a great reputation throughout the Greek world for our honesty and fairness. I took my responsibilities very seriously, as is only right – we were following in the tradition of our ancient King Iphitos, who was the first judge of the games. For the ten months leading up to the games we lived in a special building in Elis which we call the *Hellanodikeon*. At this stage, the *nomophylakes* [guardians of the law] instructed us in our duties and roles for the games. We sent out the heralds to all parts of the world to proclaim the sacred truce for the period of the games, and then spent some time inspecting the site of Olympia to ensure that all the facilities were in good working order and all the religious sites were worthy of the gods whom we worship there.

'The really busy period started a month before the games began. Now all the competitors had to come to Elis for pre-games training, which it was our duty to oversee. We had full control over all the competitors, and organised "heats" to try to sift out weaker candidates who would not be good enough to meet the Olympic standard. The athletes' training was tough in this month – we put them on a strict diet and oversaw brutal exercise regimes. If either the competitors or their trainers disobeyed us then we punished them by flogging. It may sound harsh, but it was our job to ensure that the games displayed only the highest calibre of athlete. Another key task during this month was to research the background of the athletes. We had to be sure that they were free-born Greeks – there is no place for slaves or barbarians in our games. Furthermore, we needed to decide the age category of the competitors – this was easy in many cases, but for boys with the first trimmings of a beard, it required a good deal of work to establish whether they should compete in the boys' or the men's events.

'As this month neared its end, the real festivities began. Two days before the games were due to start, we announced which competitors had been selected to compete. Then we were given the honour of heading the long procession from Elis to Olympia along the Sacred Way. On the first morning of the games, we congregated at the Altar of Zeus Horkios in the Bouleuterion. After the competitors had taken their oath, the ten of us swore that we would judge fairly and not reveal any reasons for our judgements. The rest of the games was the busiest period of my life. Of the ten *hellanodikai*, three of us oversaw the equestrian events, three the stadium events and three the combat events. However, my role was the greatest of them all – one of the ten of us had to be the chief judge of the games. My word was final.

'After we had set the order of events, we had to judge each one, hand out victory wreaths and oversee many of the sacrifices and ceremonies of the games, such as the feasts for the victors. We were also responsible for keeping order with the *mastigophoroi*. We had to keep our wits about us to check for wrong-doing, or even the presence of women at the site.

Unfortunately, there was one incident of bribery by a horse owner from Syracuse. After some investigation, we found him guilty and issued him with a large fine. At least this will go to the upkeep of the Zanes. The final day of the games was my proudest moment of all: as senior *hellanodikês*, it was my duty to crown the victors with the sacred olive wreath during the prize-giving.'

* * *

The imaginary testimony of Hippomenes shows how important the *hellanodikai* were to the games. It also reflects the high reputation of the Elean judges. The games lasted a thousand years, yet our sources record very few stories of corrupt judges (whereas there are many stories of corrupt competitors).

It was vital that the judges were held in such respect. Their decisions had to be based on eyesight alone – obviously there were no action-replays or stop-watches then – and the umpire's decision had to be final. During the games, the *hellanodikai* were allowed to wear a purple robe, a royal colour symbolising their link to King Iphitos. They could issue fines to competitors and could also have offenders whipped or beaten with rods, as Hippomenes' tale indicates.

VII. THE SPECTATORS

The spectators who travelled to Olympia from all over the Greek world must have felt as if they were on a pilgrimage. They were not just preparing to watch the greatest athletic games; equally significantly they were preparing to visit the sanctuary of their greatest god. It is estimated that some 40,000 spectators were present at the games, drawn from every colony in the Greek world. Some would come by land; many would arrive at Olympia by sailing to the north-west of the Peloponnese. Entry to the games was free.

Upon arrival at Olympia, spectators would have to find a place to sleep. Yet, as we have seen, Olympia itself was not a town or even a village; it was little more than a sanctuary with athletic facilities. While the VIPs would have stayed in the Leonidaion, the masses would either pitch tents or build huts in the surrounding fields, using the two rivers and local wells for drinking and washing.

The conditions in the late summer heat must have been appalling. Pausanias tells us that the Eleans used to sacrifice to Zeus Apomyios – Zeus 'the Averter of Flies'! There is another story of a disobedient slave being threatened with a visit to Olympia as a punishment. Despite this, many spectators would have found a visit to the games the highlight of a lifetime. Epictetus, writing at the end of the 1st century CE, comments about a visit to Olympia:

'Aren't you scorched there by the fierce heat? Aren't you crushed in the crowd? Isn't it difficult to freshen yourself up? Doesn't the rain soak you to the skin? Aren't you bothered by the noise, the din and other nuisances? But it seems to me that you are well able to bear and indeed gladly endure all this, when you think of the gripping spectacles that you will see.'

Epictetus, *Dissertations* 1.6.23-9

The whole site must have had the feel of a country fair, with stall-holders hawking their wares, while philosophers, poets and politicians made speeches and encouraged debate. Dio Chrysostom, also writing in the 1st century CE, gives a sense of this atmosphere when he narrates an imaginary visit to the Isthmian Games by the philosopher Diogenes, who is clearly unimpressed with what he finds there:

'Many miserable sophists could be heard shouting and reviling each other round the temple of Poseidon while their so-called pupils fought with one another. Writers were reading their rubbish aloud. Many poets were reciting their verses to the applause of others, many conjurers were showing off their tricks, fortune-tellers theirs. There were countless advocates perverting the law and not a few pedlars hawking everything and anything.'

Dio Chrysostom, *Concerning Virtue* 8.9

At Olympia, spectators would have marvelled at the buildings of the Altis and made sacrifices at the altars to pray for their favoured competitors. They would have also played a full part in the ceremonies, processions and feasts, adding to the colour and excitement of the occasion. Above all, a visit to the games would have made any man proud to be a Greek. Greeks would come from all parts of the world and would have rejoiced in the fact that they shared common gods, a common language and common ideals. It was at this moment that a Greek might have felt that he belonged to the most civilised people on earth.

VIII. WOMEN AND THE GAMES

Women were noticeably absent from the Olympic Games, either as competitors or as spectators. Although young girls were allowed to watch the events, any woman of marriageable age was barred. Indeed, Pausanias tells us a woman caught at the games faced the death penalty:

'On the road to Olympia ... there is a precipitous mountain ... called Typaeum. It is a law of Elis that any woman discovered at the Olympic Games will be pitched headlong from this mountain.'

Pausanias, *Guidebook to Greece* 5.6.7

Greek men believed that it was an insult to the gods for a woman to be present at the Olympics. They were also very concerned to keep their female relatives from having any contact with men outside the family (see p. 159) and it was therefore vital that they were kept away from such a large gathering.

Kallipateira of Rhodes

There is a remarkable story of one noblewoman who disguised herself as a man in order to watch the games. Kallipateira of Rhodes came from a well known Olympic family – her father was Diagoras, the famous boxer. She came to Olympia in 404 disguised as a male trainer in order to watch her son Peisirodos compete in the boys' boxing event. When he duly won it, she became so excited that she leapt over the barrier of the stadium, losing most of her disguise in the process. Although she should have been thrown to her death, she was let off unpunished because of her distinguished family. Subsequently, however, a law was reportedly passed which stated that trainers had to watch events naked, in order to prevent a repetition!

The only woman who was allowed to watch the events was the priestess of Demeter Chamyne (see p. 11 to learn more about Demeter), who had an exclusive seat in the stadium. As previously mentioned, this link to Demeter may have reflected the fact that the games were held just before the harvest time of year. Other women, such as Kyniska of Sparta, did manage to have an impact on the games through the equestrian events, even if they could not be present at the site to receive their prizes.

In fact, Olympia did host an important athletic festival for women despite the ban on them attending the men's games. This was the Games

A vase painting depicting the women's race. Note that the female athletes are fully clothed.

of Hera, or *Heraia*, which also took place on a four yearly cycle, although they only had one event, a sprint run over 160 metres. Women who won this race were allowed to inscribe images of themselves in the Temple of Hera in the Altis.

Although this attitude to women seems very strange to us, it should be pointed out that women were barred from competing in the first modern Olympics in 1896, while the first female member of the International Olympic Committee was not elected until 1981. The founder of the modern games, Baron de Coubertin, was completely opposed to female competitors, declaring: 'the true Olympic hero, in my view, is the individual adult male'. The following list records when women were first allowed to compete in certain events in the modern games:

- Tennis – **1900**
- Swimming – **1912**
- Some athletics – **1928**
- Cycling – **1984**
- Modern pentathlon – **2000**

Prejudice against female athletes was evident throughout the 20th century: for example, although the 800 metre race was introduced in 1928, it was subsequently decided that it was too difficult for women, and it was discontinued until 1960. Today, however, the only events which are not open to female competitors at the summer games are boxing and baseball; moreover, some sports, such as badminton, sailing and equestrian, include mixed events.

Review 6

1. Define the following: *hellanodikês, Heraia, nomophylakes.*
2. List the similarities and differences between the duties of ancient and modern Olympic judges. Do you think it was more difficult to judge an Olympic event in ancient Greece than it is today?
3. Why do you think the judges were so respected at the ancient Olympics?
4. Compare and contrast the experience for spectators at the ancient and the modern Olympics. Which would you have preferred to visit and why?
5. Why do you think there has been so much hostility to women taking part at (i) the ancient games; (ii) the modern games? Do such attitudes about women participating in sport still exist in the world today?
E. Imagine you are a spectator at the games. Write a letter to your relatives back home (or continue the one you wrote in Review 2) describing the atmosphere and characters you find at the festival.

IX. ANCIENT AND MODERN

During the 19th century, two different cultures began to rediscover the significance of the ancient Olympic Games. In 1820, Greece gained independence from the Ottoman Empire for the first time in hundreds of years. In order to assert its national identity, modern Greece looked to its ancient past for inspiration. During the decades following independence, there was some desire to re-establish the games. Meanwhile in Victorian Britain the Public Schools saw the benefit of competitive sport for the education of their charges. The Victorians believed that athletic excellence imbued moral virtue, and there was talk of reviving the ancient games. However, it fell to a Frenchman, Baron Pierre de Coubertin, to provide the energy and vision to restart the Olympic Games in the modern era.

De Coubertin organised the first Session of the International Olympic Committee (IOC) in Paris in June 1894. It was during this session that the city of Athens was chosen to host the first Olympiad of the modern era. A new marble stadium was built on the site of the old Panathenaic stadium, and the games were officially opened in the first week of April 1896. Only fifteen countries participated in the first games, and competition was open only to amateur men. The USA won most of the medals, although the high point of the games saw a Greek, Spiros Louis, claim gold in the marathon (despite reportedly stopping for a glass of wine during the race!).

The marathon

The marathon event was invented for the modern Olympic Games, but it recalled a famous moment in ancient Greek history. In actual fact, the legend of the first 'marathon' is a confusion of two stories relating to Athens' famous victory over the Persians in 490 near the town of Marathon (see map 5). Herodotus, writing in the 5th century, relates that before the battle the Athenians sent a runner, Pheidippides, to Sparta (a distance of about 150 miles) to ask for Spartan help. Writing many centuries later, the historian Plutarch records that after the battle the Athenians sent another runner from Marathon to Athens to announce the victory. This he did, after which he promptly collapsed and died! This journey is sometimes incorrectly attributed to Pheidippides. The modern marathon is run over almost exactly the same distance as the road from Marathon to Athens (26.2 miles).

The Olympic movement was not an immediate success and took time to gain momentum. In the early years the games were very unlike those we know today – the exclusion of women and working class men meant

Politics at the modern games

As in ancient times, the noble aspirations of the modern games have sometimes fallen foul of international politics and intrigue. Here are a few examples:

- In 1936, Hitler used the Berlin games as a showcase for his Third Reich; in fact, some of the most important symbolism of the modern games (including the Olympic torch relay) originates from these 'Nazi' games.
- In 1972, the games in Munich were marked by tragedy as Palestinian gunmen kidnapped and murdered eleven Israeli competitors.
- At the 1980 games in Moscow, the USA led a boycott by 64 countries in protest at the Soviet invasion of Afghanistan in 1979. In return, the Soviet Union led a 14 country boycott of the 1984 games in Los Angeles.
- In 1998, IOC delegates were accused of taking bribes to ensure that Salt Lake City would host the winter games of 2002. After an investigation, 10 members of the IOC were expelled from the organisation.

that it was very unrepresentative of the general population. It wasn't until the Stockholm games of 1912 that countries from all around the world started to take the games seriously. Today, however, the Olympics have become the biggest sporting show on earth. Moreover, the movement also introduced the Winter Olympics in 1924 and, in 1960, the Paralympics for athletes with physical disabilities.

In 2004, the Olympic Games returned to Athens for the first time since 1896. Competitors from 201 countries competed in 301 events. Moreover, it is estimated that 3.9 billion people around the world had access to the television coverage of the events. The modern games still emphasises its ties to the ancient past: every four years, the Olympic torch is lit amidst the ruins of the Temple of Hera, while a form of the Olympic oath is still taken by representatives of the athletes and judges. Despite these links, an ancient Greek would surely have been astonished to read the modern Olympic creed:

'The most important thing in the Olympic Games is not to win but to take part, just as the most important thing in life is not the triumph, but the struggle. The essential thing is not to have conquered, but to have fought well.'

Chapter Review

E. How important was religion to the ancient Olympic Games?

E. Do you think that the same values are reflected in both the ancient and the modern Olympic Games?

3

Athenian Drama

In the second half of the 6th century BCE, a new way of worshipping the god Dionysos emerged in Athens. People called it *drama*, a Greek word which literally meant something like 'action' or 'performance'. At this moment, European theatre was born: without Athenian drama, there could have been no Shakespeare, Molière or Goethe as we know them today.

It is difficult to know exactly how and why religious worship evolved into theatre acting. What is certain is that by the early 5th century three types of play (**tragedy**, **satyr-play** and **comedy**) were being performed at some of Athens' greatest religious festivals, most notably the City Dionysia. Religion was therefore a central element of Athenian drama, even though we would not readily link it with theatrical performance today. A second distinctive feature was the element of competition: for at each festival three (or sometimes more) playwrights presented plays which were judged in order of merit. In this sense, an Athenian dramatic festival could perhaps be best compared to a film festival or to the Oscars ceremony today.

I. THE ORIGINS OF DRAMA

The birth of drama seems to have been linked to a sudden rise in the worship of the god Dionysos at Athens. This probably happened during the middle of the 6th century, when the city incorporated into its territory Eleutherae, a town near the border with Boeotia (see map 5). Since Eleutherae was the home of a cult to Dionysos, it is possible that the Athenian tyrant Peisistratos (see p. 184) sensed an opportunity. Wishing to win favour with his people, he may well have chosen this moment to introduce to Athens festivals in honour of the god.

Dionysos was a shrewd choice. As the god of fertility he was responsible for the vine and its product, wine: festivals of Dionysos were bound to include drinking and revelry – Peisistratos was giving his people licence to party on a grand scale. Within a few years, there were four festivals in honour of the god: the *Rural Dionysia* (held in late December), the *Lenaia* (mid-January) the *Anthestêria* (mid-February) and the *City Dionysia* (late March).

The worship of Dionysos which subsequently became popular in Athens contained four elements which many believe influenced the development of drama: choral dances in honour of the god, known as **dithyrambs**; cult worship of Dionysos by two groups known as **maenads** and **satyrs**; and the tradition of the **kômos** – wild partying held in celebration of the god.

1. Choral dancing – the dithyramb

'Dancing is the loftiest, the most moving, the most beautiful of the arts, because it is not mere translation or abstraction from life; it is life itself.'
Havelock Ellis (1859-1939), British social reformer

In the western world today, dancing no longer holds the importance that it once did. Nonetheless, historically every culture has recognised dancing to be a powerful means of self-expression, perhaps believing, with Martha Graham, that dance 'is the hidden language of the soul'.

This was certainly true in ancient Greece, where Socrates reportedly learnt to dance at the age of seventy because he felt that an essential part of himself had been neglected. Dancing in a *choros* (see below) was at the heart of marriages, funerals, athletic events, military parades and religious festivals. Many of these dances, moreover, focused on the gods, perhaps recounting myths or thanking them for blessings received. In fact, dancing was one of the fundamental ways in which the Greeks honoured their gods.

Choros
It is hard to translate the Greek word *choros* effectively, since it really refers to singing and dancing as one single act. Its English derivatives reflect this double meaning: words such as 'choir' or 'choral' refer exclusively to singing, while a 'choreographer' is someone who arranges the movements of a group of dancers.

Dancing was particularly important in the worship of Dionysos. Indeed, during the 6th century, a particular type of choral dance, the **dithyramb**, developed in honour of the god, during which people would dance and sing myths associated with him. Appropriately enough, dithyrambic performances became a central feature of the new City Dionysia and the ever-competitive Athenians later established a tribal contest in the dithyramb, at which each of the city's ten tribes (see p. 189) entered choruses of fifty men and fifty boys to challenge for a prize.

Ancient sources report that at some point in the second half of the 6th century, an Athenian named **Thespis** set himself apart from his chorus. Dressed in a mask and costume, he impersonated different characters from the dithyramb and took part in dialogues with the chorus. This was the first important step to drama as we know it – Thespis had moved away from merely singing about mythological stories to actually acting them out; today his name lives on in the word 'thespian'. As drama developed, choral song and dance was to remain fundamental to Athenian plays.

It was not long before this new genre of 'drama' had its own competition at the City Dionysia: the first recorded contest was held in 534, when Thespis was victorious. Records state that he was awarded the prize of a goat, which may well explain the origin of the word 'tragedy'. For at the earliest plays, it seems, a goat – *tragos* in Greek – was either awarded as a prize or sacrificed in honour of Dionysos. The Greek word *tragôdia* was therefore a joining of *tragos* and *ôdê*, 'song', so that it meant something like 'the song of the goat-singers'. It was probably only later that the word 'tragedy' came to describe a play depicting a terrible misfortune (see p. 111).

Acting hypocritically

The early Greek word for an actor was *hypocritês*, which literally meant 'interpreter', possibly because the first actors, like Thespis, simply interpreted the stories related by the chorus. The English word 'hypocrite' has evolved from this, since it describes a person who puts on an act, pretending to be someone that they are not.

---

2. The maenads

Dionysos was a fascinating god. He was particularly associated with wild forces, be they uncontrollable forces of nature or the powerful emotional forces which can grip human beings. In Euripides' *Bacchae* (see text box), he is described as a god 'most terrible and most gracious

Maenads dancing beside an image of Dionysos.

to mankind': to those who oppose him he brings great suffering, but to those who honour him he offers release from the pains of life; his beneficial side was illustrated by two important epithets (cf. p. 6): *eleuthereus*, 'freer' and *lusios*, 'releaser'. Therefore most Greeks were understandably anxious to worship Dionysos appropriately.

One of Dionysos' most prominent cults was made up of women called **maenads**, or **bacchae** (Dionysos was also known as Bacchos). In his tragedy *Bacchae,* Euripides depicts them dressed in fawnskins, each carrying the *thyrsos* (an ivy-tipped branch) and dancing wildly in the mountains, where they catch wild animals and eat them raw: the name *maenad* actually meant 'maddened woman'. It is unclear how accurate a picture this is of the real-life cult; however, what is significant about Euripides' narrative is that, at the height of their worship, the maenads believed that they were possessed by Dionysos in a moment of ecstasy.

Dionysos' real-life worshippers certainly believed that he could offer them an ecstatic experience; in Greek, *ekstasis* meant 'standing outside oneself' and, at this moment, a follower felt that he was filled with the god, freeing him from his old personality and allowing him to take on a new identity. This idea clearly resurfaces in drama, where, for the life of a play, an actor assumes a different personality to his own (or more than one – Greek actors often played a number of roles in a play). The masks used by dramatic actors symbolised this change of identity; the idea of wearing them perhaps originated from the practice of certain cults of Dionysos, which carried a mask of the god during their celebrations.

Euripides' *Bacchae*

Just before he died in 406, Euripides wrote what is arguably his greatest play. *Bacchae* retells the myth of Dionysos' return to Thebes, his mother's city, where the people have rejected his worship. To punish them, he drives many of the city's women to nearby Mt Kithairon and maddens them into a frenzy; in this state, they mistake their king, Pentheus, for a wild animal and rip him to pieces. Pentheus' mother Agave then carries his head back into Thebes, believing it to be that of a lion. It is only when she arrives there that her madness is removed and she realises what she has done.

The play is important for many reasons. On one level, it gives an insight into how the Athenians viewed Dionysos as a god 'most terrible and most gracious'. For while the citizens of Thebes are punished horribly by the god, the faithful followers who accompany him from the east experience his ecstatic sweetness. Most brilliant, however, is the characterisation of Dionysos in the play. During the prologue, the god addresses the audience in his own character. However, he then disguises himself as a visitor from Asia, only revealing his true self at the end of the play: the god of drama himself, on stage at his own festival, chooses to leave behind his personality and assume a new identity.

---

3. The satyrs

A second group associated with Dionysos were the mythological **satyrs**, who were believed to be woodland creatures, half-human and half-animal, representing the basic human appetites for food, drink and sex. In myth, they usually accompany the god, drinking, dancing and

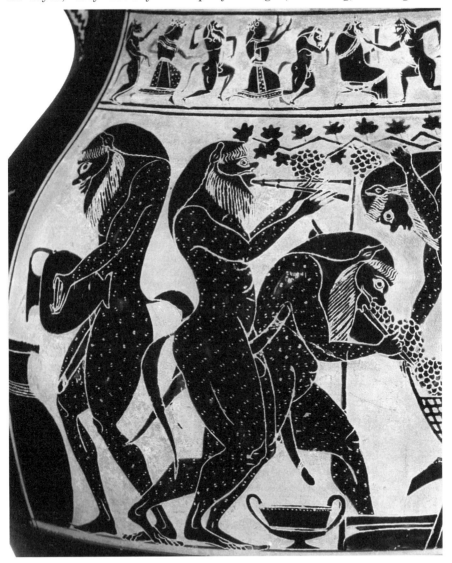

Cavorting satyrs making wine. Note the familiar symbols of Dionysos: grapes, a musical instrument (the *aulos*) and large phalluses.

revelling; artists portray them with bushy tails, snub noses, pointed ears and, most importantly, large phalluses. The satyrs symbolise the release Dionysos can offer his followers through pleasure and also point to his wild and fertile nature.

The myth of the satyrs gave rise to another type of drama, the 'satyr-play'. At the City Dionysia a tragic playwright had to offer four plays, three tragedies followed by a satyr-play. Although we know comparatively little about them since only one has survived in its entirety (*Cyclops* by Euripides), satyr-plays seem to have been light-hearted parodies of tragedy with the chorus always playing satyrs. They may have aimed to offer the audience a release after they had sat through three intensely serious tragic dramas.

Yet satyr-plays may have emerged for another reason too: for tragedies soon moved away from telling stories about Dionysos, to the extent that some complained that they had 'nothing to do with Dionysos'. In the satyr-play, however, Dionysos was a common character and his worship was at the heart of the action.

4. The kômos

A key element in festivals of Dionysos was the *kômos*, which literally meant 'revel'. Men came out into the streets of the city, drinking, singing and dancing in honour of the god. Central to the *kômos* was the icon of a human phallus. Dionysos was god of human fertility (in addition to crop fertility) and the phallus was a symbol of his power, abundance and ability to bring new life. Fertility, both agricultural and human, was particularly important in ancient Greece, which was a mountainous country with few fertile plains; moreover, life was precarious and the rate of infant mortality was high, even when a pregnancy reached full term.

During the *kômos*, revellers sang and danced and held aloft leather phalluses as a way of giving thanks to the god. From these dances and songs eventually developed comic plays: in Greek, *kômôdia* literally meant 'the song of the *kômos*' and the phallus remained a prominent symbol in many Greek comedies, where it was worn as part of the costume (see p. 125). The *kômos* illustrates how Dionysos was worshipped as a god who could relieve people of their troubles through wine and song. In *Bacchae*, the prophet Teiresias explains this aspect of the god to a sceptical Pentheus:

> 'He ... invented the liquid drink of the grape ... and introduced it to mortals, the drink which puts an end to sorrow for wretched men, when they are filled with the juice of the vine, which brings sleep to them and forgetfulness of daily troubles. There is no other antidote to suffering.'
> Euripides, *Bacchae* 278ff.

Review 1

1. Define the following and explain their relevance to Athenian drama: *choros, dithyramb, ekstasis, hypocritês, kômos, maenad, ôdê, satyr.*
2. Explain the origin of the English words *comedy, drama, thespian* and *tragedy.*
3. What was the nature and purpose of a satyr-play?
4. To what extent are the Athenian traditions of: (i) dancing, (ii) drama, (iii) festivity, comparable to other cultural traditions you are familiar with?
5. Do politicians today ever try to promote civic festivals or holidays in order to gain popularity, as Peisistratos did?
R. Read the prologue to Euripides' *Bacchae* (lines 1-62). What do we learn about Dionysos and his followers from these lines?
E. How did the worship of Dionysos influence the birth of Athenian drama?

II. THE DESIGN OF A THEATRE

Tourists today can still visit many well-preserved classical theatres dotted around the Mediterranean countries; the most famous of these is probably the theatre at Epidauros in the Peloponnese, where plays are performed even today to audiences in excess of 10,000. However, such

The view from the back of the theatre of Epidauros today.

97

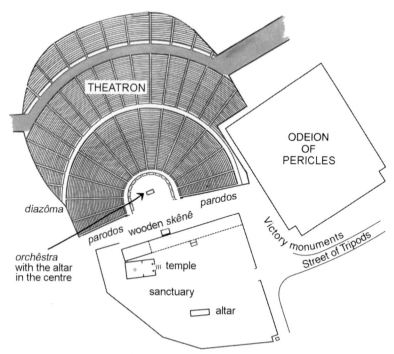

A plan of the sanctuary of Dionysos.

theatres were only built from the later 4th century, when theatres were first constructed in stone; by contrast, theatres of the 5th century (the high point of Athenian drama) were wooden and so little trace of them has survived. Despite this, it is probably fair to imagine that the wooden theatres were designed in a similar way, albeit less grandly.

The largest and most important theatre at Athens was the theatre of Dionysos, which actually formed part of a religious sanctuary to Dionysos on the south side of the Acropolis (see p. 16ff. to read about religious sanctuaries). The sanctuary also contained the Odeion (a concert hall commissioned by Pericles in the 440s) and the large temple of Dionysos. The theatre itself, which could hold an estimated 17,000 spectators, was first built in stone in the 320s and underwent significant changes over the centuries. However, today's remains still give a good idea of the view down to the stage for 5th century spectators.

The location of the theatre (see maps 6 and 7) was important for one very practical reason: the south side of the Acropolis was protected from the cold north winds which often blew in the winter months. In addition, the location had symbolic importance since the theatre was wedged between the Acropolis, the religious heart of the city, and the temple of Dionysos below. As drama developed, the area became the 'theatre district' of Athens; indeed, the street leading to the theatre, which wound around the north and east sides of the Acropolis, became known as the 'Street of Tripods', since many a festival victor built a monument to display his prize, which was often a large bronze tripod.

1. The theatron

The *theatron* (which meant 'watching area' and gives us our word 'theatre') was the area of the theatre where the audience sat. It was normally built on a hillside, which allowed engineers to create a steep viewing area full of seats. This also made the setting clearly visible to all spectators, regardless of their distance from the action. Many theatres also afforded a magnificent view for miles beyond the stage building.

The *theatron* was at least semicircular in shape, although some theatres allowed the seats to bend round further, making it nearer to two-thirds of a circle. This design created outstanding acoustics – even today a whisper in the *orchêstra* (see below) of the theatre of Epidauros is clearly audible from the top row of the *theatron*. The front row of the *theatron* was called the **prohedria** ('the seats at the front'); this was occupied by officials and dignitaries. At Athens, the central seat of the *prohedria* was the throne of Dionysos, reserved for the god's priest.

The priest of Dionysos' seat, which is still in place in the theatre today.

The design of the *theatron* allowed an enormous number of spectators to be fitted in; capacity was further increased by the lack of individual seats – there were simply rows of wooden or stone benches. With such vast numbers entering the theatre, it was important to allow easy access to and from seats. To achieve this, the *theatron* of more elaborate stone theatres was designed with a horizontal aisle half-way up, the **diazôma** ('the row across'), which created a division between the upper and lower seating areas. This also enabled more aisles to be created in the upper half of the *theatron*.

2. The orchêstra

Orchêstra simply meant 'dancing-area' in Greek. Situated at the front of the *theatron*, it was a circular area with the seats wrapped around its front half. The *orchêstra* (in the theatre of Dionysos it was about 20 metres in diameter) was where the chorus would sing and dance and remain throughout the play – they would never be seen on the stage; this allowed the audience to identify more closely with the chorus than with the actors. In the middle of the *orchêstra* was an altar to Dionysos, a reminder to all present that the god was watching over his festival.

As well as the chorus, minor characters (such as messengers or exiles) could also perform in the *orchêstra*, reserving the main stage for the leading characters. Steps up to the stage allowed actors to move between the two. On each side of the *orchêstra* pathways led in from off-stage; each pathway was called a *parodos* or *eisodos* (both meaning 'way-on') and acted as an entrance for the chorus and minor characters (and also for spectators).

3. The skênê

Behind the *orchêstra* was a low wooden stage called the *proskênê* (there is some debate about when this was introduced to the theatre; it probably didn't exist in the early days of tragedy). Behind the *proskênê* was a building called the *skênê*, a word which originally meant something like 'tent' or 'booth'. However, in a theatrical sense it described a large wooden hut with one main double-door out onto the stage (some theatres also had two smaller side-doors). The word 'scenery' is derived from *skênê*, since from the time of Sophocles its front was often painted to add atmosphere to a play.

The actors used the *skênê* as a changing room, so costumes and props were stored there. Inside, a ladder led up to a trap-door in the roof, which could be used as a third acting area (it was usually gods who appeared there in a play). The painting on the front wall of the *skênê* clearly gave some character to the setting. However, this was not nearly as ornate as that of a typical theatre set today, since it would have been difficult for most of the audience to see the scene-painting in any detail.

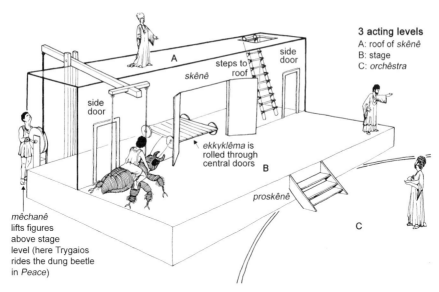

3 acting levels
A: roof of *skênê*
B: stage
C: *orchêstra*

The *proskênê* and *skênê*, showing the *mêchanê* and *ekkyklêma* and the three acting levels.

4. Special effects and props

Today, theatre-goers are asked to 'suspend their disbelief' to enable them to believe in the action on stage. A modern theatre usually relies on special effects to aid this, in particular artificial lighting, magnified sound, and (often) an intricate set. The Greek theatre had none of these; instead, it relied on daylight, acoustics and the audience's willingness to go along with the dramatic illusion. Oliver Taplin has therefore described the Greek theatre as the 'theatre of the mind'.

However, there were two devices commonly used to provide special effects. One, called the **ekkyklêma** ('something wheeled out'), was probably a wooden platform on wheels brought out onto the stage through the main door, which portrayed a scene which had happened indoors (it often presented the body of a character who had died off-stage). An ancient commentator described it as follows:

> 'It would show things which appear to be happening indoors, e.g., in a house, to those outside as well (I mean the spectators).'
>
> Scholion to Aristophanes' *Acharnians*, line 408

Some believe that the *ekkyklêma* may have been produced differently, since sources also speak of it revolving. By this system, the main door revolved around on a circular piece of floor beneath it, revealing an indoor scene.

The second device was called the **mêchanê**. This was a crane positioned on the left-hand side of the *skênê*; it was operated off-stage by pulleys and ropes and was used to hoist characters into the air above the roof. Most commonly, a god was elevated to make an appearance at the end of a play to sort out human affairs. From this we still use the phrase *deus ex machina* ('a god from the machine') to describe the intervention of some unexpected good fortune to resolve a difficult situation.

In Aristophanes' comedy *Peace*, the playwright even makes the *mêchanê* a source of humour. The play's hero, Trygaios, is an Athenian farmer who flies to heaven on the back of a giant dung-beetle in order to rescue the goddess Peace and bring her back to war-torn Greece. While riding on the *mêchanê*, which is decked out as the dung-beetle (see p. 101), the actor breaks the dramatic illusion and speaks directly to the machine operator:

> 'I'm really scared now, and I'm not joking any more either, dammit. Watch out for me, machine operator! I can feel my bowels loosening, and if you don't watch it, I'll feed the dung-beetle!'   Aristophanes, *Peace* 173-6

The *ekkyklêma* and *mêchanê* in tragedy

Two tragedies of Euripides well illustrate how the *ekkyklêma* and *mêchanê* were used. At the beginning of *Hippolytus*, Phaedra has fallen in love with her step-son Hippolytus. When he rebuffs her advances, she kills herself, claiming in a suicide note that Hippolytus has tried to rape her. Her body is revealed on the *ekkyklêma*, with the note still attached to her wrist. Theseus, Hippolytus' father, reads the letter and challenges his son to explain himself. Throughout the dialogue which follows, the body remains in full view, a symbol of how Phaedra has taken her secret with her to the grave.

Perhaps the most famous use of the *mêchanê* in tragedy is Medea's escape at the end of the play named after her. Euripides allowed her to escape punishment for killing her own children by having her carried off to her grandfather, the sun-god, in a chariot drawn by dragons. The final scene of the play is a dialogue between Medea, who usurps the place of the gods on the *mêchanê*, and Jason, who remains helpless and distraught on the stage.

Some props were commonly used on the Athenian stage. Tragedies were often set before palaces, temples or military huts, and props must have reflected this with altars, statues or shrines of the gods. In some plays, more unusual props were required; a chilling example occurs in *Bacchae*, when Agave appears on stage holding aloft the severed head of her son, which remains in full view as she begins to realise what she has done.

Extra sound effects were probably created in simple ways. Sometimes the chorus members themselves would create non-human sounds; for example, the chorus of frogs in Aristophanes' *Frogs* famously croak like frogs as Dionysos rows across the river Styx: '*brekekekex koax koax*'.

A vase painting of Medea's dramatic escape on the *mêchanê*, which has been decked out as a chariot drawn by dragons. In contrast to the plot of Euripides' play, the vase depicts her murdered sons left behind on the *ekkyklêma* while their tutor mourns over them and, to the left, Jason looks on in despair.

Review 2

1. Explain the function of the following: *diazôma, ekkyklêma, mêchanê, orchêstra, parodos, prohedria, proskênê, skênê, theatron.*
2. What similarities and what differences can you find between ancient and modern theatre buildings?
3. Why must theatre-goers 'suspend their disbelief'? Why do you think that Taplin described the Athenian theatre as the 'theatre of the mind'?
4. How might an Athenian playwright have disclosed information which would today be illustrated by extra sound, lighting, or a set?
R. Read the prologue of Aeschylus' *Libation-Bearers* (1-21). How might the actors have used the theatrical space? What information do the audience learn in these lines?
E. 'It is not possible for us to understand Athenian drama properly, since the ancient theatre-building was so different from its modern counterpart.' Do you agree?

III. THE CITY DIONYSIA

The City Dionysia (or Great Dionysia) was the most important dramatic festival in the Athenian calendar. It was held in the middle of the Athenian month of *Elaphêboliôn*, equivalent to late March (see p. 277), when the coming spring was an ideal time to celebrate Dionysos as the god of fertility and rebirth. It was also the beginning of the sailing season and so the festival attracted many visitors from the wider Greek world (conversely, since the Lenaia was held in January, it attracted only Athenian spectators). During the festival public business ceased and the law courts were closed; prisoners were even given day-release to watch the plays. In the later years of the 5th century, the main festival lasted for five days and, in addition to the theatrical contests, involved many other features, including processions, sacrifices and choral competitions.

It is probably no coincidence that the dramatic festivals of Athens began to flourish just as the city was undergoing major political changes. For in 508/7, a radical new form of government – democracy – emerged in Athens (see p. 185ff.). As a result, civic festivals tended to reflect the city's new democratic spirit. The City Dionysia, which was organised by one of Athens' elected officials, was no exception: on one level, the new democracy allowed playwrights unparalleled freedom of expression so that they could write plays which questioned and criticised their society; furthermore, the festival was democratic in that Athenian citizens could take part in various ways: 5th century Athenian drama was performed by the people, for the people.

1. Preparations for the festival

Preparations for the City Dionysia started many months beforehand in the summer of the previous year. Any tragic playwright wishing to compete could present a synopsis of four plays (three tragedies and a satyr-play) to the **eponymous archon** (see p. 178). By contrast, comic playwrights needed only to present the synopsis of a single play. We do not know how the archon made his choice, but he was said to 'grant a chorus' to his preferred playwrights (three each to write three tragedies and a satyr-play and three each to write a comedy); they then had to complete their writing as quickly as possible to allow enough time for rehearsing.

Next the archon had to select a *chorêgos* (see below) and leading actor (*prôtagônistês*) for each playwright. He chose six citizens to act as *chorêgoi* and allocated them to the playwrights. The same process took place to select the *prôtagônistês* for each set of plays: after the archon had chosen the best actors in the city, he matched them by lot to a playwright.

104

The chorêgos

The *chorêgos* ('chorus-director') was the supervisor and financial backer of a set of plays and so his input was vital to their success. Wealthy Athenians were required to perform various public services called liturgies, a kind of super-tax on the rich (see p. 213); serving as a *chorêgos* was one such liturgy. In fact, many wealthy Athenians welcomed the opportunity to become a *chorêgos* for a year: if they helped make a success of such an important festival, it allowed them to gain fame and popularity in their city. (In this sense, serving as a *chorêgos* could be compared to sponsoring a major public event today.) We know that, early in his career, the leading politician Pericles (see p. 196ff.) was *chorêgos* for Aeschylus' set of plays (including *Persians*) at the City Dionysia of 472.

A *chorêgos* required a great deal of money to make a success of the position: records tell us that 3,000 drachmas were spent by a *chorêgos* for tragedy in 410 and 1,600 drachmas by a *chorêgos* for comedy in 402 (see p. 275 for information about Greek currency values). The *chorêgos* had to pay for almost everything: costumes, props, masks, special effects, the wages of the chorus and their accompanying musician, and a party for the cast at the end of the festival. He also had to select all the members of his chorus and provide them with food, a place to train and sometimes even accommodation. Moreover, if the playwright wasn't skilled enough to train his own chorus, then the *chorêgos* had to hire a professional trainer; and, if his playwright won, he might want to pay for a victory monument, which would be inscribed with his own name, together with those of the eponymous archon, the main actors and the musicians.

Such expense seems to have shocked some. The historian Plutarch quotes an anonymous Spartan who is appalled at the amount spent by the Athenians on drama instead of on their army:

'If the cost of the production of each drama were reckoned, the Athenian people would appear to have spent more on the production of *Bacchaes* and *Phoenician Women* and *Oedipuses* and the misfortunes of Medeas and Electras than they did on maintaining their empire and fighting for their liberty against the Persians.'   Plutarch, *On the Glory of Athens* 348f-349a

2. The festival

A day or two before the festival began, the **proagôn** ('pre-contest') was held in the Odeion. In this ceremony the plays were announced; each playwright stepped forward in front of a full house and delivered a short synopsis of his four plays. Next he would introduce his *chorêgos*, actors and musicians, who all wore garlands. An actor may even have read a short passage from one of the plays – an ancient version of a film trailer! This was the only time that the actors would appear on the stage without their masks, so it was also a chance for the audience to see what they looked like.

On the evening before the festival began, a wooden statue of Dionysos was brought into the city from a shrine just outside the city on the road to Eleutherae. This **torchlight procession**, known as the *eisagôgê* ('bringing in'), was meant to re-enact Dionysos' first arrival in Athens from Eleutherae. The ephebes (the city's military cadets – see p. 203) escorted the statue to the theatre of Dionysos, where a sacrifice was made. Thereafter the statue remained in the theatre throughout the dramatic performances, a symbol of the god's presence at his festival.

Date	Event
8 Elaphêboliôn	*proagôn*
9 Elaphêboliôn	torchlight procession (*eisagôgê*)
10 Elaphêboliôn (Day 1)	*pompê*
	dithyrambic contests
	kômos
11 Elaphêboliôn (Day 2)	opening ceremony
	3 tragedies, 1 satyr-play, 1 comedy
12 Elaphêboliôn (Day 3)	3 tragedies, 1 satyr-play, 1 comedy
13 Elaphêboliôn (Day 4)	3 tragedies, 1 satyr-play, 1 comedy
14 Elaphêboliôn (Day 5)	judging and prize-giving
a few days later	the review

Day 1

On the morning of Day 1 the grand procession, or **pompê**, took place. It started outside the city and made its way through the streets to the agora, then on to the temple of Dionysos, where it culminated in the sacrifice of a sacred bull together with many other animals. Later that evening, a **kômos** was held in the streets by the men of the city. Based on the evidence available, here is an account of the day by an imaginary Athenian:

* * *

'Finally the first day of the festival was upon us and the weeks of anticipation were over. Excitedly I hurried out with my friends to the edge of the city, jostling my way through the noisy crowds. People were drawn from all backgrounds – rich and poor, citizen and foreigner, young and old, all of them laughing, shouting and joking. When we reached the city gates the procession was just beginning. It was a rich and riotous affair as we watched the throng drive the sacred bull and many other sacrificial animals through the streets. The most colourful figures were the metics [see p. 201] and the *chorêgoi*. The former wore purple robes and carried trays of sacrificial offerings; the latter proudly showed off their elaborate gowns. Of the other citizens, some hung leather wine-bottles over their shoulders, others carried loaves of bread specially baked for the sacrifice, while more still were holding up phalluses in honour of Dionysos. In the middle of it all was the *kanêphoros*, the aristocratic maiden carrying a golden basket brimful with the first fruits of spring, all offerings to the god.

'From time to time, we stopped along the route to sing and dance at holy altars. At the most important of these, the altar of the twelve gods in the agora, the singing and dancing reached its peak. Anticipation of the sacrifice was growing. We headed on the short distance to the temple of Dionysos. A friend claimed to have counted over 200 animals offered to the god – we knew we would eat well later on! I prayed that Dionysos would find favour with our city and grant us the greatest Dionysia in our history.

'That evening, as darkness fell, we feasted on the sacrificial meat and washed it down with the sweet drink of the god himself. Then we headed out into the streets and joined the *kômos*. We sang and danced our way through the streets by torchlight, led by musicians playing their *auloi* and *kitharai* [see p. 278]. I could feel Dionysos present with us and we partied long and late – perhaps too late in view of the early start in the theatre the next morning!'

* * *

As if these celebrations weren't enough, the dithyrambic competitions were probably held on the afternoon of this day too. These competitions were a key part of the festival and the performances also required a lot of rehearsal. Each tribe submitted two choruses – one of boys, one of men – to perform a dithyramb in the *orchêstra* of the theatre. Every chorus was funded by a *chorêgos*, for whom victory could bring great honour, as well as the prize of a crown and a tripod.

Days 2, 3 and 4 (the play days)
Although the programme of events changed over the years, in the latter part of the 5th century each day began with three tragedies, followed by a satyr-play, all written by the same playwright. Lots were drawn to determine whose set of plays was performed on which day. The action started very early in the morning, with a break for lunch after the satyr-play. In the afternoon the day's entertainment was concluded with a comedy – the first recorded comedy at the City Dionysia was put on in 487; however, comedy carried less importance at the festival than tragedy; in fact, the main comic festival at Athens was the Lenaia.

Before the plays began on Day 2, there was a grand **opening ceremony** in the Theatre of Dionysos. The priest of Dionysos first sacrificed a piglet on the altar in the *orchêstra*, then the ten generals of Athens poured libations (see pp. 26-7) to the twelve gods. Following this, three important presentations were made:

- **Parade of tribute**. In the years of the Athenian empire during the 5th century, all the tribute due from her subject-allies had to be paid at this time of year. The money was carried into the *orchêstra* and laid out for the audience to view.
- **Proclamation of honours.** A herald announced the names of citizens who had done outstanding service for the city and awarded them a crown.
- **Parade of orphans**. The boys and youths whose fathers had died fighting for Athens now paraded into the *orchêstra*. The state paid for their education as a mark of respect. Those who had turned 18 that year were awarded a suit of armour and declared independent citizens.

The opening ceremony was clearly a moment of great political theatre. This was particularly true of the parade of tribute: the money was brought in by 400 hired bearers, each carrying a sack holding one talent of silver (the equivalent of 6,000 drachmas). Moreover, the whole spectacle was witnessed by the largest peacetime gathering of Athenians: the only occasion when more Athenians would have come together was on the battlefield.

The audience
Entry to the theatre cost two obols per day. As this was roughly the equivalent of a day's wage for an unskilled worker, the poor were probably excluded from the festival in its early years. However, at some point in the second half of the 5th century (or possibly later), the Athenian state established the **Theoric Fund**, which paid for the poorest citizens to attend the theatre if they could not afford the entrance fee. This ensured that the dramatic contests were open to the full range of citizens, rich and poor, young and old.

The front and back of
a theatre token found
at Athens.

Upon payment of the fee, each citizen was given a token bearing the letter of his tribe. The *theatron* was divided into thirteen wedges and it seems that ten of these were set aside for the ten tribes. The other three wedges were probably reserved for metics, foreigners and possibly women (it is uncertain whether women could attend the theatre or not; however, if they did so, it would not have been in large numbers). The seats of the *prohedria* and behind were reserved for important officials: the 500 members of the council (see p. 205), the ephebes, foreign and allied dignitaries, generals, other important magistrates and the priest of Dionysos. In the following extract from Aristophanes' *Frogs*, the priest is even addressed by the character Dionysos in a moment of fright:

3. Athenian Drama

'Oh, Mister Priest, protect me, remember that drink we're going to have after the show!'   Aristophanes, *Frogs* 297

Spectators would probably have brought provisions such as cushions and food to make the day more comfortable; they may also have required suitable clothes to protect them from the elements if the weather was bad. While watching the plays, they were no doubt loud and opinionated, even though it was a religious festival. Thus, they were probably more comparable to an audience in Elizabethan England than to one today. Sources speak of spectators hissing, hooting or kicking their heels when unimpressed. A comic audience must have been especially lively, and here we can perhaps compare them to a pantomime audience today. As a result, a theatre police force, whose members were called 'rod-bearers', was employed to beat unruly spectators!

Singing for freedom

Since many Athenians probably took part in a chorus at some point in their lives, they must have been a knowledgeable and discerning audience. The historian Plutarch illustrates this with an astonishing story, which also suggests the popularity of Athenian drama in the wider Greek world.

In 415, Athens launched a failed attack on the Sicilian city of Syracuse. Many Athenians were captured and imprisoned in stone quarries, where their Syracusan captors treated them with unrestrained barbarity. However, the same Syracusans had a particular fondness for the plays of Euripides, so much so that they were prepared to feed or even liberate any Athenians who could sing his choral odes. Upon returning to Athens, those who had been set free visited Euripides to thank him for saving their lives.

Day 5 (judging and cast parties)

The Athenian system of judging plays at the City Dionysia was highly democratic and tried to avoid any unfair influence or bribery. The judges had to vote on the winning tragic and comic playwrights. From 449, there was also a prize for the leading actor, which was probably judged in the same way as the other two:

- Before the festival began, the council drew up a list of names from each of the ten tribes of the city.
- The names from each tribe were sealed in an urn and the ten urns were then stored on the Acropolis.
- On the first morning of the plays, the ten urns were placed in the theatre and the eponymous archon randomly drew out one name from each urn. These ten citizens then swore an oath of impartiality and were installed as judges for the competition.
- The judges watched all the plays and were no doubt influenced by the audience reaction. On the fifth day of the festival each judge wrote down his order of merit on a tablet. All ten tablets were then placed in a single urn.

- The eponymous archon then drew out five of the ten tablets at random and the playwright with the most votes was declared the winner. The archon announced his name and crowned him with a garland of ivy.

A drawing of part of the Athenian victors' list, a long series of inscriptions which recorded the winners in the dramatic competitions at Athens.

After the judging was over, the participants headed off to the cast parties thrown by the *chorêgoi*, a final opportunity for wine and revelry in honour of Dionysos.

The review

A few days later, the Athenian assembly met in the theatre of Dionysos to review the festival. Any citizen could make a complaint about how it had been run. If his complaint was upheld, then the eponymous archon could be fined. However, if the assembly felt that the festival had been a success, they could vote to give him a crown to thank him for his efforts.

Review 3

1. Define the following: *chorêgos, eisagôgê, pompê, proagôn, prôtagônistês, Theoric Fund.*
2. Imagine you are the eponymous archon. How would you choose the poets for the City Dionysia? What information would you want to know about their proposed plays?
3. Imagine you are a *chorêgos* for tragedy who wants to put on the best show ever. Draw up a list of ideas and expenses for your plays.
4. How are major arts projects and events funded today? How important do you think it is for a society to spend money on culture and the arts?
5. Design a poster advertising the events for the coming City Dionysia.
6. Imagine you are (i) an Athenian; (ii) an allied delegate. Describe your experience of watching the opening ceremony of the festival.
7. What do you think were the strengths and weaknesses in the system of judging the plays?
R. Read lines 1154-62 of Aristophanes' *Assembly-Women*. What do they suggest about the judging process?
E. What were the strengths and weaknesses of the organisation of the City Dionysia? Could we learn anything from the Athenians on how to organise an arts festival today?

IV. TRAGEDY

Tragic plays in the days of Thespis, it seems, had retold stories about Dionysos, perhaps particularly focusing on the sufferings of the god and his followers. However, for reasons which remain obscure, the genre of tragedy soon moved away from dealing exclusively with Dionysos. Instead, it came to examine the nature of suffering itself – playwrights began to 'put human suffering on stage'.

Why do people suffer? How far can we control our own destiny? What makes a person a hero? It was just these kind of fundamental questions about human life which tragedy set out to confront. The plays did not seek to provide easy answers by using plots which came to neat conclusions; instead, they typically ended with the intense pain of the main characters unresolved. The audience was rather invited to 'suffer with' (*sympathein*) the characters and perhaps thereby to reflect upon the suffering in their own lives.

Tragic plays, now solemn and serious, presented noble characters who bore their suffering with dignity. Playwrights therefore drew upon a variety of Greek myths for stories of heroism and suffering. With one exception (Aeschylus' *Persians*; see pp. 194-5), every surviving tragic play relates a story from Greek mythology. Thus the audience usually knew the outline of the plot in advance; the interest lay rather in how the playwright had chosen to interpret it. Indeed, playwrights often wrote plays based on the same myth; for example, we have a play about Electra from each of the three great tragedians.

Contemporary issues

Even though the plays were set in the mythological past, they could still be topical and relevant to contemporary society; various surviving plays raise issues which must have struck home to a 5th century Athenian audience. For example, Aeschylus' *Eumenides*, first performed as part of the *Oresteia* trilogy in 458, relates the origin of the Athenian legal system just as it was undergoing radical reform (see p. 196). If, as many scholars believe, Sophocles' *King Oedipus* was presented in the early 420s, then its opening, where the Thebans are enduring a catastrophic plague, must have reminded the audience of the horrific plague which had struck Athens in 430. Moreover, some of Euripides' plays, such as *Trojan Women* and *Andromache*, posed powerful questions about the nature of war at a time when Athens was engaged in a brutal conflict with Sparta.

---

1. The tragic playwrights

The variety of roles undertaken by the playwrights was extraordinary. Not only did they write every line in verse, they also composed the music; some playwrights, such as Aeschylus, also trained and choreographed the chorus as well as acting in the play themselves.

5th century Athens saw a remarkable flourishing of tragedy, at the heart of which were the works of three great tragedians: **Aeschylus**, **Sophocles** and **Euripides**. After the last two both died in 406, tragedy declined and never reached the same high standards again.

Aeschylus (*c.* 525-456)

Aristotle tells us that Aeschylus introduced a second actor onto the stage, a radical development from the one-actor tradition of Thespis. He later followed Sophocles' model of using a third actor. Although he probably wrote about eighty plays, only six survive today (he is sometimes also credited with a seventh), three of which belong to his famous trilogy, the *Oresteia* – a series of three plays (*Agamemnon*, *Libation-Bearers* and *Eumenides*) which recount the working out of the curse of the house of Atreus and the introduction of justice to Athens. Aeschylus' plays are distinctive and his language is very grand and serious. The role of the chorus and song is still fundamental: more than half of the lines in *Suppliants* are sung. Despite his artistic achievements, Aeschylus was prouder of his record as a veteran of the battle of Marathon. He wrote an epitaph for himself recording this – and made no mention of his poetic career!

Sophocles (*c.* 496-406)

Sophocles was the most innovative of the three. He introduced the third actor, he increased the number of choristers from 12 to 15 and he introduced scene painting on the front of the *skênê* to make the stage more atmospheric. He was also very successful, winning 24 contests and never coming third. Although he is believed to have written at least 120 plays, only seven survive. The most famous of these are his Theban plays (*Antigone*, *King Oedipus*, *Oedipus at Colonos*). He was also an important political figure in Athens, serving as a general alongside Pericles in 441.

Euripides (*c.* 480-406)

Euripides was more popular after his death than during his lifetime, probably because he liked to shock his audiences and be inventive with plots and characters. Aristophanes' comedies frequently parody him, portraying him as a playwright of humble birth who creates dangerous female characters and great heroes who are reduced to wearing rags – a far cry from the grandeur of Aeschylus. Euripides was particularly interested in the psychology of his characters, who are usually complex and well-developed. Eighteen of his plays have survived (he is sometimes credited with a nineteenth), although he is said to have written 92 in all.

Mutual respect

Although the playwrights were often in competition with one another, there is a moving story that illustrates their mutual respect. In 406, news of the death of Euripides was received shortly before the *proagôn* of the City Dionysia. Sophocles reportedly appeared in the Odeion in mourning clothes, leading in his chorus and actors without their customary garlands. When they saw him, the audience apparently burst into tears.

Aristophanes' *Frogs*

In 405 Aristophanes wrote a comedy called *Frogs*. The previous year, both Euripides and Sophocles had died and the Athenians perhaps feared that the standard of their tragedies would never be recaptured. In *Frogs*, Dionysos goes down to the Underworld and holds a competition to bring back one of the three great tragedians. Sophocles is too modest and respectful to challenge Aeschylus and so it is left to the other two to present their cases.

During the contest the two characters criticise one another's styles and language, and from this we can learn how their work might have been viewed in Athens. However, arguably the most interesting moment is when the two characters agree – that the responsibility of a good playwright is to educate his audience. When Euripides is asked what qualities he looks for in a good poet, he replies: 'he should teach a lesson, make people into better citizens'. Soon after, Aeschylus adds: 'from the very earliest times, the really great poet has been the one who had a useful lesson to teach'.

2. Watching a tragedy

There are some obvious contrasts between ancient and modern plays. 5th century plays were written to be performed once only, at a dramatic festival – a crucial difference from the modern theatre, where plays are performed many times, sometimes running for years. A second key difference was that a play was not written to be read and studied as a text. Everything was geared around the acting of the play on one special occasion. To analyse a Greek tragedy, it is therefore essential to reconstruct what a spectator might have experienced.

Differences between the perspectives of ancient and modern spectators are immediately clear: performances were held out of doors in daylight hours; there were only three actors who played all the main roles; all the actors wore masks over their faces; and between the scenes of the play the chorus sang and danced in the *orchêstra*. It is this final point which is most striking. Watching an ancient tragedy was perhaps similar to watching a combination of a stage-play, an opera and a ballet. Singing and dancing were as elemental to the performance as the acting itself. Moreover, they provided a direct link back to the dithyramb and Dionysos.

The music

It cannot be overstated how important music was to a Greek play – the comparison with watching an opera or musical today is worth considering. Poets used music to heighten emotional intensity – an ancient commentator called Aristoxenus observed that speech began to sound like song 'when we become emotional'. For example, in *Bacchae*, Agave moves from song during her madness to speech as she recovers her sanity. By contrast, the emotionally repressed Pentheus sings not a single line during the play.

A Greek play had three main forms of musical song:

- **choral odes**. These were perhaps comparable to the grand choruses of opera; the chorus usually danced as they sang them.
- **kommos**. This was a formal song at moments of heightened emotion involving dialogue between an actor and the chorus.
- **monody**. This was a solo song by an actor, often sung at moments of great distress, which could be compared to an operatic solo.

---

3. Structure

A tragedy was introduced by a prologue, in which the plot was outlined and the scene set. The chorus then entered the *orchêstra* via the *parodoi* and sang their entry song (known as the *parodos*). The rest of the play was a series of scenes involving dialogue between the main characters; between each scene, the chorus sang an ode. After the final ode the last scene of dialogue was called the *exodos* ('departure'). The action of the plays was usually set in the same location over a very short period of time, such as one day. This brought great intensity and allowed events to develop at a brisk pace.

One of the most powerful moments in a tragedy was the **messenger speech**. One of tragedy's rules was that violence could not be portrayed on stage (although Sophocles' *Ajax* arguably breaks this rule with Ajax's suicide). Therefore, moments of violence had to be reported to the audience by an actor whose character had heard of or witnessed the event. The lack of visual violence meant that the use of powerful language became profoundly important. These speeches were the polar opposite of many modern Hollywood films, which compete with one another in using ever more dramatic special effects. Ancient playwrights had to convey the same level of violence with words alone.

In the famous passage below, a messenger in *King Oedipus* recounts how Oedipus has blinded himself after discovering the dead body of his wife Jocasta, who has hanged herself:

The King saw too, and with heart-rending groans
Untied the rope, and laid her on the ground.
But worse was yet to see. Her dress was pinned
With golden brooches, which the King snatched out
And thrust, from full arm's length, into his eyes –
Eyes that should no longer see his shame, his guilt,
No longer see those they should never have seen,
Nor see, unseeing, those he had longed to see,
Henceforth seeing nothing but night ... To this wild tune
He pierced his eyeballs time and time again
Till bloody tears ran down his beard – not drops
But in full spate a full cascade descending
In drenching cataracts of scarlet rain.

Sophocles, King Oedipus 1264-79

4. Masks and costumes

The concept of actors wearing masks seems very strange to us today. Facial expression is a vital part of modern acting and it is hard to imagine a play without it. Yet, in the absence of artificial lighting, facial expression would not have made a significant impact in the Athenian theatre; for the majority of the audience were sitting more than 20 metres from the stage. In this context, the masks actually added something to the performance.

(a) (b) (c)

Masks for the Athenian theatre; (a) is for a young girl, (b) is for a king and (c) is for a satyr-play.

Masks were made of linen, cork or wood and had openings for eyeholes and the mouth. There was often some hair attached at the top to act as a wig. They were slightly larger than life-size to make them more visible, and tragic masks were generally painted with the grand and solemn expressions of tragic characters. In the absence of facial expression, actors must have relied on other means of expression. The use of gestures and expansive body movement took on far more significance, while actors must have changed the pitch and tone of their voices to express emotion.

In fact, the use of masks could be turned into an advantage. Since the plays were performed by three actors alone, masks allowed them to play a range of roles – men and women, rich and poor, old and young. Two other benefits wouldn't seem immediately obvious to a modern reader:

- **Actor versatility**. Occasionally, two different actors were required to play the same character; for example, in Sophocles' *Oedipus at Colonos*, the role of Theseus could not have been played by one actor throughout the play. This would have been conveniently disguised by the use of the same character mask.
- **Visual impact**. A change of mask for a character during a play could make a tremendous visual impact. When Oedipus arrived back on stage after blinding himself in *King Oedipus*, he must have worn a new, blood-spattered mask with darkened eye holes.

The costumes of tragic actors were based on the two main items of Greek clothing (see p. 157): the *chitôn*, a full-length robe, over which was often worn a shorter cloak, a *himation*, which reached down to the knees. However, in contrast to everyday clothing, tragic costumes were

Tragic actors in costume depicted on the Pronomos vase.

116

more closely fitted, had sleeves and, most importantly, were often ornate and colourful, with a rich patchwork of different patterns. Tragic costumes therefore reflected the grand and heroic characters of the genre. Alternatively, some roles required specific costumes: paupers were dressed in plainer robes, black was reserved for mourners, soldiers wore armour and barbarians trousers, etc. On their feet actors wore soft leather boots, *kothornoi*, which reached up to the thigh.

Putting the boot on the other foot

The *kothornos* which the actors wore on their feet was loose and flexible, which meant that it could be worn on either foot. The word *kothornos* was therefore used to describe someone who changed their views easily. The 5th century politician Theramenes was reportedly nicknamed '*kothornos*' when he kept switching his allegiance from one political party to another.

In the absence of stage-lighting, masks and costumes were also an important way for the playwright to give the audience information. A distinct mask and costume would have made it much easier for the audience to identify characters as soon as they arrived: gods, old men, kings, queens, paupers and slaves would all have been instantly recognisable by their garb.

Research: The Pronomos vase

The Pronomos vase, an Athenian mixing bowl (*kratêr*) dated to *c*. 400, is one of our best sources of evidence for actors' costumes and masks. It depicts actors in a satyr-play and takes its name from the *aulêtês* named on the vase, who is known to have performed in Athens in 394.

Examine a picture of the vase and consider: (i) How we can tell who the playwright is; (ii) How we can tell who Pronomos is; (iii) How we know that this must have been a satyr-play; (iv) what information the vase gives about the actors' masks and costumes.

---

5. The cast

There were two distinct groups of performers in the Athenian theatre – the professional actors who played the leading roles and the amateur chorus members who were chosen from the citizen body. Nonetheless, all the actors were male citizens, even though they might have played goddesses, women, foreigners or slaves. However, this did not prevent playwrights from creating a powerful and compelling range of characters.

Leading actors

In any tragedy, no more than three actors with speaking parts were allowed on stage at any one time (although, in practice, minor characters such as children could also appear and were sometimes given a line or two); moreover, the same three actors were used to play all the leading roles, something a playwright had to bear in mind when writing his script: plays usually contained about eight to ten different parts, and so an actor could be required to play four or even five characters. There must have been moments of rushed confusion as actors changed mask and costume inside the *skênê*. For example, in Sophocles' *Antigone*, the same actor had to play the following five roles:

- **Ismene**, the timid sister of Antigone.
- A Theban **soldier** who acts as a guard.
- **Haimon**, a noble young man engaged to Antigone.
- **Teiresias**, a blind old man who has prophetic powers.
- Queen **Eurydice**, the mother of Haimon.

Actors were also required to be good singers, perhaps in a variety of different character roles; thus, playwrights probably wrote parts with certain actors in mind, aware of their particular vocal talents.

The chorus

Nothing captured the democratic spirit of the City Dionysia more than the chorus, which was made up of fifteen ordinary citizens (or twelve in the early days of tragedy). If the dithyrambic contests are factored in, then well

The chorus performs in a modern version of a Greek tragedy.

This vase shows two lines of a chorus of soldiers singing and dancing in unison. The identical position of each dancer suggests a carefully choreographed sequence.

over 1,000 Athenians could have competed as choristers in the festival. We do not know how they were selected (talent was surely important), but selection for a chorus must have been a great honour; choristers were apparently spared military service during the rehearsal period.

The rehearsing probably took months and must have been hard work. A *chorêgos* for tragedy selected his choristers to act in all four of the plays he was financing; they would have spent hours learning and practising all the words, music, and dance steps, often wearing heavy masks and costumes. One interesting side-note to this is that, since Athens was a small and open city, the rehearsals probably took place in public, allowing other Athenians a preview of what they could expect at the coming festival.

Each chorus had a leader who was sometimes given one or two individual lines; that aside, choristers sang and danced in unison. They were accompanied by a musician (the **aulêtês**) playing an *aulos* (an instrument closely associated with the worship of Dionysos). Sadly, since we have no records of the music or dances, we can only guess at how a choral ode may have looked and sounded. However, the dancing probably involved the whole body, with movement of the arms and swirling of the body. They may have divided into formations of 3x5 (or 3x4 in the early years).

The chorus served various purposes in a play, some of which are suggested below:

- **Actor**. The chorus was usually a part of the action itself, often portraying local townsfolk. For example, in Aeschylus' *Agamemnon*, they are elders of Argos who witness Clytaemnestra's crimes; in Sophocles' *King Oedipus*, citizens of the plague-struck city of Thebes; in Euripides' *Medea*, Corinthian women who feel sympathy for Medea's plight but are horrified by her actions. Sometimes the chorus could be more sinister: in Aeschylus' *Eumenides*, they are represented as snake-haired avenging spirits.
- **Scene-setting**. Choral songs often give the audience important background information: the opening chorus of *Agamemnon* relates the sacrifice of Iphigenia, which is crucial to understanding why Clytaemnestra wants to take revenge on her husband.
- **Commentator/moral voice**. The chorus often stepped back from the actors and offered a commentary or moral opinion on the events of the play. For example, the chorus of elders in *Agamemnon* condemn Clytaemnestra's murderous actions; in *King Oedipus*, the chorus of Thebans lament the sad downfall of their king.
- **Background mood**. The chorus also offered a background setting to the action, acting much like the soundtrack of a film does today. In this way, it could build suspense before an act of violence or lament after a moment of tragedy.
- **Scene-break**. The most practical role of the chorus was to create a break between scenes, acting almost as a stage curtain can today. This allowed the actors to leave the stage and change costume if necessary.

Review 4

1. Define the following: *aulêtês, chitôn, himation, kommos, kothornos, monody, parodos*.
2. In your opinion, do modern playwrights or film directors ever try to 'educate' their audiences? Should they do so?
3. What similarities and differences can you find between the requirements of ancient and modern acting?
4. What do you think were the benefits and drawbacks of the masks for: (i) the audience; (ii) the actors?
5. Could a Greek play have existed without a chorus?
R. (i) Referring to lines 453-9 of *Bacchae*, draw or design a mask to be used by an actor playing the character of Dionysos.
R. (ii) Read lines 907-91 of Aristophanes' *Frogs*. How are the plays of Aeschylus and Euripides contrasted in this passage?
E. (i) Imagine you are a selected to be a chorister for a tragic poet. Describe your experiences of rehearsing for and competing in the City Dionysia.
E. (ii) Plutarch claimed that tragedy offered 'a wonderful aural and visual experience'. Do you agree?

V. COMEDY

Watching a comedy at Athens must have been a riotous experience. Although it shared many conventions with tragedy, comedy was a different dramatic genre, one which had emerged out of the songs and dances of the *kômos* and which thus celebrated fertility with revelry and raucous laughter. The following comments by Paul Cartledge give a flavour of the genre:

> 'It is not really surprising that no modern form of comedy ... should come anywhere near to reproducing the inimitable cocktail that was an Aristophanic play. For if we were to translate its content, tone, style and atmosphere into recent or contemporary terms, it was something like ... broad farce, comic opera, circus, pantomime, variety, revue, music hall, television and movie satire, the political cartoon, the political journal, the literary review, and the party pamphlet – all shaken and stirred into one very heady brew.'   *Aristophanes and his Theatre of the Absurd*, p. 73ff.

As Cartledge suggests here, the study of 5th century comedy really only concerns one playwright – Aristophanes. We do know a little about some of his contemporaries, such as Cratinos and Eupolis, but only Aristophanes' plays had the classic status which ensured that a number of them were preserved. It is therefore debatable to what extent Aristophanes is typical of the comic playwrights of his day.

Aristophanes (450-386)

Aristophanes was regarded as the greatest writer of what we call Old Comedy, which flourished during the second half of the 5th century. He was therefore an important contemporary of both Sophocles and Euripides. Eleven of his plays have survived, although there are fragments of many others and the total number was perhaps around 40. Most were written during the years of the Peloponnesian War (431-404), a time of vigorous political life at Athens. As we shall see, his plays tended to satirise public life and public figures and, although he was writing to entertain, his work almost certainly offers an insight into the political issues of the day. In some ways, his plays could be compared in modern western society to the British satirical magazine *Private Eye* or the *Daily Show* in the USA.

1. Themes

Above all, Old Comedy was political and focused on public life. For this reason, Aristophanes' plays are frequently cited elsewhere in this book. The following are possibly the most common themes in his works:

- **War**. One can detect particular anger and pathos in Aristophanes' plays relating to the war. One 'war-play', *Lysistrata* (see pp. 201 and 252), seems on the surface to be an amusing tale of Athenian and Spartan women plotting to end the war by holding a sex-strike. Yet, since it was written the year after Athens and her allies had lost a huge number of young men in an ill-fated expedition to Sicily, the idea of women surviving without men must have been painfully close to reality. Other 'war-plays', such as *Knights* and *Acharnians*, lampoon Cleon, an Athenian leader in the 420s (see p. 219).
- **Public life**. Other areas of public life were satirised too. In *Wasps* (see p. 217), Aristophanes makes fun of public jury-service, while *Clouds* mocks Socrates and the sophists (see pp. 50-1). Plato records that when Socrates was later put on trial, he complained that he had been unfairly represented by Aristophanes.
- **The theatre**. The theatre itself proved a rich source of humour. Aristophanes enjoyed mocking the grand pretensions of tragedy and particularly of Euripides' plays: the tragedian is actually a character in three of the eleven surviving comedies. Aristophanes also enjoyed depicting gods as cowardly and ridiculous (in contrast to the power and grandeur of tragedy's gods); for example, in *Frogs*, the slave Xanthias is far braver than Dionysos.
- **Fantasy**. Since watching a comedy offered an escape from everyday life, Aristophanes wrote some escapist 'fantasy' plays: in *Birds*, for example, two Athenians leave Athens to create an ideal city in the sky.

2. Structure, form and language

The plays of Aristophanes are much less formally structured than those of tragedy. A helpful contrast between the two is drawn by Ian Storey and Arlene Allan, who compare the carefully developed plots of tragedy to the shape of a comedy:

> '*Farce* or *fantasy* might be more appropriate descriptions of what Aristophanes created. Old comedy depends not on a complicated plot of intrigue or a subtle interaction between characters, but on the working out of a great idea, the more bizarre the better. Imagine a fantastic idea, wind it up and let it run, watch the splendidly "logical" conclusions unfold, and let the whole thing end in a riotous final scene.'
>
> *A Guide to Ancient Greek Drama,* p. 174

The last point here is especially significant: unlike tragedies, comedies typically finished in a mood of celebration and triumph, often involving a banquet or wedding. A further difference between the two genres was the setting; for where tragedy was generally based in the mythological past (and usually in cities other than Athens), comic plays involved characters from everyday Athenian life, either public figures or stock characters. Consequently, the audience were not usually familiar with a comic storyline in advance (as they were when tragedy was based on a well-known myth) and so comic prologues were longer and aimed to introduce the plot and main characters.

Comic plots usually revolved around a conflict. A good example occurs in *Acharnians*, written by Aristophanes in 424 after Athens had been at war with Sparta for six years. The leading character, Dikaiopolis ('Just-city') tries to convince the Athenians to come to terms with their enemies. When they refuse, he makes his own private peace with the Spartans. At this point the chorus runs in singing its *parodos* and hunting Dikaiopolis; they are Acharnians from a farming region in the front line of the war in Attica. Furious with what they see as his treachery, they bay for his blood. Dikaiopolis, however, is unmoved:

> *Dikaiopolis*: Oh, I know we always say hard things about the Spartans, but are they responsible for all our troubles?
> *Chorus Leader*: The Spartans not responsible? You dare say that, bold as brass, to our face, and you expect to escape with your life?
> *Dikaiopolis*: Yes, not entirely responsible, not entirely responsible ... and if the people (*indicating the audience*) don't think I have justice on my side, then – I'm willing to speak with my head over a chopping block!'
>
> Aristophanes, *Acharnians* 309ff.

Dikaiopolis goes on to make a speech in his defence with his head across a chopping block! It proves so successful that he manages to win himself a reprieve and does indeed make his own personal peace. As the play progresses, he bears the fruits of his peace, while others around him suffer from war. The final scene depicts him boozily celebrating a festival in the arms of music-girls.

The passage above typifies comedy in various ways: in its development of a humorous conflict, in the amusing yet macabre image of Dikaiopolis' head on a chopping block and in the direct involvement of the audience. However, despite the humour, the topic raised here is deadly serious – the prosecution of the war with Sparta. This was the essence of old comedy: important issues treated in the context of farce and fantasy.

The *parabasis*

One interesting feature of comic plays was the *parabasis* ('stepping-forward'). This was a speech by the chorus, or the chorus leader, in which the playwright would put forward his own views to the audience. When *Frogs* was written in 405, Athens was in terrible trouble in the war. Aristophanes used the *parabasis* to argue for the forgiveness of certain Athenians who had previously betrayed their city. The poet clearly felt that the Athenians needed all the help they could get. In *Clouds*, Aristophanes even uses the *parabasis* to complain about the fact that an earlier version of the same play had not won a prize.

Language

The language of Aristophanes offers a paradox. On the one hand, he was often incredibly crude, using the Greek equivalents of English four-letter words to describe sex, bodily functions and even the characters themselves. This was in stark contrast to the very formal language of tragedy and satyr-plays (in fact, this was a major difference between comedies and satyr-plays).

On the other hand, Aristophanes could use language sublimely and wrote some of the finest choral lyrics to have survived from Athenian drama. He was also very inventive, and his linguistic flair is perhaps comparable to that of Oscar Wilde or Noel Coward in English. One famous example of this cleverness occurs in *Birds*: when the two leading characters think about a name for their new city, they come up with *Nephelococcygia*, or 'Cloud-Cuckoo Land', as we still say today.

3. Staging and acting

Although comedy had the same distinction between leading actors and chorus, there were some important differences in staging:

- It is likely that comedy allowed a fourth leading actor to appear on stage (although some scholars dispute this).
- A comic chorus consisted of 24 members rather than 12 or 15.
- Comic costumes and masks were designed to make the actors look ridiculous and build up the element of farce in the play.
- Comic actors often broke the dramatic illusion of the theatre by acknowledging the presence of the audience (as we have seen in the passage from *Acharnians*) and, at times, even addressing the spectators directly (as Dionysos does his priest in *Frogs*).

The *ekkyklêma* and *mêchanê* in comedy

Aristophanes enjoyed making extensive use of the *ekkyklêma* and *mêchanê* in his plays. We have already seen how *Peace* begins with the leading character, Trygaios, setting off into the sky to look for the elusive goddess Peace. The opening 170 lines of the play see him sing an aria while suspended on the dung-beetle. *Clouds* also uses the *mêchanê* to add humour. When Socrates first appears, he is suspended in mid-air in a basket on the *mêchanê*. When asked what he is doing so high up, he replies that it helps him to think higher thoughts. Aristophanes often satirised Euripides as the tragedian who made most (and perhaps excessive) use of both devices. In *Acharnians*, a caricatured version of Euripides even arrives on stage on the *ekkyklêma*!

The Choregoi vase (see opposite) clearly illustrates how different comic costumes were from tragic ones. A comic actor wore a short tunic, a cloak (reaching just below the waist) and tights. The whole costume

This scene on the Choregoi vase is particularly rare and instructive since it depicts a tragic actor (left) arriving on stage in a comedy; the vase therefore illustrates the contrast between tragic and comic costumes: the former noble and ornate, the latter ridiculous and oversized.

was thickly padded, especially around the belly and buttocks, which made an actor seem shorter and rounder than in real life. It also enabled him to fall and roll around, as comedies often relied on physical humour and slapstick. At such moments, a comic actor behaved more like a circus clown.

The costume's most iconic element was the oversized leather phallus, which may well have been attached by a string to the tunic so that an actor could simulate an erection. In some plays, the phallus was a key element in the plot, most famously when the women of Athens stage a sex-strike in *Lysistrata*. In *Wasps*, Philocleon even offers his phallus to the music-girl as a hand-rope for her to pull herself up onto the stage! Yet the phallus was more than just an entertaining prop – it was a direct link to the *kômos* and a celebration of Dionysos' role as god of fertility.

The costumes of a comic chorus ranged from the colourful to the ridiculous. The titles of some comedies refer to their choruses, and names such as *Birds*, *Clouds*, *Frogs* and *Wasps* suggest that costume designers were kept very busy. The costume designer for *Birds* even

Terracotta statuettes of comic actors.

A chorus of horsemen performing to the music of the *aulêtês*. This vase may depict a scene in Aristophanes' *Knights*.

needed to be an expert ornithologist since the chorus was made up of 24 different types of bird! As these lines illustrate, the arrival of the chorus in the *orchêstra* must have been astonishing:

> *Peisthetairos*: Help, look at this mob of birds coming in now!
> *Euelpides*: Lord Apollo, what a swarm! You can't see the gangways for them.
> *Peisthetairos*: A partridge and a francolin; a mallard; and that's a halcyon.
> *Euelpides*: What's that behind the halcyon?
> *Peisthetairos*: The halcyon's barber, of course.
> *Euelpides*: A barber's not a bird.
> *Peisthetairos*: Isn't he? My barber's called Sparrow and he's a very queer bird indeed. And here's an owl ... Look at them all! Jay, turtledove, crested lark, reed warbler, wheatear, pigeon, merlin, sparrowhawk, ringdove, cuckoo, stockdove, firecrest, rail, kestrel and – oh look – a dabchick! Waxwing – vulture – woodpecker – and that seems to be the lot.
>
> Aristophanes, *Birds* 294ff.

As this passage suggests, comic masks were also distinctive. Facial features were grossly exaggerated and mouths often ridiculously large. Some plays satirised public figures (e.g. the politician Cleon, the philosopher Socrates or the playwright Euripides) and the masks of these characters may have parodied their real looks: the real Socrates, who was present to watch himself portrayed in *Clouds*, reportedly stood up during the performance so that the audience could compare the likeness!

Review 5

1. Outline the differences between costumes and masks worn by comic actors and those worn by tragic actors.
2. How do you think watching a comedy was different from watching a tragedy?
3. Imagine you are the costume designer for Aristophanes' *Birds*. How would you dress up the chorus?
4. Are there satirists today who could be compared to Aristophanes? Is there an equivalent to the *parabasis* at any cultural events today?
R. Read the opening lines of *Frogs* (1-37). What do we learn about the typical nature of comedies from this passage?

Chapter Review

E. To what extent was the City Dionysia related to the god Dionysos?
E. How could an Athenian citizen take part in the City Dionysia? Is there any equivalent festival in the modern world?
E. 'Watching a play at the City Dionysia would have been a far more rewarding experience than going to the theatre today.' Do you agree?

4

Athenian Society

By the 5th century BCE there were hundreds of Greek settlements dotted around the Mediterranean (see map 1) 'like frogs round a pond', in the words of Plato. Although these communities were united by a common language, literature and religion, there were often many differences between them. Despite this, we can get a clear picture of what life was like in only one city, Athens. Since Athens provides us with the great writers of the classical age, it is the city about which we know by far the most.

The study of Athenian social life can be divided into three groups of people: Athenian men, Athenian women, and slaves. Each of these groups lived widely different lives with very contrasting rights and responsibilities. Athenian men lived much of their lives in the public areas of the city, such as the gymnasium, the agora and the assembly. Athenian women generally remained at home, where they oversaw the daily life of the household. Slaves operated in both spheres under the command of their masters.

This chapter is designed to reflect these three distinct lifestyles. It begins by looking at the structure of Greek houses and households; it then moves on to sections on male citizens, female citizens and slaves; finally, it concludes with an examination of how Athenians approached death and funerals.

I. THE OIKOS

The Greek name for a house, *oikos*, was also used to describe more than the physical building where a family lived. Indeed, it is sometimes better translated as 'household' since it could also refer to all the people who lived in the house and to all the property attached to it. At the head of the household was the master of the house, the *kyrios*, though day to day management was overseen by his wife, the *kyria*. The *oikos* consisted of the whole of their family and all their slaves – the wealthier the family, the more slaves they were likely to own; only the poorest families would have no slaves at all.

The *oikos* was seen as both a domestic and an economic unit, since Athenian households aimed as far as possible for self-sufficiency – the production of their own food and material goods. Many households owned farmland outside the city; if the plot was large enough, surplus food could be sold in the market. Moreover, the home itself was a centre of economic activity, since women and slaves spent much of their time spinning and weaving in order to produce all the cloth required by the *oikos*. The distinct lives and aspirations of men and women were defined by the clear division of labour between the two groups – men worked outside the house while women toiled within its walls.

The first economy

The meaning of the Greek word *oikos* as 'household' survives through its legacy in the English language. For the English prefix 'eco-' is simply a developed form of the Greek 'oiko-', so that the word 'economy' originally meant 'the organisation of the household'.

It is interesting to note that in English 'economy' can also describe the saving of money or indeed of anything (e.g. an economy of effort). This surely refers back to the Athenian idea that the successful running of the household required careful management of all the resources available.

---

1. Attitude to houses

The Greeks spent far more on their public buildings than they did on their private houses. Buildings such as temples (see pp. 17-18) and theatres (see p. 97ff.) were often elaborately designed to display civic wealth. By contrast, private houses were generally modest and unremarkable. There are various possible reasons for this: first of all, since Greek men did not spend much time at home, they were less concerned with what their houses looked like; secondly, Greece is a region prone to earthquakes and so it made little sense to construct grand houses which might be reduced to rubble in a matter of minutes; finally, it is also possible that the democratic Athenians of the 5th century valued the sense of equality provided by modest housing, an idea suggested by the 4th century orator Demosthenes:

'The private houses of those in power then were modest and in keeping with our democratic ideas of equality.'   Demosthenes, *On Organisation* 13.29

However, it would be wrong to say that the houses of Athens were all uniform. As today, the wealthy could afford a larger living space, while there were clear differences between urban and rural dwellings.

2. Design

The same basic design for private houses was used in the city, village and countryside. While their foundations were of stone, their walls were constructed of sun-baked clay bricks, which were so easy to cut through that burglars were commonly known as 'wall-piercers'! The roofs of houses were made with clay tiles. Houses were rectangular and often had a

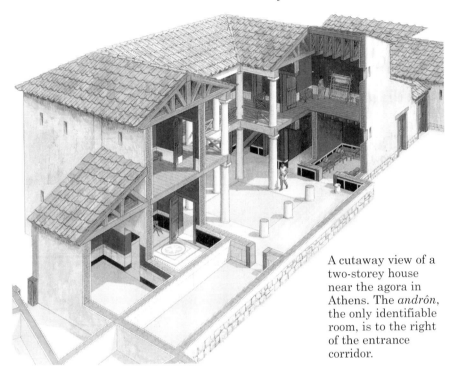

A cutaway view of a
two-storey house
near the agora in
Athens. The *andrôn*,
the only identifiable
room, is to the right
of the entrance
corridor.

smaller second floor reached by a ladder. The few, glassless windows in the house were small and high up; this had the benefit of keeping the heat and dust out of the rooms as well as discouraging burglars. The floors were either hard beaten earth or covered with tiles or blocks of stone.

Entry into the house was usually through a large, impressive wooden front door which led into the courtyard, the focal point of the house, from which most of the rooms led off. The courtyard was paved and often contained a well or a cistern for collecting rainwater; pits to collect waste for manure were also common. Many of the household tasks were carried out here, allowing the women of the house to sit in the open air. Verandas were often built to one side to allow them to sit in the shade if need be. In the countryside the courtyards tended to be larger in order to accommodate animals and farming equipment; many also contained large storage towers.

The most important room of the house was the **andrôn** ('the men's area'). Every type of house excavated in Greece (rich and poor, urban and rural) seems to have had an *andrôn*, which was usually located near the front door. It was essentially a large dining room, where the *kyrios* would host *symposia* (see p. 146). Athenian women were banned from this room; the only women allowed in were slave-girls or foreigners. The cement floor was slightly raised around all four sides and couches were

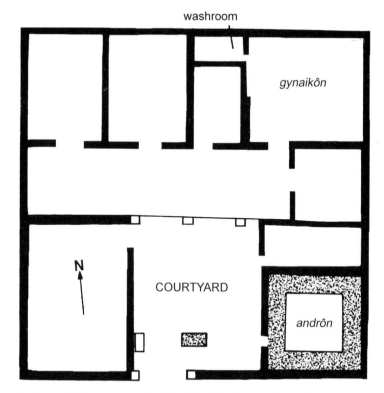

A plan of a house excavated in Olynthos in northern Greece.
This is one house in a block of ten.

A drawing and plan of a 5th century country house.

placed on this elevated area. In the centre of the room, the lower rectangle was often decorated with pebble mosaics. The walls of the *andrôn* could be ornately decorated, perhaps with paintings of men or gods themselves drinking and feasting. In Aristophanes' *Wasps* a son advises his ill-educated father on how to behave at a dinner-party:

> 'But now you must say something complimentary about the bronze ornaments – look up at the ceiling – admire the rugs on the wall.'
> Aristophanes, *Wasps* 1214-15

In another part of the house was the **gynaikôn** ('the women's area'). The *kyria* might well have had a bedroom of her own, but the main room in this area was the loom room, where the women of the house would spin and weave. The *gynaikôn* was often found either at the back of the house or on the first floor, out of the way of the front door. The other rooms off the courtyard were bedrooms for children, slaves' quarters and storerooms. The latter were particularly important for storing the goods and produce of the household.

Wealthy houses might also have had a kitchen and a bathroom. In other cases, food was cooked in the courtyard, as cooking equipment was small and light and could be easily set up there. If a house lacked a bathroom then each bedroom had a jug and basin for occupants to use. Large pots acted as toilets, and slaves regularly had to empty these into the gutter outside the house. As Athens had no sewer system, there were public slaves who washed the streets down on a daily basis.

Decoration and furniture were quite sparing. Interior walls were typically plastered and painted simply, often in red and white. Wealthier families may have decorated their houses with tapestries or statues of dead ancestors. For furniture, couches were used to dine and sleep, while there were also stools, chairs and tables. Clothes were stored in chests or cupboards, but all other goods were hung on hooks on the walls. A tidy and well-ordered house was clearly a source of pride for this Athenian:

> 'How good it is to keep one's stock of utensils in order, and how easy to find a suitable place in the house to keep each set in! What a beautiful sight is created by boots of all sorts arranged in rows! How beautiful it is to see cloaks of all sorts kept separate, or blankets or bronze vessels or table furniture!'
> Xenophon, *Oikonomikos* 8.19

3. Domestic religion

The Greek gods were worshipped at every level of society (see pp. 1-2) and each *oikos* had its own religious shrines. For example, at the front of a house's courtyard was a stone altar to **Zeus Herkeios**, with a snake engraved on its side. The epithet *herkeios* (see p. 6 to read about epithets of the gods) was originally derived from the Greek word for a fence, and so Zeus Herkeios referred to 'Zeus who protects the boundaries of the house'. Zeus was also invoked in the home as *ktesios*, the protector of the *oikos'* property.

Another important religious shrine in the house was the **hearth**, which may well simply have been an altar dedicated to Hestia, goddess of the hearth (see p. 13). It was normally located in one of the communal rooms and symbolised the health and cohesion of the household; at the start of every meal, offerings of food would be thrown into the flames to give thanks to the goddess; the hearth was also the scene of the *amphidromia* a few days after the birth of a child (see opposite).

A Herm.

The Herms

Outside the front door of a typical house could be found a Herm, a four-cornered pillar with a bust of Hermes on its top and an erect phallus on its front, symbolising male strength and fertility. These Herms were believed to be symbols of good fortune and were often also seen at the entrances of public buildings and along roadways.

In 415, in the middle of the war with Sparta, a scandal involving Herms erupted in Athens. The Athenians awoke one morning to discover that nearly every Herm in the city had had its face and genitalia mutilated and disfigured. This was taken to be a terrible omen for the naval fleet about to set sail for a major campaign in Sicily – which ended in a humiliating defeat for Athens.

Review 1

1. Define the following terms: *andrôn, gynaikôn, Herm, kyrios, kyria, oikos, Zeus Herkeios, Zeus Ktesios.*
2. Imagine you are an estate agent responsible for selling a medium-sized house in ancient Athens. Design a pamphlet advertising the house.
3. Do we give more importance to the design of our private houses or our public buildings today? How does this compare to ancient Athens?
4. Why do you think that Xenophon's character is so keen on tidiness at home? How important do you think this is in a home?
5. How well decorated was a typical Greek house in comparison with your house? How important do you think this is for a house's character?
6. List the religious elements in an Athenian home. Do people today have similar religious shrines or artefacts at home?

II. THE LIFE OF A MALE CITIZEN

Male citizens were the privileged elite of Athenian society (you can read more about the political rights of citizens on p. 203). As such, they were accorded great freedom within their society, and many 5th century Athenians spent a great deal of time involved in the politics of their city. However, even within the citizen class there were great contrasts in education, wealth and lifestyle, all of which depended to some extent on whether a man lived in an urban or a rural area.

1. Childhood and education

i. The early years

As soon as a baby was born (see pp. 158-9 for childbirth) it was laid on the ground; its father and a midwife inspected it. If its father refused to accept it, the baby would be taken out of the city and exposed (see below). There was particular delight at the birth of a son, who could inherit the family name and estate. The front door of a house was decorated with a wreath of olives for a baby boy (and a wreath of wool for a baby girl).

However, a child was not introduced to the rest of the family for five days (presumably to reduce the chances of infection). On the fifth day after birth, the father formally accepted the infant in a ceremony called the **amphidromia**, literally meaning 'running around', so called because the father would carry it around the family hearth at a run. However, the most important day for the family was the naming day, which took place ten days after birth. This date would be celebrated in future much as we celebrate a birthday.

135

Exposure

Babies who were unwanted at birth were taken outside the city and abandoned, either to die or to be rescued and enslaved. There was a variety of reasons why a baby might be exposed: perhaps the family couldn't afford to feed another mouth; often it must have been the result of an unwanted pregnancy for a slave-girl or prostitute. It is impossible to know how many babies were exposed in this way, but the number is likely to have been very significant.

It is interesting that some Greek myths feature the exposure of an infant who grows up to be an important figure, such as Oedipus or Paris. In fact, this phenomenon was not confined to the Greeks, as can be seen in the well known stories of Moses and Romulus in Jewish and Roman culture respectively.

A child's early years were spent at home in the care of its mother, who might have been helped by slaves or a nurse. Although sparse, the evidence suggests that the patterns of early childhood bore many similarities to those of today. Some vases show a baby in a terracotta high chair, while a father in Aristophanes' *Clouds* shows off his knowledge of his son's baby talk:

> 'wah-wah meant you wanted a drink ... ma-ma meant you were hungry and as for ca-ca – well the moment you said that I had you out of the house and held you at arm's length ...'   Aristophanes, *Clouds* 1382-5

A vase painting showing a mother with her baby in a high chair.

As children grew, parents may have told them stories such as Aesop's fables, which the philosopher Socrates could still remember in his death cell at the age of 70. Archaeologists have discovered a variety of toys: spinning tops, dolls and dolls' houses, hobby horses, small carts, as well as board games. In one popular game, knucklebones, a child threw some small bones into the air and then attempted to catch them on the back of his hand. Vase paintings also portray children playing ball games which look a little like football or hockey.

ii. Education

At the age of 7 boys could be sent to school for a formal education which lasted for up to ten years. However, there was no state education system, so children went to school only if their parents could afford it. Nevertheless, teachers were not highly valued in society and so education seems to have been fairly cheap. As a result, a majority of Athenians were probably literate; in fact, they needed to be so, since the democratic process required some basic skills in reading and writing.

Finding time for school

The word 'school' is directly derived from the Greek word *scholê*, which literally meant 'leisure'. This is because originally the only Greeks who read, discussed and learnt about intellectual matters were those who had enough leisure time to do so. Learning was therefore seen as an activity for those wealthy enough to be able to indulge in it.

Even today, education should not be taken for granted. In 2007, UNICEF estimated that 14% of girls and 10% of boys globally would receive no education whatsoever. The same organisation estimated that, globally in 2004, 28% of women and 16% of men were illiterate – amounting to more than one billion people.

In addition to formal schooling, a typical boy must have learnt a great deal from his father. At home, he would observe how his father acted as the *kyrios*, learning how a man should treat the family members in his charge. Outside the home, a father would probably teach his trade to his son, or else how to manage and run a farm estate out of the city. These practical lessons were very important for the son as he developed into a young man.

The paidagôgos

In organising his son's education, a father first appointed a tutor, known as a *paidagôgos*, who would be a family slave, preferably with some academic training. The *paidagôgos'* duties were various:

- To supervise the boy at home and at school, escorting him between the two and carrying his school bags.
- To sit in on the lessons and to help him with any homework.
- To teach good manners and discipline and to set a good example. If his charge behaved badly then the *paidagôgos* was allowed to cane him.
- To report to the father on a regular basis, keeping him up to date with his son's progress.

A tombstone of an Athenian boy, resting his hand on the head of his (actually much older) *paidagôgos*. The inferiority of the slave is indicated by his much smaller size.

Despite the importance of their role, *paidagôgoi* were generally looked down on. On seeing a slave fall out of a tree and break his leg, Pericles is supposed to have said: 'He's only fit to be a *paidagôgos* now.'

Schools and teachers

Athens did not have schools as we understand them. In fact, boys were sent to study with a teacher, who would work in a room somewhere. The quality of the schoolroom depended rather on its location. Many teachers used rooms in private houses, and these schoolrooms were probably sparsely furnished. A boy would sit on a stool or bench and perhaps have the use of a table, but there would be little decoration on the walls, although a simple wooden board may have been used like a blackboard. Some schools were attached to an exercise-ground (palaistra) where there were better facilities. School would start early in the morning and finish by the middle of the day.

Teachers were poorly paid and held low status in society, probably because they were either slaves or foreigners to Athens. Moreover, anyone could go into business as a teacher without having any qualifications. It is unlikely that many were specialists in the more advanced areas of the curriculum. The Athenian orator Demosthenes gives us a flavour of how teachers were viewed when he tries to insult his opponent Aeschines, whose father had been a teacher:

'You were brought up in total poverty. You actually helped your father sweat it out in the schoolroom, grinding the soot for the ink, scrubbing down the benches, and sweeping the room. Aeschines, I suggest that you calmly ... compare your background with mine and then ask the jury whether they'd rather have been you or me. You were booed at – I did the booing; you taught the ABC – I was the pupil.'

Demosthenes, *On the Crown* 285

The low status of teachers is curious, considering that Greeks believed that education was so important for their children.

A boy's education was divided into three areas: **academic studies**, **musical studies** and **physical education**. While some schools offered all three, parents would often use a different school for each discipline.

Academic studies

At the age of 7, a boy was sent to an academic teacher known as a *grammatistês*. At first he studied the Greek alphabet and learnt how to read and write. The style of teaching at this stage was very monotonous – there was lots of learning by heart, many hours of practising writing on a tablet, together with endless reciting aloud of words and letters. Reading was harder then than now: there was neither punctuation nor gaps between words! If a boy lost concentration or misbehaved then he was likely to be beaten with a sandal or a cane.

To write, he used a tablet full of wax and a type of pen called a stylus. The pupil could write in the wax with the sharp end of the stylus and then use the blunt end to rub over the wax, allowing him to start again with a fresh surface. If he made good progress he was allowed to use ink and papyrus instead of a wax tablet. The boy probably also had some education in basic numeracy, for which an abacus was used.

Once a boy had mastered these basics, academic education moved on to its most important stage, outlined as follows by Protagoras, a respected educationalist, in one of Plato's dialogues:

'When the children have learnt their letters and are beginning to understand the written word as well as the spoken, they are made to learn by heart the famous poets, whose works contain sound advice and good stories, as well as praise of the heroes of old, so that the child is inspired to imitate them.'
Plato, *Protagoras* 325E

The learning by heart of great literature, particularly the *Iliad* and the *Odyssey*, was very important. Some boys may even have learnt the whole of them by heart. Greeks believed that these works provided great moral lessons and taught them what it meant to be a Greek. Famously, Alexander the Great always carried his copy of the *Iliad* with him wherever he went and read from it frequently.

It is hard for us to know how much progress pupils made in this system. For one thing, there was no formal examination system with results for us to analyse. Secondly, although the class sizes were relatively small (perhaps about twelve), a class would have contained boys of a variety of ages and levels of ability.

Musical studies

Two or three years later the boy began his musical education under the tutelage of a music teacher, the *kitharistês*. Music was a fundamental mark of a well-educated man in Athens, and it was at the heart of the adult society into which boys would be introduced – at religious festivals such as the City Dionysia (see Chapter 3), at *symposia,* or even in military parades. It is therefore regrettable that historians know comparatively little about musical sound and notation (you can read about Greek musical instruments on pp. 278-9).

The cultured man

The belief that music was the mark of a cultured man is often seen in Greek literature and history. Achilles, the greatest and toughest of the heroes in the *Iliad*, is an accomplished musician; when the Greeks come to beg him to return to battle, they find him 'delighting his mind with a clear-toned lyre'. The historian Plutarch also tells a story about the Athenian Cimon, a prominent general during the 460s. He visited a friend for dinner and was asked to sing after the meal. According to Plutarch 'he sang – and most charmingly too, with the result that all the guests began to say how much better educated he was than his rival, the general Themistocles'.

Boys first learnt to play an instrument, usually the *kithara*, by ear, and then to accompany it in song. Some boys may also have learnt to play the *aulos*. Musical education clearly dovetailed neatly with the boy's academic studies, since poems such as the *Iliad* and the *Odyssey* were composed to be recited in song. The importance of musical education in classical Athens was outlined by Protagoras:

> 'The *kitharistês*, by using similar methods to the *grammatistês* when he introduces the boys to Homer, tries to teach the boys moderation and to lead them away from doing wrong. The *kitharistês* teaches the boys to play the lyre and then to sing lyric songs to their own accompaniment. In this way they become more cultured, more controlled and better balanced people, and their behaviour is all the better for it.'
> Plato, *Protagoras* 326A

Protagoras here makes an explicit connection between music and morality, a belief which has emerged repeatedly during history. In the 1960s, for example, many traditionalists blamed the emergence of an age of sexual permissiveness on the new 'popular music'. As recently as 1984, the Soviet leader Yuri Andropov said: 'It is intolerable to see the occasional emergence on a wave of popularity of musical bands with a repertoire of dubious nature. Their activity is ideologically and aesthetically harmful.' No doubt he would have agreed with Plato's view, expressed 24 centuries earlier:

A vase painting showing teachers instructing boys in music and reading.

> 'A new style of music is to be guarded against at all times. For whenever new styles of music are introduced they bring with them new styles of behaviour and new beliefs.'
> Plato, *Republic* 424C

As Plato suggests, the Athenians believed that teaching a boy the right sort of music was also a way of teaching him the right sort of behaviour.

Physical education

Greek cities needed their men to be fit and strong in order to make excellent soldiers, so physical education was fundamental to a boy's upbringing; thus, most cities funded public gymnasia, which also acted as public meeting places with a variety of uses – the Academy, Plato's famous philosophical school, was located in a gymnasium. One feature of such a gymnasium was the palaistra, an exercise ground where physical training took place.

The physical education teacher was known as a *paidotribês* ('the exhauster of boys'); he was easily recognised by his purple cloak and forked stick, which he used to cane any pupils who stepped out of line. Boys were taught many of the sports practised at the great Greek games (see pp. 67-74): running, long jump, javelin, discus, as well as the combat sports of boxing and wrestling. Protagoras goes on to give two reasons why physical fitness was considered so important:

> '... so that by improvement their bodies may be the servants of their minds, which are now in a healthy state, and so that the boys are not compelled to be cowardly in wars and their other duties, because of the weakness of their bodies.'
> Plato, *Protagoras* 326A

Thus, as well as valuing physical exercise as a form of military training, Greeks also saw the link between a healthy body and a healthy mind, surely recognising that physical fitness promotes mental well-being.

Higher education and the sophists

A boy's traditional education finished at about the age of 14. However, during the 5th century a new intellectual movement brought a form of 'higher education' to Athens (this intellectual movement, which started with thinkers and scientists in the region of Ionia, is described in more detail on pp. 50-1). As the movement developed, some educated men tried to popularise the new thinking and lectured widely about ideas which had previously been confined to a small number of intellectuals. These teachers were known as sophists, or 'wise men'.

The sophists were professional teachers who made their money either by teaching privately or by giving public lectures for which there was an admission fee. Most of them travelled widely, taking their knowledge to whoever would listen. One famous sophist was Hippias of Elis, who discussed fields as diverse as ethics, history, geography, literature, astronomy and geometry; Protagoras was another, and he specialised in law and government. However, without doubt the most popular subject in 5th century Athens was rhetoric – the art of public speaking.

Rhetoric was a vital skill in the new democratic system; for people realised that a persuasive speech in the assembly could bring great political influence; as the orator Antiphon observed, in a democracy 'victory goes to him who speaks best'. When Gorgias, the father of rhetoric, came to Athens in 427, he was given star billing and his lectures sold out. He taught people how to argue equally well for either side of a case, much as a lawyer today might argue either for the prosecution or for the defence.

Sophistication or sophistry?
Opposing views about the sophists are still reflected in the English language today: on the one hand, we say that a person of advanced thinking is 'sophisticated'; however, the word 'sophistry' is used to describe someone employing false and deceptive arguments to win their case.

Yet such lessons were really limited to the sons of the rich who could afford to pay the sophists' fees, and this exclusiveness was a serious limitation of the sophistic movement. Moreover, not all these young men apparently used their new skills in honest ways; consequently, the sophists became controversial figures in Athens. Aristophanes wrote a play, *Clouds*, which satirised them as teachers of deceit who, rather than equipping their charges to search for truth, instead showed them how to win an argument at all costs, using as much deception and dishonesty as might be necessary. His portrayal of them is neatly summed up in the following lines from a character called the 'Unjust Argument':

'The point is this: if you slip up, and sooner or later you will, you're tongue-tied and can't begin to defend yourself. But if you're educated in the new style there's nothing you can't talk your way out of.'

Aristophanes, *Clouds* 1076ff.

Aristophanes made his career out of satirising public life and so it is hard to know how much truth there is in this portrayal. Indeed, it is difficult to make any sort of balanced judgement about the sophists, since the sources left to us are likely to be biased against them. However, it is perhaps fair to say that, whatever faults they may have had, they represented an important movement in offering a liberal and rationalist education. For this reason, some have even referred to them as the founding fathers of higher education.

Review 2

1. Define the following: *amphidromia, grammatistês, kitharistês, paidagôgos, paidotribês, sophist.*
2. How common is infanticide in the world today? What are the reasons for it and have they changed since the age of classical Athens?
3. Why do you think that education was valued so highly but the teachers themselves were not? Do such attitudes still exist?
4. Write an imaginary school report on an Athenian boy (although such reports did not exist) including remarks from all three of his teachers.
5. Draw a table charting the similarities and differences between Athenian education and the education you are receiving today.
6. Do you agree with Plato that new styles of music bring new styles of behaviour and belief?
7. Why do you think that rhetoric was so important in classical Athens?
E. Read the account of the Spartan education system on pp. 240-3. How do the two systems compare? Which one would you have preferred to go through and why?

---

2. Adult life

A boy was brought up in preparation for his role as the **kyrios**, who had various responsibilities. He needed to ensure that his wife was running the domestic affairs and finances effectively, and to speak often to the *paidagôgos* about the progress of his son. He would have bought slaves in the slave-market as well as being the main representative for the family at public events such as weddings, funerals and festivals. Moreover, his image would have been greatly enhanced if he was able to host a successful drinking-party, or *symposium*, for friends and associates. Finally, the *kyrios* was ideally a role model for the rest of the family, not least for his sons who would look up to him.

Work and politics

As a male citizen in a city like Athens, the *kyrios* would have wanted to be very involved in the politics of the city. If a man was wealthy then he had a real advantage – he would not have to work so much and so would have more time to attend meetings, debates and votes. In fact, Athenians who had to work hard seem to have been looked down on by the wealthy, as these comments of Xenophon illustrate:

> 'Jobs in craft and industry have a bad reputation and are regarded with contempt. For they ruin those who do them both physically and mentally. For those low-class jobs do not allow people enough time to be with their friends or to take part in public life, with a result that such workers are obviously bad at social and political activities.'
>
> Xenophon, *Oikonomikos* 4.2-3

This passage illustrates the importance of social and political life to Athenian men. If a man was not at work during the day, then he was likely to be found socialising in public places such as the *agora*, the assembly, the law courts or a gymnasium. However, in reality, most citizens had to work to some extent in order to provide for their families.

Farming

In Athens, a large number of the citizens were also farmers who owned small estates outside the city. These estates were a crucial part of providing self-sufficiency for the *oikos*. One of the most important crops was the olive (see below). However, other crops included fruits such as grapes (particularly important for the production of wine), apples, pears, figs and pomegranates as well as grain such as barley, rye and wheat. Some estates also reared animals, such as cattle, sheep and goats, which provided wool, dairy products and meat. Bee-keeping was also important, as honey was the main way of sweetening food and drink.

Olives

It is not hard to see why Athenians believed that the olive tree was a sacred gift to them from their patron goddess Athena (see p. 13). They used olive oil in an amazing variety of ways and it is difficult to imagine how they could have lived without it. It was needed for cooking, lighting lamps, preserving food, making perfumes and medicines, as well as washing the body. Certain olive trees in Attica were protected by the state and, according to Aristotle, anyone found guilty of digging one up could be sentenced to death.

Olive oil was highly prized and a family would store it in large pottery jars called amphorae. Indeed, at the Panathenaic festival at Athens the winners of the sporting events were paid not in money but with amphorae of olive oil (see pp. 31-2). There was also a great deal of profit to be made from exporting or selling olive oil if a farm could produce a surplus.

---

4. Athenian Society

The region around Athens, Attica, had advantages and disadvantages as a farming area. The fertile land was sun-drenched and close to the large market in the city. Moreover, its proximity to Piraeus, the harbour of Athens (see p. 270), meant that it was an ideal location for trade and export. Set against this was the threat of drought, thin soil on the mountainous terrain and the fact that grazing goats often harmed the crops. There is good evidence that 5th century Athenians therefore imported many foods from overseas.

Crafts and trades

By the 5th century the majority of Athenians living in the city were employed in a trade or craft. However, there was no 'heavy industry' as we know it, supported by large factories. Instead, there was a myriad of small businesses which used stalls or workshops. The following lines from a character of Aristophanes suggest the variety of the working life at Athens:

'When the cock sings his dawn song, up they all jump and rush off to work, the bronze-smiths, the potters, the tanners, the shoemakers, the bath-attendants, the corn merchants, the lyre-shapers and shield-makers, and some of them even put on their sandals and leave when it's still dark.'

Aristophanes, *Birds* 489-92

A similar indication of the trades practised in Athens is given in Plutarch's description of Pericles' building programme (see p. 198). Most workshops and shops were rooms hired out at the front of private houses where just a handful of people could work. The largest factory we hear

A vase painting showing a bronze-smith's workshop. The tall furnace is typical of this period. Large bronze statues were cast in pieces and brazed together.

145

of employed 120 slaves to make armour. However, evidence suggests that workshops were usually far smaller; for example, the father of the famous orator Demosthenes owned two workshops, one with 32 knife-makers and the other with 20 carpenters.

The main hub of trade and commerce in the city was the market-place, known as the **agora** (see pp. 272-3). Stretching out from there to beyond the Dipylon Gate was an area known as the **kerameikos** (see p. 274), perhaps the nearest thing Athens had to an industrial area. This was the potters' quarter – Athens was famed throughout the Greek world for the quality of its pottery. Athenians used pottery products in various ways; as well as storing food and drink, they were used as ornaments in the home, as votive offerings to gods (see pp. 27-8), at ceremonies such as weddings and funerals and even as prizes at athletic festivals (see pp. 31-2). Pottery was one of Athens' main exports, alongside silver, oil and wine.

3. The symposium

The main occasion when a Greek would entertain at home was a symposium. 'Symposium' literally meant 'drinking together', and it was essentially an elaborate dinner party. Holding a successful symposium was very important for the image of the *kyrios* since he gained a reputation for being a good host, ready to provide excellent food, wine and entertainment for his guests.

Preparations
The preparations for a symposium started some days before the event. The *kyrios* sent out slaves with invitations – these were typically small statues made of limestone which depicted people walking to a party or feasting. The women of the house were also involved in the preparations, making garlands for the guests to wear and decorating the *andrôn* with flowers, as well as long streamers of vine or ivy.

It was obviously vital to order the best food and drink. The *kyrios* would hire a professional cook to produce the meal and would discuss the menu with him. If the *kyrios* wanted a certain type of dish served, he would try to find a cook who had a high reputation in this field. The cook would normally bring his own cooking equipment with him. The host also had to organise the wine, since its quality was of crucial importance. Some of the most famous wines came from the islands of the Aegean Sea, such as Chios and Lesbos.

Entertainers also needed to be hired. These came in various forms – musicians and dancers were common, while acrobats might also appear. Since citizen women could not enter the *andrôn*, the only women present at a symposium would be slaves, entertainers or courtesans (see below).

Arrival and dinner

The festivities usually started in the early evening and continued late into the night. Upon arrival at the *oikos*, guests were led into the *andrôn*, where they took their places on couches. There were usually between seven and eleven couches at a dinner party, all of which were laid out on the raised outer part of the floor of the *andrôn* (see pp. 131-2). Two people could recline on each couch, leaning on the cushions with their left elbows, which left their right arms free for eating and drinking.

Before the prolonged drinking of wine took place, a dinner was served. It was brought in by slaves and served up on small three-legged tables (which could stand well on an uneven floor). There were normally three courses: an appetiser such as olives, dates or onions, followed by the main course, usually an elaborately cooked dish of meat or fish; finally a sweet desert was served, such as a mixture of fruit, honey and pastry.

Drinking

At the end of dinner slaves removed the tables and swept the floor clean. The guests washed their hands in water, after which they were garlanded with flowers and anointed with scents and perfumes. The drinking stage of the symposium then began with the pouring of a libation (see pp. 26-7) and the singing of a hymn to the 'good divinity'. The guests also drank a toast of unmixed wine to the god.

One member of the symposium was elected its president, or *symposiarch*, and he had responsibility for the wine. His first duty was to decide the strength of the drink, since Greeks always watered down their wine. The most common strength seems to have been five parts of water to two of wine, which gave a mixture of about the strength of modern beer. The two liquids were added together in a mixing bowl known as a *kratêr*, the capacity of which would typically be between 18 and 36 litres. The *symposiarch* then had to decide how many *kratêrs* were to be mixed for the symposium – three seems to have been a typical number.

After this, it was up to the *symposiarch* to choose the size of the drinking cups, the number of toasts and the frequency of rounds. Wild drunkenness does not often seem to have been the aim; indeed, in the following lines from a play by Eubolos, the god Dionysos gives some amusing advice to fellow drinkers at a symposium:

'Three *kratêrs* only do I propose for sensible men, one for health, the second for love and pleasure and the third for sleep; when this has been drunk up, wise guests head for home. The fourth *kratêr* is mine no longer, but belongs to pride; the fifth to shouting; the sixth to revel; the seventh to black eyes, the eighth to legal summonses; the ninth to bile; and the tenth to madness and people tossing the furniture about.'   Eubolos, fr. 94

A vase painting of a symposium in full flow. The figure on the right is playing *kottabos*.

When the drinking started, the entertainers would arrive. Girl musicians were normally hired to play the *aulos*, while dancers, acrobats and mimers were also common. Xenophon's account of a symposium sees a Syracusan man introduce three entertainers: a girl who was an expert *aulos*-player; another who was an acrobatic dancer; and a boy who was a gifted lyre-player and dancer. The acrobat performs as follows:

> 'After this, a hoop was brought in, bristling with sharp swords. The dancer did somersaults in and out through these, until the spectators were terrified that she might hurt herself, but she coolly completed her performance without accident.'   Xenophon, *Symposium* 2.2

The guests could also provide their own entertainment, joining in with the singing or dancing, telling anecdotes, or playing games. Some guests might sing **skolia**, or drinking-songs, which were composed to be sung at symposia. Another common source of fun was a game called **kottabos**. After draining their cups, the guests tried to flick the dregs of the wine at a target. Sometimes this target was a disc balanced on a stand, at others it was a bowl or cauldron which would hiss when the wine landed in it. Evidence suggests that to win the game, the style of your throw was as important as hitting the target.

Intellectual discussion was a central element of many symposia. Guests might listen to poetry or music and then discuss philosophical matters. In Plato's account of a symposium, the guests agree at the start that they wish to discuss philosophy. As a result, they send away the female entertainer and decide on a weak mixture of wine. It must have been important for the *kyrios* to ensure intelligent conversation at his symposium; a passage in Aristophanes' *Wasps* which describes a symposium emphasises that the participants at such events should be well-bred and well-educated.

Plato's *Symposium*

The most famous account of a symposium occurs in one of Plato's dialogues involving Socrates. Entitled simply *The Symposium*, it relates a discussion about the nature of love at a symposium hosted in 416 by the tragic poet Agathon after his victory at the Lenaia drama festival. Written some time around 380, it remains one of the most famous studies of love in western literature; in it, Socrates advocates a profound, non-sexual love between friends, which today we call 'platonic love'.

Courtesans

A unique group of women in Athenian society were the courtesans, known as *hetairai* (which literally meant 'companions'). In effect, these were high-class prostitutes, although they were hired for their conversational or musical skills as well as for their undoubted sexual allure.

Hetairai were never from Athenian citizen families – they were either slaves or (more likely) foreigners who had come to Athens to make money. This allowed Athenian men to draw a sharp distinction in their sexual attitudes between Athenian women and others, a distinction neatly summed up in the words of Demosthenes:

> '*Hetairai* we have for the sake of pleasure ... but wives to bear us legitimate children and to look after the house faithfully.'
>
> Demosthenes, *Against Neaera* 122

Although these words illustrate the obvious enthusiasm which Greek men felt for beautiful women, it is important to remember that they took bisexuality for granted; indeed, the youthful male was generally considered to be the finest specimen of physical beauty.

Hetairai tended to be the most educated women at Athens and could hope to earn a lot of money in their own right. Aspasia, the most famous woman in classical Athens, was almost certainly a *hetaira*. Although she grew up in the city of Miletos, she came to Athens at a fairly young age. Here, she became the mistress of the leading politician and general Pericles (see pp. 196-9), living with him for about fifteen years. Plutarch tells us that Pericles valued Aspasia for her intelligence and political acumen and he even claims that Socrates would bring his pupils to listen to her. Some Athenians were so concerned about the effect that Aspasia might be having on Athenian politics that they brought an unsuccessful prosecution against her.

Review 3

1. Define the following: *hetaira, kottabos, kratêr, skolia, symposiarch, symposium.*
2. How does working life in Athens compare with working life today?
3. How does a symposium compare to a modern dinner-party or formal social occasion?
4. How would you summarise the Greeks' attitude to drinking alcohol? How does it compare to attitudes to alcohol consumption today?
5. To what extent do you think that Greek male attitudes and assumptions about women and sex still survive in the modern world?
E. (i) Imagine you are a *kyrios*. Write a diary for a typical week in your life.
E. (ii) Imagine you are a slave who has to organise a symposium for your master. Describe all the arrangements you make.

III. ATHENIAN WOMEN

It is very hard for us to know about the lives of Athenian women with any certainty. For, according to Thucydides, Pericles once said:

'The greatest glory of a woman is to be least talked about among men, whether in praise or blame.'   Thucydides 2.46

The only female writer who has survived from ancient Greece is the love poet Sappho, who tells us little about the everyday lives of women. Therefore the written evidence we have comes exclusively from men; even the great female characters of Greek drama are male inventions. In spite of this, the sources do allow us to develop some idea of what a woman's life must have been like.

1. Childhood

The wreath of wool left hanging outside the front door after the birth of a girl symbolised her economic destiny as a housewife (the wreath of olives was equally symbolic for a baby boy). The birth of a daughter was often a cause of disappointment; whereas a son could inherit the family property and earn a living, a daughter would have to be married off with an expensive dowry. Baby girls were therefore more likely to be abandoned at birth than boys. Even if they were accepted, daughters were treated as inferiors at home; for example, a girl would usually be given a smaller portion of food than her brothers at mealtimes.

As children grew, the lives of boys and girls took widely different paths. A daughter was not sent to school; instead, she remained at home and learnt from her mother the roles and duties expected of an Athenian wife: spinning, weaving, cookery and managing the finances. She may

A young girl cradles a hare; she is a bear in the service of Artemis at Brauron.

also have helped to care for younger siblings. A few girls probably learnt to read, since some vase paintings show women holding scroll-books, but it is likely that most women were illiterate. Likewise, there was probably only a small minority of girls who learnt musical skills such as lyre-playing or singing.

One area in which girls could play a role outside the home was in performing certain religious tasks in honour of the city's goddesses. In the following lines, a chorus of Athenian women in a comedy of Aristophanes reflect on a girl's childhood:

'When I was seven, I carried the sacred symbols; then at ten I was grinder of Athena's barley; then at the Brauronian festival of Artemis I was the Bear-girl in the saffron robe; and when I was grown up handsome, I carried the sacred basket ...'   Aristophanes, *Lysistrata* 641ff.

One of the cults mentioned here is that of Artemis at Brauron on the east coast of Attica, where girls served as *Arktoi* (bears), perhaps marking their journey into adolescence. Other girls might have served as *Arrêphoroi* (bearers of secret things), living for a while on the Acropolis and performing secret rites for Aphrodite at her sanctuary below. Both the *Arrêphoroi* and the *Ergastinai* (workers) wove the robe for Athena at the Panathenaic festival (see pp. 29-30), while many religious processions were led by *Kanêphoroi* (basket-bearers), who carried baskets of sacred emblems.

These rituals were important for girls since the same goddesses would oversee their lives as adults: Artemis as goddess of childbirth, Aphrodite of sexuality and Athena of spinning and weaving.

2. Marriage

A woman's marriage was usually arranged to take place as soon as she reached puberty at the age of about 14. The arrangement was made between the *kyrioi* of two families; the girl was normally pledged to a man about twice her age. No thought was given to love or romance; instead, a marriage was seen as a pragmatic social and financial agreement between two families. The bride usually had little or no say about the man she was going to marry; indeed, some couples did not meet until their wedding day.

For many young women in their early teens, marriage must have been a very traumatic experience. A bride had to leave behind her own family to live with her new husband and his family. Some women were forced to move to another region of Attica, so losing regular contact with their relatives. It is, therefore, perhaps unsurprising that marriage was sometimes equated with grief. A fragment from a lost tragedy of Sophocles gives voice to a woman's feelings:

> 'It is my belief that young women in their fathers' homes live the sweetest life of all. For ignorance always keeps children secure and happy. But when we reach womanhood and reach some understanding, we are thrust out and sold away from our ancestral gods and our parents. Some go to live with strangers, some with foreigners, some go to joyless homes, some to unfriendly ones. All these things, once a single night has yoked us to our husbands, we are obliged to praise, and consider a happy outcome.'   Sophocles, fr. 524

Forced marriage

Even today, our society has to contend with the awful spectre of 'forced marriage'. This should not be confused with 'arranged marriage'. Many cultures worldwide practise the custom of arranging marriages for their sons or daughters, but these marriages go ahead only with the consent of both bride and groom. Such marriages can be happier and longer lasting than the 'love marriages' which have become normal in western society.

Crucially, a forced marriage takes place without the consent of the bride or groom. In the UK, some two hundred cases of people taken abroad to marry against their will are reported to the Foreign and Commonwealth Office each year; the number unreported is likely to be much higher and the vast majority of cases involve young women who are forced into marriage. Some campaign groups define this as a modern form of slavery; for its part, the United Nations declares that 'a woman's right to choose a spouse and enter freely into marriage is central to her life and dignity, and equality as a human being'.

The betrothal (enguê)

A girl could be betrothed at any age and was in fact legally married from this date. However, it was not uncommon for a betrothal to occur years before a girl reached marriageable age. Often the bride wasn't even present at the betrothal ceremony, which was an exchange of oaths between her father and the groom. The word for betrothal, *enguê*, which literally meant 'pledge' or 'security', reflects the sad truth that women were often treated as little more than items of property. The betrothal was a verbal contract between the two men as follows:

> 'I give you this woman for the ploughing of legitimate children.'
> 'I agree.'
> 'I agree to provide the dowry of ...'
> 'I accept that too, with pleasure.'

The two men next shook on the agreement in the presence of as many witnesses as they could muster. The latter were important since there were no formal legal or civil documents to be signed. Marriage was simply a private agreement between two families.

The dowry

The dowry was central to the marriage contract. Figures from law-court speeches suggest that the dowry was usually set at between 5% and 20% of a *kyrios'* wealth. Although it belonged to the husband, it was meant to give protection to a wife; for if a man wanted a divorce, he had to return the dowry in full to his wife's family. If he did not do so, then he was charged 18% interest per annum on the value of the dowry.

A dowry's influence

Unmarried women whose *kyrioi* could provide a large dowry were highly sought after. Once married, these women could also use their dowry as a powerful bargaining tool: for a husband was more likely to treat his wife well if he feared losing such a prized financial asset. Some Greek writers were unimpressed by women holding such power: Plato commented that dowries could cause husbands to behave slavishly, while a fragment of Euripides' *Phaethon* describes a free man who has become 'a slave of his marriage-bed, having sold his body for a dowry'.

If a woman's husband died, then her dowry passed onto her sons; if there were no children, then it was handed back to her family. There was also a particular law for the death of a man who left a daughter (or daughters) but no sons. His wealth and property were legally attached to the daughter, who became known as an *epiklêros*. Her name was read out in the assembly and she was married to the closest available male relative of the deceased. This ensured that wealth stayed in the immediate family.

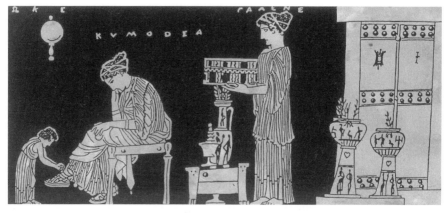

A vase painting showing a bride dressing for her wedding. A girl is fastening her special sandals, while a maid brings in a decorated box, possibly containing the wedding veil. A *loutrophoros* can be seen behind the chest in the middle.

The wedding ceremony

The wedding itself took place over a period of three days, each of which had a name: the **proaulia**, the **gamos** and the **epaulia** (-*aulia* probably derives from the verb *aulisdesthai*, 'to spend the night'; thus the *proaulia* was held the day before the wedding night, and the *epaulia* the day after it). In the days leading up to the *proaulia* the bride would spend time at her home, preparing for the ceremony with her mother, other female relatives, friends and slaves.

The most important event of the **proaulia** was the making of sacrifices and offerings to the gods, in particular to Artemis, the virgin goddess (see p. 13). The bride would offer a lock of hair, childhood toys and clothing to the goddess to thank her for the protection which she had given during the bride's childhood and to ask for her support in leaving the sphere of virginity; moreover, Artemis as goddess of childbirth would also be important in her future life. An anonymous author records the dedication of a girl named Timarete:

> 'Timarete, daughter of Timaretos, before her wedding, has dedicated her tambourine, her pretty ball, the net that shielded her hair, a lock of hair, and her girl's dresses to Artemis of the Lake, a virgin to a virgin, as is fit. Daughter of Leto, hold your hand over the child Timarete, and protect the pure girl in a pure way.'   *Palatine Anthology* 6.280

The day of the marriage ceremony, the **gamos**, started with the bride's ritual bath in holy water, which was meant to enhance her fertility. Water was drawn from a sacred spring and carried by a young child in a *loutrophoros*, a double-handled, painted vase especially used for wedding ceremonies.

Next came the dressing of the bride. She was adorned in the most expensive clothing possible; many families even hired the services of a professional wedding dresser. Her hair was arranged, and she was then bedecked with robes, a crown, jewellery and perfume. However, the most important item was the veil, which symbolised her virginity and was not removed until the marriage ceremony was over. Once the bride was ready, there followed the wedding feast in her father's house. Both families were present, although the men and the women dined at different tables. Expensive food was served, after which a libation was poured and musicians and singers performed. As the following lines suggest, the question of who to put on the guest list could be as controversial then as it can today:

'There is no occasion for a feast that is as conspicuous and much discussed as a wedding ... therefore, since there is no one who is unaware that we are entertaining and have invited people, we are ashamed to leave out anyone, and we invite all of our relatives and friends and connections of any type.'
Plutarch, *Moralia* 666ff.

The feast was one of the only public social occasions in ancient Athens which involved women, and jokes about their drinking were common. For example, in Menander's comic play *Dyskolos*, the women at a wedding feast apparently soak up wine 'like sand'!

The procession
The day's most important event was the procession from the bride's house to the groom's house; this symbolised the bride's transfer from one *oikos* to another. It began in the evening with the groom symbolically dragging the bride from her mother, and then leading her to a cart, in which she rode between the groom and the best man. The procession was a loud and raucous affair, attended by all the wedding guests and often many other townsfolk. It was conducted by the light of torches (believed to ward off evil spirits) and men with musical instruments sang marriage songs while women threw fertility symbols such as fruits and flowers at the couple. The bride's mother walked behind the cart carrying torches.

A wedding procession. The bride and groom are in a chariot, two men carry torches, while two women follow behind carrying presents.

In the *Iliad*, Homer describes a series of wedding processions in a scene on the shield of Achilles:

'... there were marriages and feasting, and they were escorting the brides from their houses through the streets under the light of burning torches, and the wedding-song rose loud. The young men were whirling in the dance, and among them *auloi* and lyres kept up their music, while the women all stood at the doors of their houses and looked on admiring.'

Homer, *Iliad* 18.491-6

When the cart arrived at the groom's house, the bride was welcomed by her mother-in-law, who was also holding torches. The bride ate a quince, while the groom's friends burned the axle of the chariot to show that the bride could not now journey back to her old home. The couple were led to the hearth of the house, where they were showered once more with symbols of fertility: a mixture of dates, coins, dried fruits, figs and nuts.

The focus of the ceremony now moved to the marital bedroom: for the bride's loss of virginity was a key element of the wedding. Friends would prepare the bedroom with flowers and decorations and the groom would lead his bride in, after which the doors were closed. A friend of the groom would stand guard outside the doors, while friends of the bride would stand with him and sing songs, perhaps throughout the night, to reassure her and offer their support. They might also beat on the door to ward off evil spirits.

Early the next morning the couple were woken by friends singing outside their bridal chamber. The **epaulia** centred around the presentation of gifts to the bride, mainly by her new relatives. This was perhaps done to bind her more closely to her new home, although some have suggested that it was a compensation for her lost virginity of the previous night. One source records that brides were given items such as 'unguents, clothing, combs, chests, bottles, sandals, boxes, myrrh and soap'.

3. The kyria

A married woman automatically became the leading female in the family and assumed her role as the *kyria*. She was responsible for overseeing all the household tasks and carried a bunch of keys to symbolise her control of the storerooms, which contained all the food and resources required for the cold winter months. In the following lines, Xenophon relates instructions from a husband to his new wife:

'You must stay at home, and make sure that if the servants have to go out of doors they all leave at the same time. As to those who stay in, you are in charge of them, and all duties they perform within the house. You also have to see to all goods brought into the house. You must budget carefully for future needs: don't spend in a month what is needed for a year. When your slaves bring you wool, you must make sure that clothes are made for anyone who needs them. Then you must keep a close watch on the store-room, to see that the grain stays fresh enough to eat; and when a slave falls ill, you must take care that he is looked after properly.'

Xenophon, Oikonomikos 7.35ff.

One of the most important of these duties was the spinning and weaving of cloth, which would take place in the *gynaikôn*. Cloth was very expensive in the ancient world as it was all made by hand. Therefore it saved the household an enormous amount of money if it provided all its own cloth. Cloth was used not just for clothes, but for other household items such as curtains and sheets.

Clothing

Greek clothing was relatively straightforward. For a man the main item was the tunic, known as a *chitôn*. Over the top of this he often wore a cloak, a *himation*, which was a large rectangular piece of woollen cloth. Footwear ranged from light sandals to sturdy boots.

Women wore a type of *chitôn* which fell to the ankles and was fastened by brooches. Wealthy women could afford to wear linen rather than wool. The *himation* was often also used as a shawl, while many vase paintings depict women wearing it as a veil covering their faces. Indeed, it seems likely that women were expected to wear a veil when they went out in public.

A reconstruction of women's dress. The figure on the right is wearing the long tunic covered by a *himation* and a head-scarf. The figure in the centre has her *himation* wrapped around her.

Women working at the loom. To the right, two women weigh out the wool in preparation for spinning, while to the left, two other women work an upright loom; the finished portion of the woven material is rolled up at the top of the loom.

Women would start with wool or flax stalks, which ideally came from their own animals or farms. A lot of work went into cleaning and preparing this raw material and rolling it into loose balls of wool, which was now ready for spinning. Vase paintings show women using knee-guards for this rolling process. The wool was then spun into a thread with a distaff and spindle. After this it was often dyed using various substances such as earth, leaves and berries. The most expensive dye was a purple dye from shellfish found in ancient Phoenicia. Once enough wool had been spun and dyed, the women would work at a loom weaving it into clothing or any other resource. This time-consuming process was central to the working life of women.

4. Childbirth

The first duty of a Greek wife was to produce a male heir who could inherit his father's estate. The central importance of this duty is shown by the language used to describe adult women. An unmarried woman was a *parthenos* (maiden) until she got married when she became a *nymphê* (a married woman without children), but the real mark of womanhood was when she bore her first child – she was now known as a *gynê*.

Childbirth is difficult enough in the modern world. If a pregnancy survives complications, there follows the intense pain of labour. These difficulties were magnified many times for women in ancient Greece. Healthcare was extremely rudimentary and pain prevention was far less developed: women had to endure labour pains without anaesthetic.

Miscarriage and death during labour were thus far more common than they are today. Medea, in Euripides' play of the same name, famously compares women giving birth to men fighting in battle:

> 'Men say of us that we live a life free from danger at home while they fight wars. How wrong they are! I would rather stand three times in the battle line than bear one child.'   Euripides, *Medea* 248-51

Midwifery

For a long time women were barred from playing any role in the medical profession, including childbirth. However, a remarkable woman called Hagnodike apparently brought about the legalisation of midwifery in Athens. As a young woman, she disguised herself as a man in order to study medicine. Later, still disguised, she gained such a reputation as an obstetrician (doctor of childbirth) that some of her rivals grew jealous and brought a criminal charge of sexual corruption. For they believed that 'he' must have been seducing 'his' patients to have won such approval. A writer called Hyginus (*Fabula* 274, 10-13) takes up the story:

> 'At the point when she was about to be sentenced by the court, Hagnodike lifted up her tunic and demonstrated to the jurors that she was a woman. Her prosecutors then became even more vigorous in their accusations. But some of the wives of the jurors came to court, and announced: "You are no longer our husbands but our enemies, if you are prepared to condemn a woman who has done so much for our health." After this the Athenians changed the law, so that women of Athenian birth were allowed to study medicine.'

---

5. Rights and lifestyle

Although the *kyria* undoubtedly had a great deal of power at home, she also had great limitations imposed on her. She was legally the possession of her husband and had to obey his commands. She had no right to vote or take any part in the political system of the city (see p. 201). Indeed, a woman's freedom was severely limited once she stepped outside the front door.

Women were discouraged from leaving the house and would usually need to be escorted by a male relative. This was to prevent unwanted attention from other men who might have provided a threat to the *kyrios*. Women could not buy or sell land, while at Athens they were prevented from buying anything worth more than a *medimnos* of barley, an amount which would support an average family for about six days. Although they could acquire property through gift or inheritance, it was always put under the management of the *kyrios*.

In the case of poorer women, it was less practical for them to be so hidden away. They might have no choice but to leave the house regularly in order to perform basic tasks. Many women would have made a trip to the fountain on a daily basis, while there is evidence that some poor women had to take jobs as stall-holders at markets or washer-women in order to make ends meet for their families. Such women were looked down on by the rest of society; for example, the comedies of Aristophanes frequently make fun of the tragic playwright Euripides by claiming that his mother used to sell vegetables in the *agora*.

Divorce

In legal terms, divorce was relatively straightforward in Athens, since no court case was required. If a man wanted to divorce his wife then he would just send her back to her own family, along with the dowry. The most common reason for divorce was probably the inability of a woman to produce a child (infertility was not often attributed to a man); a husband might also divorce his wife if he had the chance to marry an *epiklēros* in his own family. In practice, the divorce rate in Athens does not seem to have been high, partly because loss of the dowry would often have been a serious financial blow.

It was very unusual for a woman to initiate a divorce. In legal terms, all she had to do was to return to live with her own family; however, if they did not want to accept her back then they could return her to her husband. This might happen if the family feared that it would be hard to find her a new husband. A further factor which discouraged women from seeking divorce was that any children usually remained living with their father; by walking out on a husband, a woman was probably also walking out on her children.

Euripides himself produced one of the most famous passages which highlight how desperate women may have felt about their plight. In *Medea*, the heroine has fled to Corinth with her new husband Jason, with whom she has two children. After he divorces her in order to marry the princess of Corinth (a younger woman) she tears into him with a searing indictment of the treatment of women:

'Of everything that is alive and has a mind, we women are the most wretched creatures. First of all, we have to buy a husband with a vast outlay of money – we have to take a master for our body. The latter is still more painful than the former. And here lies the most critical issue – whether we take a good husband or a bad one. For divorce brings shame on a woman's reputation and we cannot refuse a husband his rights. We come to new ways of behaviour, to new customs – and, since we have learnt nothing of such matters at home, we need prophetic powers to tell us specifically what sort of a husband we shall have to deal with. And if we manage this well and our husband lives with us and bears the yoke of marriage lightly, then life is enviable. But if not, death would be welcome.

For a man, when he has had enough of life at home, he can stop his heart's
sickness by going out – to see one of his friends and contemporaries. But
we are forced to look to one soul alone.'   Euripides, *Medea* 230-48

By the end of the play, Medea is reduced to such rage and desperation
that she murders their two children in order to exact on Jason the most
painful revenge possible. Most controversially of all, Euripides allows
Medea to escape punishment for her crimes by having the sun god carry
her away to safety (see p. 103).

The Thesmophoria

Perhaps one occasion when woman could have some freedom came with
the one annual festival at Athens exclusively for women. It took place in
the autumn and was a fertility festival at which women commemorated
the myth of Demeter and Persephone (see pp. 11-12). Known as the
Thesmophoria (*thesmophoros* or 'law-giver' was an important adjective
for Demeter), only married women were allowed to take part; they
camped out for three days and two nights in an area near the Pnyx, the
hill where the Athenian assembly met (see map 6). This location was
clearly symbolic: for a few days, married Athenian women took
possession of the city's seat of government.

The rites of the festival were a closely guarded secret, but we do know
the outline of events:

- **Day 1**: The women set up shelters; some of them then went down into a
  nearby cave to retrieve the bones of piglets and images of male genitalia
  (fertility symbols) which had been left there. These were placed on the
  thesmophorion, the altar to Persephone and Demeter; later, they were
  scattered on the fields to promote fertility.
- **Day 2**: They fasted and sat on the ground, perhaps as an act of mourning
  in imitation of Demeter's grief for her daughter.
- **Day 3**: They celebrated the gift of children and prayed for blessings on
  them and on future families, as well as for good crops.

Such a festival may seem strange in a society where women's movements
were normally so carefully controlled by their menfolk. However, there was
an ancient belief in the link between female and crop fertility. Many Greek
men would have believed that these rites were vital to the prosperity of their
society. Moreover, there was no danger of a woman being unfaithful, since
the exclusion of all men from the festival was strictly enforced.

For women, the festival must have been a welcome chance to make
new friendships and experience welcome freedoms. Aristophanes even
wrote a play, *Women at the Thesmophoria*, in which the women plot to
punish the playwright Euripides for misrepresenting the female sex in
his plays. The women are portrayed in festive mode: drinking wine,
complaining about their husbands and gossiping about sex.

Review 4

1. Define the following: *enguê, epaulia, gamos, gynê, nymphê, parthenos, proaulia.*
2. Which aspects of an Athenian wedding also feature at weddings today? Which aspects seem strange to you?
3. Draw up a table listing the similarities and differences between the ancient and modern attitudes to the institution of marriage.
4. Are there 'women-only' events in your society? Could any of them be compared to the *Thesmophoria*?
5. To what extent can male attitudes towards women in Athens still be seen in your society and other parts of the world today?
6. Compare the passage quoted from Sophocles on p. 152 with the passage quoted from Euripides on pp. 160-1. Make a list of the complaints each makes about a woman's place in society. How many of them are common to both passages? Do they contradict each other at all?
R. Read chapter 8 of Plutarch's biography of Alcibiades. What do we learn about Athenian divorce from this passage?
E. 'The institution of marriage in Athens was designed to keep wealth and power in the hands of men.' Do you agree?

IV. SLAVERY

Slavery was a fact of life in Ancient Greece, something which jars with our perception of the Greeks as among the most enlightened of ancient peoples. It is impossible to know exactly what proportion of the population was enslaved; however, it might be estimated that if 5th century Attica had a population of between 300,000 and 350,000, then there would probably have been a slave population of between 80,000 and 100,000.

Today, we are rightly horrified by slavery. However, in judging the 5th century Athenians on this issue, it is important to bear in mind two things. The first is that slavery was a fact of life in every ancient society; indeed, only in the last two centuries have serious campaigns of abolition been waged (slavery was abolished in the British Empire only in 1833 and in the USA in 1863). Secondly, it is fair to say that the Athenians generally treated their slaves better than almost any other ancient people.

One important attitude to slaves is illustrated in the words of Xenophon: 'those who can do so buy slaves to share their work with them'. Indeed, the *Erechtheion* on the Acropolis was built by a combination of slaves, metics and citizens; all those who worked on the project were paid one drachma per day, whether slave or free (see pp. 275-6 for information about Greek currency values). This no doubt

162

appalled the Spartans, who gave tasks to their slaves which they felt too demeaning to perform themselves (see p. 235ff.). A further indication of the Athenian treatment of slaves is suggested by the complaints of one conservative Athenian:

> 'There is a very great lack of discipline among the slaves ... in Athens. You are not allowed to strike a slave there, nor will a slave step aside for you ... If there were a law that permitted a free man to strike a slave ... you would often find yourself hitting an Athenian on the assumption that he was a slave. For ordinary citizens there wear no better clothes than slaves ... and look no different.'   *Constitution of the Athenians* 1.10

Despite these views, it would be wrong to say that slaves had an easy life in Athens. In fact, there were so many different types of slave that it is impossible to make one statement regarding their treatment. Yet the comments above do suggest that the Athenians had a more progressive attitude to their slaves than other contemporary peoples. Moreover, the comic plays of Aristophanes contain various examples of quick-witted slaves who out-think their masters; it is hard to imagine that Athenians could have found such characters entertaining if they did not have a basis in truth.

The ethics of slavery

Although slavery was rarely questioned in ancient Greece, it seems that some sophists of the late 5th century did challenge the institution. The plays of Euripides often portray slaves as noble characters; some plays, such as *Trojan Women*, also present with great pathos the suffering of noble Trojans who are captured and enslaved at the end of the Trojan War.

However, such insights were rare. Even Plato and Aristotle, two of the most influential philosophers in European history, both firmly believed in slavery. Indeed, Aristotle even wrote an extensive justification of the practice, arguing that slavery was 'natural' for some people and describing slaves as 'living machines'.

---

1. Routes into slavery

There were various ways to become a slave in the Greek world. Some were born into slavery, since their parents were already slaves. Other babies were brought up as slaves after being exposed at birth. Herodotus even tells us that some peoples, such as the Thracians, sold their children into slavery. However, it would have been expensive for a Greek family to look after slave children and so their numbers were probably not large.

Undoubtedly the main route into slavery was as a captive of war. This applied not only to men who were on the losing side of a battle but also to their womenfolk and children, a common theme in Greek literature.

In the *Iliad*, Achilles and Agamemnon quarrel over possession of a captive woman, Briseis, who is to serve as a slave-girl. Later in the poem, the Trojan prince Hector movingly reflects on his wife Andromache's future life as a slave should Troy be conquered:

> 'You will live in Argos, weaving at the loom at another woman's command, and carrying water from a foreign spring ... and for you there will be renewed misery, that you have lost such a husband to protect you from the day of slavery. But may I be dead ... before I hear your screams and the sound of you being dragged away.'   Homer, *Iliad* 6.456ff.

These lines illustrate a key point about Greek slavery; for Greeks felt much easier about enslaving foreigners – barbarians, in their eyes – than they did about enslaving fellow Greeks. It is likely that the majority of slaves in classical Athens were foreigners, even if some could speak Greek.

Yet there were other ways for people, Greek and barbarian, to end up in slavery. Travelling in the ancient world was particularly dangerous, and it was not uncommon for travellers to be captured by pirates and sold at the nearest slave market. In some cities, though not in Athens, people who fell into ruinous debt could also be sold into slavery.

2. The slave trade

Once captured, potential slaves were taken to the slave-market, which took place in the agora. The cost of slaves varied dramatically according to their age, talent, education and gender. One document dated to 415 lists the prices paid at the compulsory sale of sixteen slaves belonging to a man convicted of sacrilege:

> The property of Kephisodoros ... living in Piraeus: slaves – Thracian female, 165 drachmae; Thracian female, 135; Thracian male, 170; Syrian male, 240; Karian male, 105; Illyrian male, 161; Thracian female, 220; Thracian male, 115; Syrian male, 144, Illyrian male, 121; Kolkhian male, 153; Karian boy, 174; little Karian boy, 72; Syrian male, 301; Maltese (?) male, 151; Lydian female, 85.

It is interesting that so many slaves were from Thrace, a region to the north of Greece. Thracians tended to have lighter skin than Greeks and this may explain why Xanthias, meaning 'blondie', was such a common name for a slave.

The average price in this list is 160 drachmas and this seems to be fairly typical. However, there were exceptions; for example, one very rich Athenian, Nikias, paid 6,000 drachmas for a Thracian slave to manage his mining interests – clearly a highly skilled slave!

A slave carrying two
amphorae.

3. Types of slave

Slave labour was employed in a wide variety of ways and different slaves were bought with different talents. There were three main types of slave: domestic slaves, wage-earning slaves and public slaves.

- **Domestic slaves** lived in the *oikos* with the family and performed all the tasks related to it. These may have included answering the front door, supervising the children, collecting water from the fountain or doing the shopping. Male slaves would also work on the family farm. More specialist roles included wet-nursing and acting as a child's *paidagôgos*. Domestic slaves were often treated as part of the extended family; as such, they could develop close working relationships with family members. This was particularly true of female slaves, who shared the women's work of the house with their *kyria*. In Euripides' *Medea*, it is to her nurse that Medea turns when she is deeply troubled and needs emotional support, while in the *Odyssey*, the slave Eurycleia is one of the most loyal and trusted members of Odysseus' household.
- **Wage-earning slaves** usually belonged to wealthier families who wanted to make a profit on their slaves. Unskilled slaves were hired out for menial work in areas such as the docks, farms or in the mines at Laureion (see p. 167). The same Nikias is said to have hired out 1,000 slaves for one obol a day to a man who fed them and sent them down the silver mines, replacing any casualties; this gave Nikias a profit of 10 talents per year (one talent was worth 6,000 drachmas). Slaves with particular skills in crafts such as pottery, shoe-making, building and boat-making were highly valued. Most valued of all, however, were those who had the training and ability to handle financial matters. Attractive female slaves and young male slaves could also be hired out as dancers or prostitutes for parties and festive occasions.

- **Public slaves** were not owned privately but by the state, and there were many roles for them in Athens. Perhaps most remarkably, the Athenian police force was made up of slaves, known as the Scythian Archers. Although they were far less powerful than a modern police force, they were still important for the successful running of the city (see pp. 207-8). Other state-owned slaves included the public executioner, employees of the public mint and the street-sweepers who were responsible for removing the piles of effluent from the streets on a daily basis.

4. The treatment of slaves

The quality of a slave's life depended on his owner and the job to which he was assigned. However, legally, all slaves were treated as the property of their owner and had few rights; for example, slaves could neither vote nor marry; a slave of any age was routinely addressed as *pais*, or 'child'; and commonly slaves seem to have been used for the sexual gratification of their owners. However, some slaves could buy their freedom if their masters allowed it, particularly if they were wage-earners; such slaves would save for years to buy their freedom, after which they held the status of a metic (see p. 201ff.). Nonetheless, the freeing of slaves was not common, far less so than in the subsequent Roman Empire.

Some slaves clearly lived appalling lives, not least those who worked as miners or agricultural labourers. It seems that all slaves were liable

Agricultural workers picking olives.

to physical punishment. In Aristophanes' *Frogs*, the slave Xanthias is able to sustain far more flogging than the god Dionysos as he is so used to being flogged! Moreover, a slave's evidence could only be used in a court of law if it had been extracted under torture, since this was believed to make him more frightened of the law than of his master.

The mines at Laureion
Undoubtedly the worst conditions for slaves were those found at the lead and silver mines at Laureion, 35 miles from Athens (see map 5). These mines became very important to the Athenians in the 480s when they needed to fund their naval fleet (see p. 194). There was a slave-market near the mines and slaves newly arrived to Attica were often bought and packed straight off to the mines. There were at least 10,000 slaves working in these mines; at times there may well have been at least twice this number.

Conditions in the shafts were grim – they were dark, narrow and prone to collapse. Fumes from the smelting of the metals were highly noxious, posing a further health risk. The personal lives of mine slaves were also harsh; they lived together in barracks near the mines, which were guarded by Athenian soldiers in watchtowers. No other family members were allowed to live there since their masters did not want to feed extra mouths. Without doubt, working in the mines was the very worst end of slavery.

However, some slaves clearly had a reasonable quality of life. According to Xenophon, Socrates placed slaves alongside houses, land, farm animals and equipment as 'things that are both acquired and looked after with care'. Although they were classified as property, there were some rights which humanised them to a small extent:

- **Welcome**. Upon joining a family, slaves, like new-born children and new wives, were formally accepted into the *oikos* with religious ceremonies at the family's hearth.
- **Legal protection**. A 5th century writer tells us that it was illegal to strike another man's slave. Moreover, if a master killed his slave, he was believed to be polluted before the gods and had to purify himself (see p. 16).
- **Asylum**. A slave could seek refuge at a religious altar or sanctuary if he felt his master was treating him unfairly; the shrine of Theseus near the Acropolis was a popular place for such refugees. A state official would hear his complaints and could force the master to sell the slave or perhaps to swear an oath promising to treat the slave better in future.
- **Eleusis**. Slaves could be initiated into the Eleusinian Mysteries (see p. 44ff.).

Besides these basic rights, the lives of slaves might have had some compensations: a domestic slave could take part in the life of the family, sharing the family's food and perhaps worshipping its gods. A skilled wage-earning slave was based in a workshop and so usually lived apart from his master, allowing him some freedom in his private life.

Again, it must be emphasised that we should be careful when judging slavery in ancient Greece. In classical Athens, many slaves were able to live as part of a family, where they were fed, clothed, housed and valued. Today, many practices continue around the world which are tantamount to slavery, such as sweatshop labour, people-smuggling and enforced prostitution. It would be dangerous to believe that slavery belongs to an uncivilised past.

Review 5

1. How many different jobs might each type of slave have done in Athens?
2. How would you define 'slavery'?
3. Why do you think slavery has been such an accepted part of life until fairly recently? Why has this attitude changed in the last two centuries? What aspects of our society do you think might horrify people in future?
R. (i) Read about how the Spartans treated their slaves (the helots) on pp. 236-8. What differences are there between the Spartan and Athenian attitude to slaves?
R. (ii) Read Aristophanes' *Frogs* 738-56 and *Knights* 1-73. What do these passages tell us about the comic portrayal of slaves?
R. (iii) Read the 'Slavery Today' section at www.anti-slavery.org. How many modern forms of slavery are listed? How do they compare to what you have read about slavery in ancient Athens?
E. To what extent do you think that an Athenian's lifestyle and prosperity depended on his slaves?

V. DEATH AND FUNERALS

Death was far more visibly present in ancient Athens than it is in the western world today. Some estimate that as many as half of children born died before their fifth birthday. Consequently, the Greeks had a highly developed set of rituals relating both to funerals and to the subsequent respecting of the dead. As we shall see, Greeks believed that the lack of a proper burial could prevent the soul from passing safely to the Underworld; it would then be doomed to wander aimlessly for ever, a notion which filled them with horror.

Death could also have social and political consequences for a family, although this depended to some extent on who had died. The death of a *kyrios* or a son might have serious financial or social implications, since men were both the bread-winners and the family's representatives in the city. Conversely, the death of a female relative was often viewed less gravely, particularly if she had married and produced children.

168

Nonetheless, it seems that a woman's funeral was accorded equal status to that of a man.

The ceremonies after death consisted of four stages: the **preparation** of the body; the **prothesis**, the equivalent of a modern wake; the **ekphora**, when the body was carried in procession to the burial ground; and finally the **burial** of the body in a grave or tomb. Professional undertakers were very rare; rather, the organisation of the funeral was entirely the responsibility of the family's women. This was a critical job, since it was very important for a family's public image to hold a respectful funeral and give the deceased a proper send-off.

1. Preparation

As soon as a person died, the eyes and mouth were immediately closed and the body was prepared for the *prothesis*. Only women over the age of 60 or an immediate female relative could take part in this process. They first washed the body, dressing any wounds if a violent death had occurred. The corpse was then anointed with perfumes, dressed in a long white shroud and garlanded with flowers, after which it was laid out on a bed with the feet facing the door of the room, so that its soul could depart. A coin was placed in its mouth, which was held closed by a linen chin-strap. It was believed that the coin would be needed by the dead person's soul to pay Charon, the mythological ferryman who rowed the dead over the river Styx and into the Underworld.

2. The prothesis

For two days the body was laid out in a room of the house (*prothesis* meant 'laying out') and a vigil was kept beside the body as friends and relatives came to pay their respects. Greeks believed that death automatically brought religious pollution upon both the house and its occupants. For this reason, a bowl of spring water was placed outside the front door, alerting passers-by and enabling visitors to cleanse themselves as they left.

The most important element in the *prothesis* was the ritual lament, which was performed by the women of the house. They would cut their hair short, mark their heads with ashes and, dressed in filthy, torn clothing, move round the body as they sang their lament, beating their breasts and scratching at their cheeks until they drew blood. Some families also hired professional mourning singers to lead them in their dirges.

A vase painting showing a woman laying out a corpse on a bier while two other women raise their arms in lament.

3. The ekphora

The funeral took place before sunrise on the third day. It began with the *ekphora* ('carrying out'), the procession from the house of the deceased to the grave or tomb. In the 7th century, funerals had become so extravagant that Solon (see p. 181ff.) introduced laws limiting excessive displays of grief; one such law limited the number of women who could attend (only close relatives or those over 60), since a funeral was one of the only times when a woman might meet a man outside her own family.

The corpse was either carried by a horse-drawn cart or by pall-bearers. Men walked in front of the hearse, women and children behind; an *aulos*-player typically accompanied the procession with a sombre tune. The main cemetery in Athens was in the area of the kerameikos outside the walls, a location designed to prevent pollution or disease from entering the city. Alternatively, some families buried their dead on their own private estates in the country.

4. The burial

Once at the burial site, the body was either cremated or buried – as today, both practices were common. However, the shortage of wood in Attica made cremation more expensive. If it was to be cremation, then a pyre

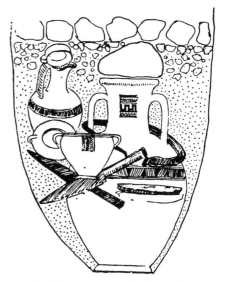

A cremation burial in the Athenian agora. A bent sword is wrapped around the neck of the amphora, which contains the ashes of the deceased.

was built beforehand and, once the body had burnt completely, wine was used to put out the flames. The closest relative would gather the ashes and place them in a funerary urn, which was then placed in the grave.

The importance of burial

Since Athenians were horrified by the thought of a body going unburied, they even made laws supporting the right of burial: if a Greek saw an unburied body then he was legally obliged to bury it; in this situation, three handfuls of earth were enough to constitute a burial. In 406, after the Athenian army had won an important sea-battle at Arginusae, a storm caused them to abandon their attempts to retrieve the bodies of their dead. Back in Athens, the Athenians were outraged and voted to execute all the generals who had been involved in the battle.

Greek literature also offers two famous examples of disputes about the burial of a body. After Achilles has killed Hector in the *Iliad*, he seeks to inflict further punishment by refusing to return the corpse to his family for burial. The gods who look on are horrified by Achilles' behaviour and cause him to relent and release the body. Athenian theatre-goers would have been reminded of this dispute when they watched the first performance of Sophocles' *Antigone* in the 440s. In this drama, Antigone is forbidden by the state to bury her brother Polynices. However, she remains true to her conscience, gives him a burial and is executed for treason.

Once the body or funerary urn was in the grave, relatives would add offerings and gifts. Food and drink was provided to nourish the soul on its journey into the afterlife. Private possessions were sometimes included, reminders of the dead person's life which might comfort them

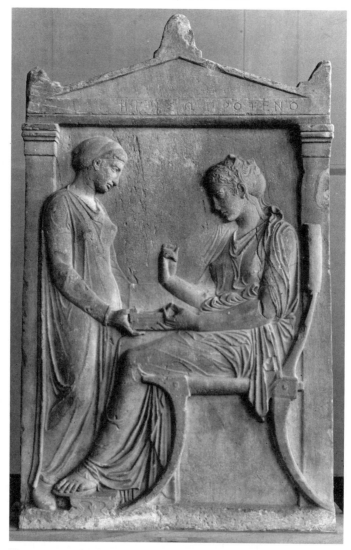

The grave *stêlê* of a woman called Hegeso, who sits at the right
selecting an ornament from a box held by a slave girl.

as they moved on. A child might be buried with dolls or toys; a male
citizen with the tools of his trade; jewellery and clothing were often
added to a woman's tomb. Most poignantly, girls who died before
marriage were typically buried in wedding clothes together with a
loutrophoros: such girls were now brides of death. Libations of wine and
sometimes oil were also poured into the grave.

A further element of the graveside ceremony was the sacrifice of an

172

animal, meat from which was later shared out as part of a funeral feast at the family home. To complete the process, a tombstone known as a **stêlê** was placed above the grave. Its centrepiece was usually a carefully worked relief or painting of the deceased, often in company with other family members. Most tombstones were then simply inscribed with the dead person's name together with his father's name (for a male) or her husband's or father's (for a female). A few surviving *stêlai* also display personal messages, such as this tribute to a young boy:

'Philostratos, son of Philoxenos,
Your grandfather's name you bore,
But to your parents "Chatterbox",
Once their joy, now mourned by all,
By a spirit you were carried off.'
Greek Inscriptions 12974

5. Tending the dead

In common with many societies, the Greeks emphasised the importance of respecting and honouring their ancestors, and feared haunting or ill omen if they did not do so. In fact, ancestors were still considered very much part of the family and worshipping them properly was vital to an Athenian's image and reputation.

The importance of ancestors
Two examples illustrate the importance of ancestors to the Athenian mind. When the Persians invaded Greece in 480, the battle cry for the Athenians was to free their 'native land, wives, shrines of the ancestral gods and tombs of the ancestors'. On a more practical level, when a citizen wanted to stand for political office, one of the questions he had to answer at his interview for candidacy (see p. 204) was 'whether he had any family tombs, and if so where they were'.

The period of mourning lasted for 30 days after burial; family members were expected to visit the tomb on the third, ninth and thirtieth day. Thereafter, the grave was visited every year on the anniversary of death. At such visits the *stêlê* was adorned with ribbons and wreaths of flowers, while food and drink offerings were offered over the grave. Often, special oil jars known as *lêkythoi* were left on the tomb. These had a white background and were usually painted with scenes depicting death. The importance of tending a grave even caused some childless Athenians to adopt an heir just for this purpose.

In addition to private days of remembrance, the city set aside days annually for the communal worship of the dead. There were days of the dead (*Nekysia*) and days of the forefathers (*Genesia*), when graves were

The painting from the *lêkythos* on the right. Note the *lêkythoi* on the steps of the tomb and hanging on the wall at the back.

adorned, special food eaten and drink offerings poured into the graves – barley broth, milk, honey, wine, oil, or even the blood of sacrificial victims. A further day of remembrance was the third day of the *Anthestêria*, a festival celebrating new wine. On this day it was believed that the dead roamed the earth, and Athenians cooked pots of mixed vegetables which they dedicated to Hermes, the god who escorted the dead down to the Underworld.

Review 6

1. Define the following: *ekphora, prothesis, lêkythos, stêlê.*
2. Why do you think the Greeks placed so much importance on burial?
3. In your opinion, why were women given such a prominent role in the ceremonies surrounding death?
4. What similarities and what differences can you find between Athenian funerals and those of other societies with which you are familiar?
5. Why do you think it was important for Athenians to remember and respect their dead? Are such attitudes still important today?
R. Read *Iliad* 24.776-804. What typical elements of a funeral occur here?
E. 'The Athenian ceremonies of death were all designed to give proper honour and respect to the deceased.' Do you agree?

5

Athenian Democracy

'We here highly resolve ... that government of the people, by the people, for the people shall not perish from the earth.'

Abraham Lincoln, 19 November 1863

When Abraham Lincoln delivered these words at Gettysburg during the American Civil War he captured the political spirit of his age, since an enormous change was taking place in western political thought. For the first time since the collapse of the ancient world, democracy had come back into fashion and was fast becoming accepted as the fairest – and therefore the best – form of government.

Democracy had been invented some 25 centuries earlier in 6th century Athens where, although it was often a highly controversial system, it lasted for 186 years between 508 and 322. During this period there were only two brief interruptions to the democratic system, when the city was taken over by groups of oligarchs (see p. 186) for a few months in both 411/10 and 404/3. Athenian democracy was thus a remarkable achievement – the city was the first in recorded history to give the vote to such a large number of its people.

However, the 'democratic' system in place in classical Athens was not democracy as we would understand it in the 21st century. For one thing, two large groups of the population – women and slaves – were completely excluded from the political process; in fact, less than a fifth of the adult population could actually participate (although we should also be aware of the history of modern democracy: for example, the US Constitution gave African-Americans the right to vote only in 1870, while women won the right to vote in most countries only during the 20th century). Secondly, Athenian democracy was 'direct' rather than 'representative': today, we elect politicians to represent our views in government; in Athens, every single citizen could vote on every single issue – what we would call a 'referendum'.

The principle of democratic government is rarely questioned in the western world today. Yet in classical Athens it was highly contentious, and even loathed by many leading citizens and intellectuals, who believed that it gave too much power to the ill-educated poor. The embodiment of this attitude was Plato, arguably the most influential philosopher in European history, who was appalled by a system he believed to be no more than 'the rule of the mob'.

> **Politics**
> The English word 'politics' is linked to the Greek *polis*, meaning 'city'. During the 7th and 6th centuries, communities in Greece were developing into independent city-states (such as Athens, Sparta, Thebes and Corinth) which began to establish their own political structures. As a result, *ta politika* came to describe 'the affairs of the city', giving us words such as 'politics', 'policy' and 'police'. It was in this context that Aristotle made his famous observation that 'man is a political animal'.

Evidence and sources

Our sources of evidence for Athenian democracy are both archaeological and written. Much useful archaeological evidence has been gleaned from the excavation of ancient Athens – most notably in the area around the agora and Pnyx. However, the strength of the written sources is more mixed. We have very little written evidence from the 8th to 6th centuries, when the main reforms which produced democracy occurred. In fact, perhaps our only important written source from this time is the poetry of Solon (see p. 181ff.), which survives only in fragments. Most writers on Athenian democracy are dated to the late 5th and 4th centuries. A further problem is that many are believed to have had an anti-democratic bias.

The following provide the most important written sources:

- **Herodotus** of Halicarnassos (490-c. 420) primarily gives an account of how the Greeks repelled the Persian invasions of the early 5th century. However, he gives as background important information about the history of Athens in the 7th and 6th centuries, albeit from the distance of many years.
- **Thucydides** (c. 460-400) was an Athenian who wrote about the Peloponnesian War of 431-404 between Athens and Sparta. We can learn a good deal from him about the workings of democracy during these years; however, he is usually assumed to be hostile to the democratic system and so his accounts of the conduct of some democratic leaders cannot be taken to be objective.
- **Aristophanes** (450-386) was a comic satirist also writing during the years of the Peloponnesian War (more detail is given about him on p. 121ff.). Great care must be taken not to assume that his work represents historical fact since he was writing to entertain. However, it is probably fair to say that, in order to create humour, his work must have been based on truth, even if it was greatly exaggerated.
- **The Old Oligarch** is the name given to the author of a pamphlet called *The Constitution of the Athenians*, which was probably written in the 420s. Little is known about the author's identity, but he puts forward the views of an old-fashioned conservative who disapproves of the democratic system. Some have even argued that it is a piece of satire designed to mimic the attitudes of conservative Athenians. Whatever the case, it is a useful source of information about democratic Athens in the late 5th century.
- **Aristotle** (384-322) was one of the great thinkers of the ancient world. He came from Chalcidice in northern Greece but was educated in Athens,

where he remained for much of his life. He was fascinated by political systems and wrote a book, *Politics*, examining them. Most important to the understanding of Athenian democracy, however, is the *Constitution of Athens* (which some believe to have been written by one of his pupils), a detailed account of the origins and workings of the democracy from a 4th century perspective.

- **Plutarch** (*c.* 50-120 CE) came from Boeotia in central Greece, lived during the period of the Roman Empire, and wrote biographies of many famous Athenians, including Solon, Themistocles and Pericles. He was writing many centuries after the events which he described and so, although he was sourcing his work from earlier historians, we cannot be certain of the accuracy of all his material.

I. THE EMERGENCE OF DEMOCRACY

The path to democratic government in Athens can perhaps be traced from the merging together of communities in Attica, which probably happened during the 8th century. However, it wasn't until the mid-5th century that it arrived in its fullest form. In the intervening years, certain key moments marked its development, each of them linked to a personality. In 594/3, **Solon** was the first to lay the foundations of the later democratic system; in 508/7, there followed the far-reaching reforms of **Cleisthenes**; in the 5th century, first **Ephialtes** in 462/1 and then **Pericles** in the 450s brought about changes which produced the 'radical democracy' for which classical Athens remains so famous. The table outlines the key events in this process.

Date	Event	Details	Pages
8th cent.	synoecism in Attica	9 archons selected from *eupatridae*; all ex-archons sit on Areopagus Council	178
7th cent.	social unrest in Attica	threat of tyranny; Draco's law code	179-80
594/3	Solon's reforms	political, economic and legal	181-4
561-510	Peisistratos and his sons rule as tyrants	cultural development of Athens	184-5
508/7	Cleisthenes' reforms	structures of government, political constituencies and possibly ostracism	185-93
462/1	Ephialtes' reforms	Council of Areopagus loses many of its powers	196
450s	Pericles' reforms	payment for magistrates; archonships opened to members of *zeugitai*; tighter citizenship laws	196-9

1. Synoecism in Attica

Athens was in fact only the largest city in an agricultural region of south-east Greece known as Attica (see map 5). Originally, the diverse communities of Attica had governed themselves, but at some point in the 8th century the region seems to have been united under the leadership of one king. This process of unification was known as *synoecism*, or 'living together'; the Athenians liked to believe that the much earlier mythological hero Theseus had unified Attica and provided a central council where the lords of the region could meet. Theseus, so the story went, became the first king of Attica and made Athens its capital city (politically 'Athens' came to refer to the whole of Attica, and so those who lived in Attica were all known as 'Athenians').

8th century Attica was a feudal society in which the vast majority were impoverished farmers owing their livelihoods to a few wealthy, land-owning families. In times of peace, these farmers worked the land owned by their lord; in times of war, they were expected to follow him into battle. Political control of Attica was in the hands of these powerful land-owning families, who were known as the *eupatridae*, literally 'the sons of noble fathers'.

By the 7th century, the political structure of Athens had begun to evolve; monarchy had been abandoned in favour of a small board of **archons** (which could be translated as 'rulers' or 'magistrates'). There were nine such archons in all:

- **The king archon** held the religious responsibilities which were originally attached to the earlier office of king.
- **The polemarch** (ruler of war) was responsible for the army and all military affairs in Attica.
- **The eponymous archon** was responsible for a wide range of administrative matters in Attica. He was given the title 'eponymous' since the civil year was named after him (e.g. 'in the archonship of Solon' referred to 594/3).
- **The thesmothetai** (law-givers) were the six junior archons, who were responsible for the legal affairs of the state.

These archons were selected only from the *eupatridae*; once an archon had served his year in office, he automatically became a life member of the **Council of the Areopagus**, named after the Areopagus (literally: 'the crag of Ares'), the hill in Athens where the council met (see map 6). It was responsible for selecting and supervising the archons, as well as acting as a court of law.

At this stage, Attica was a typical aristocratic society; the wealthy nobles ensured that they held all the power and there was no way for the poor majority to take part in government. However, during the 7th century various changes combined to ferment political upheaval and challenge the power of the aristocrats in many parts of Greece.

2. Social unrest in Attica

Three key factors challenged the status quo in Greece during the 7th century and allowed people to challenge the power of the aristocrats: **(i)** the growth of trade and commerce with other Mediterranean peoples; **(ii)** the development of hoplite fighting; **(iii)** the growing inequality between rich and poor.

(i) As trade and commerce grew, a merchant class started to emerge in many Greek communities; some men who were not members of the old land-owning families started to become very wealthy. This 'nouveau riche' community resented the fact that, in spite of their economic success, they could hold no power in their home cities. They might also have returned with tales of more prosperous societies, causing the poor to question their poverty.

(ii) Warfare also changed dramatically in this period. Until the 8th century, it was the fighting of individual nobles which had won battles. Homer's poems, dated to the 8th century, describe a world of individual heroism comparable to the age of chivalry in medieval Europe. But in the following century a new battle formation called the phalanx emerged (see p. 253ff.). This relied on soldiers working together in an interlocking team and winning battles by teamwork. Such soldiers were known as **hoplites** (from *hopla*, the Greek word for 'weapons'), and they belonged to the growing middle class who were able to buy their own weapons. Since a society's safety now rested on its hoplites, they too began to resent the exclusive power of the nobles.

(iii) The growing inequality between rich and poor was also creating anger and resentment as more and more of the poor were being ruined by debt. In Attica, many farmers had to give one sixth of the produce of the land they tilled to the rich estate owners. Known as *hektemoroi*, or 'sixth-portioners', these farmers and their families could be enslaved by the landowner if they did not pay their dues. They were then made to work the land without reward, or else sold abroad. Many farmers were forced to take extreme measures in order to repay their debts, such as selling their children into slavery.

At the same time, the wealthy landowners were turning to foreign trade to make money. Rather than sell grain to the common people, they were able to get better prices overseas in exchange for wine and olive oil. Famine therefore fell on many families. The spirit of the age was captured by Hesiod, a poet from Boeotia:

'Don't you realise, you nobles, that justice will one day be done? For the gods are watching over us always, and they can see when one of you takes unfair advantage over other men, ruining them completely and not giving a damn about what the gods think ... justice sees, and justice carries this message to the gods: the mass of common people have to pay for your greed and wickedness.'   Hesiod, *Works and Days* 248ff.

Draconian measures
Evidence of some unrest in Attica can be gleaned from the law code introduced to Athens in 621 by a man called Draco. According to Aristotle, the new constitution gave rights to those Athenians 'who provided their own armour', suggesting that the hoplite class was starting to make its political weight count. Draco's laws are proverbial for their harshness – they give us the word 'draconian' – and later Athenians liked to say that they had been written not in ink but in blood. Plutarch's account illustrates their severity:

'Under the Draconian code, almost any kind of offence was liable to the death penalty, so that even those convicted of idleness were executed, and those who stole fruit and vegetables suffered the same punishment as those who committed sacrilege or murder ... Draco himself, when he was once asked why he had decreed the death penalty for the great majority of offences, replied that he considered the minor ones deserved it, and so for the major ones no heavier punishment was left.'

Plutarch, *Solon* 17.1-2

Tyranny

In some cities, these social conditions caused some men to attempt to overthrow the aristocrats and put themselves into power with the help of a popular uprising. If they succeeded, such men were known as **tyrants**, although this word did not necessarily have its modern association with cruelty. The word 'tyrant' simply referred to a ruler who had taken power by means other than inheriting it from his father. Tyrants were typically drawn from the new merchant class who had enough wealth to support their rise to power. Cities near to Athens, such as Corinth and Megara, were taken over by tyrants in the middle of the 7th century. At Athens, a man named Cylon tried to seize power as a tyrant in 632, although he did not get enough popular support to succeed.

However, some of the Athenian *eupatridae* realised that the conditions were still ripe for revolution and tyranny. In order to prevent this, in 594 the Athenians turned to a man called Solon to reform their constitution, as the author of the *Constitution of Athens* explains:

'In this political situation, when the majority were the slaves of the few, the people opposed the leaders of the state. When the strife was severe, and the opposition of long standing, both sides agreed to give power to Solon as mediator, and entrusted the state to him.'
Constitution of Athens 5.1-2

Review 1

1. Define the following: *archon, eupatridae, hektemoroi, hopla, synoecism, ta politika.*
2. Explain how the system of government worked in Athens after synoecism.
3. Can the social tensions in 7th century Greece be compared to those in any parts of the world today?
4. Are there any societies today whose laws you would describe as 'draconian'?
R. Read the story of Cylon as told by Herodotus (5.71) and Plutarch (Solon 12). How did this revolt affect subsequent Athenian politics?
E. Why were conditions at Athens ripe for revolt and tyranny in the late 7th century?

---

3. The reforms of Solon

Solon was a very interesting character. Although he was of noble birth, he didn't inherit great wealth. Therefore he turned to trade to make money, travelling widely in the Mediterranean. He was also an intellectual who wrote poetry, some of which survives for us to read today. He often gave public recitals of his poems, many of which expressed his political views: sympathy for the poor and anger at their treatment by the wealthy, as these lines illustrate:

'Restrain in your breasts your mighty hearts;
you have taken too much of the good things of life;
satisfy your pride with what is moderate,
for we shall not tolerate excess,
nor will everything turn out as you wish.'
Constitution of Athens 5.3

Solon's appeal to the Athenians was surely his ability to see things from three perspectives: although noble by birth, he had made a living as a merchant, while his poetry sympathised with the predicament of the poor. When he was appointed eponymous archon in 594, Solon tried to create a fairer society by a series of economic, political and legal reforms.

Economic reforms
To alleviate the poverty of Attic farmers, Solon introduced a series of economic reforms called the *seisachtheia* (the 'shaking off of burdens'):

- The practice of paying one sixth of one's produce to a landowner was abolished. From now on, farmers were able to own all the land which they tilled.
- It was forbidden to enslave anyone unable to repay his debts. Those who had previously been enslaved under this practice were freed; those who

181

had been enslaved and sold abroad were allowed to return to Attica and reclaim their citizenship.

- It was forbidden to export all agricultural products apart from olive oil, thus ensuring that the people did not starve.

In addition to these reforms, Solon tried to diversify the economy of Attica. He encouraged people to develop skills aside from farming in order to increase trade with other Mediterranean peoples. He therefore introduced laws benefiting people who learnt trades and he even offered citizenship to immigrants who were skilled craftsmen.

Political reforms

Solon also saw the need for political reform in order to break the power of the *eupatridae*. He therefore redefined the class system of Athens, basing it on wealth rather than birth. Each citizen was placed in one of four classes depending on how many measures – *medimnoi* – of grain, olive oil or wine his land produced each year. One *medimnos* was approximately equivalent to 55 litres.

Official measures.

The names of the four classes give an indication of their status. At the top were the super-rich, the *pentacosiomedimnoi*, those 'with 500 *medimnoi*'; next were the *hippeis*, the 'knights', who could afford to maintain a horse; the third class were the *zeugitai*, the 'yoke-men', who could afford their own armour and were thus yoked together in the phalanx; finally the *thêtes*, the 'menial workers', were society's poor. The table opposite illustrates the rights of each class.

Solon did not introduce democracy to Athens, which remained a class-based city where the majority had minimal rights. However, he did try to transform the city from an aristocracy into a meritocracy by allowing his top two property classes to qualify for selection as archons (the selection may have included an element of allotment to improve the chances of those who were rich but not noble); ex-archons continued to hold life-membership of the Council of the Areopagus. The vice-like grip on power maintained by the *eupatridae* had been broken.

Further encouragement was given to the two lower classes: the

Class	Annual income (medimnoi)	Political eligibility
pentacosiomedimnoi	500+	archonships & Areopagus Council state treasurers members of assembly
hippeis	300+	archonships & Areopagus Council lesser offices of state members of assembly
zeugitai	200+	lesser offices of state members of assembly
thêtes	< 200	members of assembly

zeugitai were allowed to serve in the lesser offices of state, such as tax-collecting and management of the state prison, while even the *thêtes* had the right to attend the assembly, where important matters of state were discussed, even if it had little formal power. There may also have been a council of 400 members, drawn from the top three classes, which prepared business for the assembly.

Legal reforms

Solon realised that, in the interests of social justice, Athens' legal system had to be reformed. Before 594, justice was in the hands of the archons and the Council of the Areopagus; under this system, the *eupatridae* were able to rig the law in their favour and ignore the claims of the majority. Solon made the following reforms:

- **Law code**. He created his own law code to replace Draco's, legislating in fields as diverse as inheritance, funerals, the location of public wells and the planting of trees. His laws were inscribed on wooden tablets so that any literate citizen could consult them.
- **Right of appeal**. Although lawsuits were still decided by the archons, he gave citizens the right of appeal to a jury, which was made up of members of the assembly. Citizens in all four property classes were eligible to sit on these juries.
- **Public lawsuits**. He created a category of 'public lawsuits', whereby any citizen could prosecute an offence, in contrast to the 'private lawsuits' in which only the injured party or his family could prosecute.

Perhaps the most critical aspect of these reforms was the introduction of juries to Athens, so placing the legal process in the hands of the whole citizen body. Moreover, Solon's introduction of 'public lawsuits' encouraged citizens to identify with the rights of others. According to Plutarch, Solon was once asked which city he considered best governed of all, to which he replied:

> 'The city where those who have not been wronged show themselves just as ready to punish the offender as those who have.'   Plutarch, *Solon* 18.5

The results of Solon's reforms

When Solon had served his year as archon, he made the Athenians swear a solemn oath not to change his reforms for ten years in order to give them time to work. He then left Athens and travelled the world, partly to get away from those men who wanted to consult him on every minor detail of his new system.

Solon's reforms were clearly an attempt to find a compromise between rich and poor. Like many other mediators, Solon ended up pleasing neither party. Plutarch explains why both sides felt let down:

> 'The rich were angry at being deprived of their securities, and the poor even more so, because Solon did not carry out a redistribution of the land, as they had expected, or impose a strictly equal and uniform style of living upon everybody.'
> Plutarch, *Solon* 16.1

As a result, the unrest in Attica continued; in 561, a military hero called Peisistratos took control of Athens as a tyrant. In the ensuing years, he was twice thrown out of office by his political foes, but both times returned stronger. From 546 until his death in 527 he was the uncontested ruler of Athens.

Peisistratos

In fact, the years of Peisistratos' rule were prosperous ones for Athens. He was shrewd enough to retain the support of the people; loans were offered to impoverished farmers, while grand engineering projects were also undertaken, such as the repair of the city's water-supply system.

Moreover, Peisistratos was a passionate patron of the arts. He encouraged the great poets of the Greek world to visit Athens and established two of the city's most important festivals, the City Dionysia (see Chapter 3) and the Great Panathenaia (see p. 29ff.). The city itself was given a make-over; the Acropolis was transformed into a great cult site for religious worship, the centrepiece of which was a large stone temple to Athena (destroyed by the Persians in 480).

However, perhaps Peisistratos' most significant legacy was his consolidation of Solon's reforms. All the structures implemented by Solon remained in place; the tyrant simply ensured that his own supporters were selected for the archonships. While this was undoubtedly corrupt, it did at least give Solon's new structures of government time to bed down. Writing two centuries later, Aristotle (who admittedly may not have been an unbiased source) provided a positive assessment of Peisistratos' leadership, claiming that he 'ran the state moderately and constitutionally rather than as a tyrant'.

When Peisistratos died in 527, his son Hippias took over Athens, closely supported by his younger brother Hipparchos. They soon seem to have become tyrants in the modern sense of the word, and Hipparchus was assassinated in 514. After this, Hippias' rule became increasingly cruel, and in 510 a group of Athenian aristocrats, aided by King Cleomenes of Sparta (a city traditionally opposed to tyranny), successfully plotted to drive him from Athens. The stage was set for another power struggle.

Review 2

1. Define the following: *medimnos, seisachtheia.*
2. How do the names of Solon's four classes reflect their social status?
3. Which of Solon's reforms do you most approve of and which do you most disapprove of? Explain your reasons.
4. Have there been any political leaders in the modern world who, like Solon, have tried to introduce a drastic set of reforms? If so, how successful have they been?
5. Why do you think that Solon's reforms didn't settle the unrest in Attica?
6. Are there any modern leaders who would see themselves as 'benevolent dictators' like Peisistratos? If so, how benevolent do you think they are?
R. Read Herodotus' account of Peisistratos' rise (*Histories* 1.59-60). Do you agree that he used 'the silliest trick that history has to record' to reclaim power?
E. To what extent do you approve of Solon's reforms? What do you think he could have done better?

---

4. The reforms of Cleisthenes

Two aristocratic factions soon emerged in this new power struggle. On one side was Isagoras, described by Aristotle as 'a supporter of the tyrants'; in opposition to him was Cleisthenes, who belonged to one of Attica's oldest aristocratic families. When Isagoras was chosen as archon in 508, he seemed to have won the support of the wealthy elite.

Cleisthenes then took what was probably the only option left to him. Realising that he could win power only with the support of the lower classes, he promised them 'control of the state' through a series of far-reaching reforms. In the words of Aristotle, Cleisthenes 'won the support of the people'; tellingly, the Greek word used for 'people' was *dêmos*. Democracy was born in a moment of political pragmatism.

The revolution was almost snuffed out in its infancy as Isagoras enlisted the help of the Spartans to win back power. But the Athenians were having none of it; they defended their new freedoms passionately, inflicting a humiliating defeat on their enemies. Herodotus summarised the victory with these famous words:

'Thus Athens went from strength to strength, and proved, if proof were needed, how noble a thing equality is, not in one respect only, but in all; for while they were oppressed under tyrants, they had no better success in war than any of their neighbours, yet, once the yoke was flung off, they proved the finest fighters in the world. This clearly shows that, so long as they were held down by authority, they deliberately shirked their duty in the field, as slaves shirk working for their masters; but when freedom was won, then every man amongst them was interested in his own cause.'

Herodotus, *Histories* 5.78

The language of power

Democracy was one of four political systems commonly practised in the Greek world during the 6th and 5th centuries. Two others, aristocracy and tyranny, have already been mentioned; the fourth is oligarchy, a form of government which briefly replaced democracy in Athens in the late 5th century.

The Greek language has left a lasting impression on the naming of political systems, most of which end in either *-cracy* or *-archy*. Both suffixes are derived from Greek words; *kratos* simply meant 'might' or 'power', while *archê* in turn meant 'rule' or 'command'. The four systems can be defined as follows:

- Aristocracy (*aristos* = noble): power to the nobles.
- Tyranny (*turannos* = ruler): one man takes power and rules.
- Democracy (*dêmos* = the people): power to the people.
- Oligarchy (*oligos* = few): rule by a small group of people.

The reforms attributed to Cleisthenes can be divided into three groups: (i) structures of government; (ii) political constituencies; (iii) ostracism.

i. Structures of government

In fact, Cleisthenes left Solon's structures of government largely untouched. The roles of the archons, the Council of the Areopagus and the law courts remained the same; in particular, the Council of the Areopagus seems to have retained control over most of the legislation. However, those alterations he did make were significant:

- A **Council of 500** was introduced (50 men from each tribe) which was to prepare business for the assembly.
- **Assembly meetings**. Although the assembly did not yet have many formal powers (these were to come after the reforms of Ephialtes in 462/1), it did now hold regular meetings each month.
- **Selection by lot**. Cleisthenes made selection by lot the usual process by which candidates were chosen for official posts (the selection of archons and of generals were two important exceptions). He believed that this was the most democratic way to choose a government; from this moment on, most government officials were chosen randomly from the citizen body.

186

ii. Political constituencies

Where Cleisthenes was most radical was in his reform of the political constituencies of Attica, a move designed to break the power of the aristocrats for good. He completely overhauled the Athenian tribal system and made the local village, or **deme**, the basic unit of his new political structure.

The deme system

Cleisthenes realised that most of Attica could naturally be divided into demes, which were either small towns or villages. The city of Athens, far too large to be regarded as a single deme, was divided into districts, each of which held deme status.

A map showing the three divisions created by Cleisthenes (1 coastal; 2 inland; 3 city) and the distribution of demes in Attica.

---

dêmos

The word *dêmos* originally meant something like 'township' or 'village' and it could refer to the people who lived in these settlements too. As democracy developed, the word also came to refer to the whole citizen body of Attica; for example, writers such as Thucydides and Aristotle often used the word when describing the decisions taken by the assembly.

Each deme (there were 139 in all) had its own council, with an assembly, officers, treasurers and an annually elected leader called a *dêmarch*. Thus a deme managed local affairs and functioned rather as local government does today. This encouraged Athenians to involve themselves in their local communities; it also gave citizens experience of democratic government, which they could then draw upon when they served in the central government (as most citizens did at some point in their lives).

Moreover, the deme was to be the fundamental building block of citizenship. In 508/7, each Athenian had to register in what he regarded as his local deme. Thereafter, membership of a deme was hereditary, even if a man moved to another part of Attica (this may have been to keep the tribes roughly equal in size). Deme officials were required to keep a record of all men in the deme registered as citizens and, at the age of 18, a young man had to register in his father's deme and pass a citizenship test (see p. 203).

As part of the new system, Cleisthenes persuaded the Athenians to identify themselves by their deme rather than by their father's name. Thus, where a citizen might once have called himself 'Callias, son of Isocrates', he would now call himself 'Callias from Brauron'. Under the old system, a man's name had immediately indicated how well connected his family was in Athenian society. By contrast, the new naming system was classless; moreover, a man's political identity had switched from his family to his local community.

Athenian literature offers various examples of citizens who felt a deep loyalty to their deme. In Aristophanes' comic play *Acharnians*, the main character is Dicaeopolis, a farmer who 'hates the city and loves his deme'. The play was written in 425 during the war with Sparta, a few years after the Athenians had decided to move all the inhabitants of Attica into the city while their land was being invaded. Thucydides describes how painful the move was for the rural population:

'They were deeply distressed at abandoning their homes ... and their hereditary holy shrines, at having to change their way of life and at leaving what each regarded as no less than his own native city.'

Thucydides, *History of the Peloponnesian War* 2.16

5. Athenian Democracy

The tribal system

One area which Solon had not tackled was the Athenian tribal system.
There were four ancient tribes of Attica, each made up of smaller clans
and households. This system allowed the wealthy to retain great power
since they could dictate to other tribe members which leaders they
should support. The tribes were also geographically based, creating
regional rivalries within Attica. Cleisthenes therefore disbanded these
old tribes and created ten new ones.

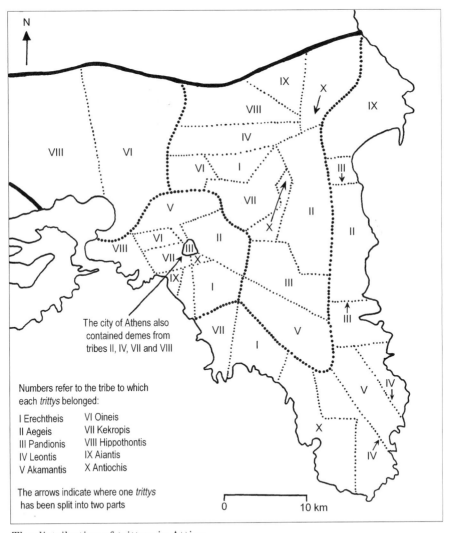

The city of Athens also
contained demes from
tribes II, IV, VII and VIII

Numbers refer to the tribe to which
each *trittys* belonged:

I Erechtheis	VI Oineis
II Aegeis	VII Kekropis
III Pandionis	VIII Hippothontis
IV Leontis	IX Aiantis
V Akamantis	X Antiochis

The arrows indicate where one *trittys*
has been split into two parts

0   10 km

The distribution of *trittyes* in Attica.

189

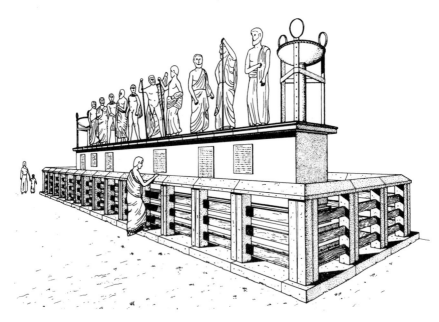

A drawing of the shrine of the eponymous heroes in the Agora. Under each hero was a public notice board relating to the respective tribe's affairs.

Cleisthenes recognised that a tribe needed to contain a wide cross-section of Athenian citizens, and he wanted each to contain demes from across Attica. He therefore divided Attica into 30 zones of roughly equal population, known as *trittyes* (meaning 'thirds'). He saw that these 30 *trittyes* could naturally be divided into three equally-sized regions of Attica – ten *trittyes* constituting the area around the **city**, ten the **inland** region and ten the **coastal** region. Each tribe was then made up of three *trittyes*, one from each region, taking care that the three *trittyes* in a tribe did not border with one another. In this way, every tribe had an equal number of men from three distinct parts of Attica.

The ten tribes were each given the name of one of Athens' legendary heroes, which had been chosen by the Pythia at Delphi (see p. 35ff.). These heroes were known as the 'eponymous heroes', since they each lent their name to their tribe. A statue of each of the ten eponymous heroes was placed in the agora in Athens. Each tribe had its own priest who performed sacrifices at a shrine to its eponymous hero.

The tribal system oiled the wheels of the democracy. Each tribe had to provide quotas of men for the Council of 500, the army, boards of officials and the law courts. Each had its own treasury, as well as elected officials and an assembly. Moreover, many sporting and musical contests at important festivals, such as the Panathenaia and the City Dionysia, were run on a tribal basis.

The ten generals

Another important innovation introduced in about 501/0 was the creation of a board of ten generals. Each tribe had to elect one of its men annually to serve as a general (*stratêgos*) of the army; there was no limit to the number of years a citizen could serve. At first it was unclear which would wield more power, the new board of generals or the old office of *polemarch*, but the generals soon proved that popular support gave them real power. Moreover, this was a position which was theoretically open to any Athenian citizen, unlike the archonship.

---

iii. Ostracism

As a further safeguard against tyranny, the Athenians invented a process known as ostracism. Aristotle credits Cleisthenes with this invention, although this is disputed – the first recorded ostracism was not until 487, some twenty years after his reforms. Nonetheless, ostracism became a significant feature of the democratic system for most of the 5th century.

Under the rules of ostracism, each year the assembly was allowed to banish one public figure for a period of ten years. Candidates for ostracism were typically perceived to be growing too powerful, so posing a threat to the democratic government. However, to ostracise a citizen was not to convict him of any crime. It was really a device to allow for a 'cooling-off period' which aimed to prevent civil unrest and a return to tyranny. Significantly, an ostracised citizen did not lose his property and

This *ostrakon* bears the words 'Kallias Kratio[u]' ('Kallias, son of Kratios') written on one side; on the reverse is an image of a Persian archer; thus Kallias seems to have been put up for ostracism on the grounds that he was a Persian sympathiser.

191

his family were allowed to remain in Attica. When the ten years were up, he could return with the full rights of a citizen.

The process worked as follows. Once a year, the assembly was asked if it wanted to hold an ostracism. If the answer was affirmative, then a further meeting of the assembly was scheduled. Plutarch takes up the tale:

'Each voter took a piece of earthenware (*ostrakon*), wrote on it the name of the citizen he wished to be banished and carried it to a part of the agora which was cordoned off with a circular fence. Then the archons first counted the total number of votes cast, for if there were fewer than 6,000 votes, the ostracism was invalid. After this they sorted the votes and the man who had the most votes recorded against his name was proclaimed to be exiled for ten years, with the right, however, to receive the income from his estate.'

Plutarch, *Aristides* 7.4-5

The term 'ostracism' was thus derived from the *ostrakon*, the broken piece of pottery upon which a citizen cast his vote. A quorum (the minimum number of votes required for a decision to be valid) of 6,000 was required for important decisions of the assembly; less important matters could be decided by a smaller turnout.

Aristides the Just

One weakness in the system of ostracism was the voting process itself. For a significant number of Athenian citizens would not have known how to write (see p. 137ff. to read about the levels of education of Athenian citizens). The famous story of Aristides the Just illustrates this point.

Aristides was an Athenian aristocrat whose reputation for fairness earned him the title 'the Just'. However, some began to resent the esteem in which he was held and in 482 he was ostracised. During the vote, according to Plutarch:

'An illiterate and uncouth rustic handed his *ostrakon* to Aristides and asked him to write the name 'Aristides' on it. The latter was astonished and asked him what harm Aristides had ever done him. "None whatever," was the reply, "I do not even know the fellow, but I am sick of hearing him called 'the Just' everywhere!" When he heard this, Aristides said nothing, but wrote his name on the *ostrakon* and handed it back.'

Plutarch, *Aristides* 7.5-6

There is no doubt that ostracism was a powerful political weapon; in its earliest years, the Athenians ostracised two prominent relatives of Peisistratos, fearing that they wanted to restore a tyranny. Over 10,000 *ostraka* have been discovered around the Athenian agora and the potters' quarter (the kerameikos – see p. 274); most interesting was the discovery of 190 ostraka in a well on the north slope of the Acropolis, all of them bearing the name 'Themistocles' and written by only a few hands, suggesting that they were prepared for distribution by the opponents of Themistocles, who was indeed ostracised in about 470.

In fact, Themistocles' story is a good example of how the mighty of Athenian society could fall. In the 480s he was an influential archon and general who earned the lion's share of the credit for the Athenian naval victory over the Persians at Salamis in 480. However, the people later resented his success and he was ostracised in 471, going to live in Argos; a few years later he moved to Asia Minor and fell in league with his old enemies, the Persians, who made him a governor of one of their provinces!

Review 3

1. Define the following: *dêmarch, dêmos, ostrakon, stratêgos, trittyes.*
2. What were the advantages of: (i) the deme system; (ii) the new tribe system? Do you think they had any disadvantages?
3. How are political constituencies divided up in your country? Do you think that this could be done more fairly?
4. What were the strengths and weaknesses of the system of ostracism?
5. Could a form of ostracism be used today? If so, which public figure would you like to ostracise from your society and why?
R. Read Herodotus' account (*Histories* 3.80-2) of the 'Persian debate' about the respective merits of monarchy, oligarchy and democracy. What arguments are advanced for and against each system?
E. Why do you think Cleisthenes introduced his reforms? Could he be called 'the father of democracy'?

---

5. The Persian Wars

Just as the infant democracy was finding its feet, the entire Greek world was faced with the threat of invasion from the vast and powerful Persian Empire to the east. Tensions between the two races grew during the 490s, culminating in two invasions of Greece – the first in 490, followed by a second ten years later. The astonishing victories achieved by the Greeks proved to be the making of democratic Athens.

In 490, the invading Persians were met by a much smaller army of hoplites (the vast majority Athenian) on the plain of Marathon in north-eastern Attica. The hoplites' superior fighting skills sealed a remarkable victory: at the end of the battle, 192 Greeks lay dead in contrast to 6,400 Persians. The victory had a deep political impact: since the hoplites had largely been drawn from the *zeugitai* class, the top two social classes realised that the *zeugitai* were crucial to their own safety.

The 480s were nervous ones for the Greeks, who believed (correctly) that the Persians would return for revenge. The Athenian general Themistocles convinced his people that the way to defeat the Persians was at sea. Athens, a city with no history of naval warfare, quickly built a large navy of triremes (see p. 211). Each trireme required 200 men, many of whom were *thêtes*. Themistocles was proved right when the Athenians won another unlikely victory at a sea-battle in the bay of Salamis in 480. The *thêtes* were also now indispensable to Athenian freedom. Even the highly conservative Old Oligarch accepted that:

> '... it is right that in Athens the poor and the common people should have more power than the nobles and the rich, because they provide the rowers for the fleet and thus give the city its strength.'
>
> *Constitution of the Athenians* 1.2

A wise decision

In 483, the Athenians had an outrageous stroke of good fortune. As Themistocles continued to argue for the construction of a navy, miners struck a rich seam of silver at Laureion (see p. 167). A debate followed in the assembly about how to use the windfall (which apparently amounted to more than 100 talents). Herodotus records that, while some men proposed that each citizen should receive 10 drachmas, Themistocles convinced the assembly to invest in 200 ships. The young democracy had shown that it could vote with foresight and wisdom.

Another important consequence of the Persian Wars was the growth in importance of the ten generals, whose influence now eclipsed that of the archons. This process speeded up after 487, when it was decided to choose the archons by lot rather than by election. Although the office of archon was still open only to the top two classes, there was now no opportunity for the wealthy to campaign (and perhaps attempt bribery) to ensure that their preferred candidates won.

In the wake of Salamis, many of the Greek city-states formed an alliance on the island of Delos in 478. Named the **Delian League**, it was designed to provide the Greeks with the naval power to withstand further Persian attacks. Athens became the most important city in the League and took command of its navy, while her allies had either to pay tribute or to supply ships. This confirmed Athens as the most important city in the Greek world and the defender of Greek freedom. As time went by, however, this great exponent of democracy at home increasingly tyrannised the members of the League until it effectively became an Athenian empire.

Consequently, this was a time of great pride in Athens, as is reflected in the literature of the period. In 472, the Athenian playwright Aeschylus wrote *Persians*, a play which celebrates the victory at

The Athenian tribute list. This fragment records the tribute paid in 440/39 by cities surrounding the northern Aegean.

Salamis. In the following lines, Atossa, the mother of the Persian king, questions the chorus about the victorious city of Athens:

Atossa: Tell me, in what part of the world is this Athens situated?
Chorus: Far away to the west, where the sun sinks down.
Atossa: But did my son wish to conquer a place so far away?
Chorus: Indeed he did; for were Athens but defeated, all Greece would fall before him.
Atossa: Is the Athenian army so enormous then?
Chorus: So powerful is the Athenian army that it has caused havoc among the mighty host of our Persian army.
Atossa: And are they a wealthy people as well?
Chorus: Their land produces silver.
Atossa: Do they fight with a bow, as we do?
Chorus: Why, no; they fight hand-to-hand, with shield and spear.
Atossa: And who is their Lord and Master?
Chorus: Madam, they are neither slaves nor servants to any man.

Aeschylus, *Persians* 231ff.

Ephialtes

In the aftermath of the wars, leaders emerged who wanted to create a democratic system of full equality for every citizen, regardless of economic class. Two rival factions now dominated the politics of the city; on the one hand were many aristocrats who wanted to keep control of the city in the hands of the wealthy and educated elite; on the other were men, styling themselves 'radical democrats', who tried to enlist the support of the poorer Athenians in order to effect more reforms.

In 462/1, one such radical, Ephialtes (who was closely supported by Pericles), managed to push through a reform which had a huge impact on the nature of Athenian politics. At this time, the Council of Areopagus was the last major barrier to equality for all citizens, since it retained control of many law-making powers. This body now seemed to belong to another age, when a wealthy elite had held power. Moreover, its aristocratic status had probably diminished since 487/6, when the archons (its future members) were first chosen by lot.

Ephialtes' reform deprived the Areopagus of all its duties except for jurisdiction over homicide, arson and the destruction of sacred olive trees (these held great religious importance – see p. 144). All other powers, such as responsibility for the Athenian law code and scrutiny of public officials, were transferred to the other bodies – the assembly, the law courts or the council. Ephialtes paid for his reform with his life when he was assassinated the following year.

6. Pericles

After the death of Ephialtes, one of his closest allies emerged to lead the radical democrats. Pericles came from the same aristocratic family as Cleisthenes (his great-uncle) and he was to become the most influential Athenian of his age. Over the next few years, he introduced the final reforms which produced radical democracy:

- **Archonships**. In 457/6, the archonships were opened up to the *zeugitai*, although in practice all citizens, including the *thêtes*, seem to have been able to hold public office after this date.
- **Payment**. Soon after the death of Ephialtes, payment was introduced for citizens who served one of the political institutions: the council, the law courts, the archons and the lesser magistracies. This allowed poorer citizens to play a full role in the democracy.
- **Citizenship**. By now Athenian citizenship was highly prized. In response to this, Pericles introduced a reform in 451/0 tightening up the citizenship laws. Henceforth, citizenship was confined to the legitimate sons of an Athenian mother as well as an Athenian father. This xenophobic legislation would actually have disqualified many eminent Athenians, not least Themistocles, from citizenship.

Pericles.

In addition to these political reforms, Pericles invigorated the economy of Attica. In 454, the treasury of the Delian League was moved to Athens; moreover, peace had been concluded with the Persians and less money was required for the defence of the League. Pericles convinced the people to divert large amounts of the League's tribute into a building project for the city of Athens.

The Athenian Empire

The relocation of the treasury of the Delian League to Athens illustrates how much power Athens had come to wield over its allies. Indeed, when the Peloponnesian War broke out in 431, the Spartans claimed that they were fighting to 'free the Greeks'. One indication of Athens' influence is that trials involving allies had to take place in Athens before an Athenian jury. The Old Oligarch lets slip the real effect of this by commenting that 'the Athenian state benefits from the fact that trials for the allies are held at Athens ... because of this, the allies have become even more the slaves of the Athenian state.'

The Acropolis, which had been sacked and had its buildings torched during the Persian invasion of 480, was adorned with the spectacular sacred buildings for which it remains famous: the Parthenon, the Erechtheion and the temple of Athena Nike; a monumental gateway, the Propylaia, marked the entrance to the site. The project had a double benefit of glorifying Athens (Pericles claimed that the city was 'an education to Greece') and providing work for its citizens. Plutarch records that the materials used were 'stone, gold, bronze, ivory, ebony, and cypress-wood' and that craftsmen of all types were employed.

This programme was not uncontroversial. One of Pericles' main political rivals, Thucydides, the son of Milesias (not to be confused with the historian of the same name), who led the aristocratic faction in the assembly, opposed the policy of spending tribute raised for military defence on beautifying the city of Athens.

The 'first citizen'

Pericles was the most influential citizen in Athens until his death in 429, to the extent that the city in this period is often referred to as 'Periclean Athens'. Yet how could this be so? Pericles himself had brought about the final reforms which ensured that the city was run equally by all its citizens.

Politically, Pericles was frequently elected general from 454; indeed, between 443 and 429 he held the post for fifteen consecutive years. This gave him a platform from which to put forward his views, and no doubt it helped that his main political rival Thucydides, the son of Milesias, was ostracised in 443 following his opposition to the building programme. Ultimately, it seems that the people respected him and were happy to trust him as their leader.

This is an important point – Pericles was only able to have the influence he did because the people gave him their blessing at the ballot box each year. At times, they did lose patience with him, such as when they fined him for the way he conducted the war with Sparta in 430. However, the historian Thucydides (an unabashed admirer of Pericles) summed up the relationship between the general and the people as follows:

5. Athenian Democracy

'Pericles, because of his position, his intelligence and his known integrity, could respect the liberty of the people and at the same time hold them in check. It was he who led them, rather than they who led him, and, since he never sought power from any wrong motive, he was under no necessity of flattering them: in fact, he was so highly respected that he was able to speak angrily to them and to contradict them. Certainly, when he saw that they were going too far in a mood of over-confidence, he would bring back to them a sense of their dangers; and when they were discouraged for no good reason, he would restore their confidence. So, in what was nominally a democracy, power was really in the hands of the first citizen.'

Thucydides, *History of the Peloponnesian War* 2.65

Athens now took great pride in its democratic system. Perhaps the greatest statement of what it meant to be Athenian at this time was made in the funeral speech which, according to Thucydides, Pericles delivered in 430 for the soldiers who had fallen in the first year of the war with Sparta. In the following lines, Pericles praises the Athenian system of government:

'Let me say that our system of government does not copy the institutions of our neighbours. It is more the case of our being a model to others than of our imitating anyone else. Our constitution is called a democracy because power is in the hands of the whole people rather than of a minority. When it is a question of settling private disputes, everyone is equal before the law; when it is a matter of putting one person before another in positions of public responsibility, what counts is not membership of a political class, but the actual ability which the man possesses. No one, so long as he has it in him to be of service to the state, is kept in political obscurity because of poverty.'

Thucydides, *History of the Peloponnesian War* 2.37

Review 4

1. Explain why: (i) the battle of Marathon; (ii) the battle of Salamis, were so important to the development of Athenian democracy.
2. What was the Delian League? How did it get its name?
3. How are Athenian values and pride reflected in the passage from *Persians* quoted on p. 195? Does any modern literature celebrate political achievement in a similar way?
4. Are there any modern examples of a democratic country which has tried to rule an empire? If so, how successful and popular have they been?
5. Why were the reforms of (i) Ephialtes; (ii) Pericles, so important in bringing radical democracy to Athens?
6. Are there examples of other countries who have established a great building programme to celebrate political progress? What benefits have they sought to get from this?
7. How true do you think was Thucydides' claim that 'power was really in the hands of the first citizen'? Why do you think that Pericles had so much influence?

II. THE INSTITUTIONS OF DEMOCRACY

The second half of this chapter examines the institutions of Athenian democracy as they worked from the second half of the 5th century. At the heart of the system was the **assembly**, the city's legislative body; business for the assembly was prepared by the 500 members of the **council**, an administrative committee without legislative power; there were many other boards of **magistrates** which took charge of different areas of government business – everything from street-sweeping to managing the state treasury. The legal safeguard for the whole system was found in the **law courts**, where any citizen could serve as a juror.

Body	Responsibility	Number	Pages
magistrates	boards of 10 each supervising an area of public life	any full citizen who had passed his *dokimasia*	203-4
council	(i) prepare legislation for assembly (ii) diplomacy (iii) supervision of magistrates	500 annually allotted (50 per tribe)	205-7
assembly	pass legislation	all full citizens (quorum of 6,000 for important votes)	207-10
dikasts	hear and judge court cases	pool of 6,000 annually allotted (600 per tribe)	214-18

1. Citizenship

Pericles' reported claim that in democratic Athens 'power is in the hands of the whole people rather than of a minority' seems astonishing to a modern reader, for probably less than 20% of the adult population of Attica was eligible to play any part in the democratic system.

It is hard to state accurately how many inhabitants there were in Attica during the 5th century. However, one estimate for the start of the Peloponnesian War in 431 runs as follows:

- 50,000 adult male citizens.
- 25,000 male foreigners (metics – see below).
- 100,000 slaves, male and female (see p. 162ff. for more on the lives of slaves).
- 75,000 women (Athenian and metics).

200

If children are factored in, the population may have been in the region of 300,000 to 350,000 (less than 5% of the estimated populations of London or New York City in 2007). Thus, Pericles' claim seems nonsensical. However, his argument would have made sense to an Athenian; slavery and the suppression of women were a fact of life in ancient Greek society, just as they have been in many other societies throughout time.

Before looking at the political role of citizens, it is worth considering the political status of women and foreigners (you can learn much more about women's wider role in Athenian society by reading p. 150ff.).

Women

Although it seems strange to us that women were given no political role in Athens, it is worth remembering when some modern democracies gave women the right to vote: 1920 (USA), 1928 (UK), 1944 (France) and 1971 (Switzerland). Indeed, before the 20th century the idea of allowing women to vote was generally thought to be ludicrous.

Two comedies of Aristophanes at least suggest that Athenian women had political views and were keen to impress them on their menfolk. *The Assembly-Women* and *Lysistrata* both revolve around plots where women try to take over the government of Athens. The following lines from *Lysistrata*, which is set during the war with Sparta, give an insight (albeit through the eyes of a comic satirist) into how women might have reacted to the decisions of their husbands in the assembly:

> 'Ever since this war started, we women, with a great deal of difficulty and strain, have somehow managed to control ourselves despite everything you men have done ... day after day we'd listen to your pompous pronouncements; but, hiding our horror at this war, we'd smile sweetly, and innocently ask whether there was any talk about peace in the assembly that day. And you would reply with a snarl: "Don't meddle in men's affairs." ... Obediently I kept quiet. But then you'd make some decision which was even more absurd, and, unable to control myself completely, I'd give a little sigh and say: "But did you *have* to make a decision like that?" And what was your reply? "Get on with your spinning. That's a woman's job. War is men's business." '
>
> Aristophanes, *Lysistrata* 507ff.

Metics

Foreigners who were resident at Athens were known as metics (from the Greek *metoikos*, meaning 'one who lives with us'). The metics were a large and important group of people in the city; as the figures above have shown, they may have accounted for as much as a third of the free male population in 431. The majority of metics probably came to Athens seeking economic opportunities; a number may have been fleeing from political persecution at home. Most came from nearby Greek cities, although there are also records of immigrants from non-Greek regions such as Thrace and Lydia.

After a foreigner had lived at Athens for more than a month, he (or she – there was a significant number of metic women in Athens) had to register as a metic in the deme where he was living (freed slaves were also given metic status, but their number was small). Each metic required an Athenian patron (*prostatês*) and had to pay a monthly tax of one drachma, or half a drachma for independent metic women (see p. 275 for information about Greek currency values); moreover, a male metic was expected to fight for Athens in times of war. Wealthier metics served as hoplites, but a significant number of them must have rowed in the fleet. The Old Oligarch emphasised the importance of this role:

'The city needs metics because of the multiplicity of skills and for the fleet.'
Constitution of the Athenians 1.12

The author here also highlights the important economic role played by the metics. A few managed to become very wealthy, but these were the exception rather than the rule. Metics could not own property in Attica, and so they were generally found in non-farming industries such as crafts and commerce: a list from 401 describes metics working in trades as varied as baking, gardening, fulling, nut-selling and mule-driving. Many lived in Piraeus (see p. 270), where they made money in areas such as foreign trade, banking, or armament production. Some female metics were successful *hetairai* (see p. 149).

Metics had a limited status in the city. They had no political rights, but were given some legal rights in the courts. They were also allowed freedom of religious worship; for example, the Thracian goddess Bendis was worshipped in a sanctuary in Piraeus. Metics could also take a full part in the cultural life of the city: they played major roles in religious processions (see pp. 33 and 106), while the wealthiest of them were eligible for the *chorêgia* (see p. 213). Occasionally, a metic was awarded citizen status if he had performed outstanding service for the city.

A famous metic family

A rich Syracusan called Cephalos was invited by Pericles to settle at Athens as a metic. He became one of the richest metics in Athens, thanks in part to his shield factory in the Piraeus which employed 120 slaves. Plato also set the dialogue in his seminal work, the *Republic*, at the house of Cephalos' eldest son, Polemarchos, suggesting that the family moved in the city's highest intellectual circles. When the democracy was briefly overthrown in 404/3, the city's new rulers conducted a purge against metics, who were seen to be supporters of the democracy. Polemarchos was forced to drink poison, but his brother Lysias narrowly escaped death and went on to become one of the greatest speech-writers in Athenian history.

Citizens

At the age of 18, a young Athenian, whose parents were both Athenian citizens, could present himself to his deme-council to register as a citizen. He had to prove his age and that he was free-born. If his application was accepted, then he served for two years as a military cadet known as an **ephebe**. Little is known about the programme for the ephebes in the 5th century, but in the 4th century they underwent military training, during which they guarded the borders of Attica and were introduced to its main religious sanctuaries. A similar system of national service survives in some countries today, including modern Greece.

Upon completing these two years, the young man became a citizen of Athens and could now speak in the assembly; however, full citizenship rights did not come until the age of 30, when he could serve as a magistrate or a juror. The rights of a full citizen were as follows: (i) he was free from direct taxation; (ii) he had the right to own land; (iii) he could bring lawsuits and serve as a juror; (iv) he had full political rights. When Aristotle defined citizenship, he emphasised the last two:

> 'What effectively distinguishes the citizen proper from all others is his participation in giving judgement [i.e. in the law courts] and in holding office [i.e. by sitting in the assembly, serving on the council or serving as a magistrate].'
> Aristotle, *Politics* 1275a22

The most important point about citizenship in ancient Athens is that it was participatory. There were few politicians in the modern sense of the word; instead, the city relied upon its ordinary citizens to vote in the assembly, serve as state officials, sit on juries and serve in the military. Indeed, the contemptuous Athenian word for a private citizen who kept to himself was *idiôtês*, from which we derive 'idiot'. Once again, the spirit of the age was captured by Thucydides' Pericles:

> 'We do not say that a man who takes no interest in politics is a man who minds his own business; we say that he has no business here at all.'
> Thucydides, *History of the Peloponnesian War* 2.40

2. Magistrates

Athens had no professional civil service; instead, all civic jobs were administered by boards of magistrates selected from the citizen body to serve for one year. According to Aristotle, in addition to the 500 councillors, there were about 700 magistrates serving Attica each year, the vast majority of whom were chosen by lot to serve on a board of ten men (one from each tribe). A citizen could hold a specific magistracy only once, meaning that most citizens served as magistrates at some point in their lives. However, there was no bar to citizens going on to hold other magistracies in subsequent years.

Each board was responsible for a specific area of civic life; the board of archons was the most famous, but we also hear, for example, of *astunomoi*, who were responsible for keeping the streets and highways clean, *agoranomoi*, who supervised markets, and *metronomoi*, who checked weights and measures against official government standards. A particularly important board was called the Eleven, which was in charge of administering legal punishments and managing the state prison.

At the heart of the magistrate system was a series of checks and balances. When a citizen (who had to be over 30 to serve) applied for a post, he was examined for good character by the council in a test called the **dokimasia** ('scrutiny'). The *Constitution of Athens* lists the questions posed by the council in the *dokimasia*:

> 'They first ask: "Who is your father and what is your deme? Who was your father's father and who was your mother, and her father and his deme?" Then they ask whether the candidate is enrolled in a cult of Apollo Patroös and Zeus Herkeios, and where the shrines are, then whether he has family tombs and where they are; whether he treats his parents well, pays his dues, and has gone on campaign when required.'
>
> *Constitution of Athens* 55.3

Of the two gods mentioned here, Apollo Patroös was worshipped by the Athenians as the father of Ion, one of their earliest ancestors, while Zeus Herkeios was honoured as the protector of the home (see p. 133). Membership of the two cults therefore indicated both a man's Athenian ancestry and his ownership of a house in Attica. After the hearing, the council voted on whether to put the candidate forward for a magistracy.

Accountability

Magistrates were held to account both during and after their year's service. At each month's sovereign assembly (see p. 208) a vote of confidence was held in the performance of the magistrates. A complaint could be made against any magistrate and, if upheld, he could be removed from office. At the end of his year's term, every magistrate had to give an account of his performance to the council; this report was called the **euthunai** ('accounts'). If any citizen felt unhappy about a magistrate's conduct, then he could bring a charge of misconduct to the law courts. A magistrate convicted of mismanaging state finances was fined twice the amount he had mismanaged; moreover, an official convicted of embezzlement or of taking bribes was fined ten times the amount involved in his fraud.

Review 5

1. Define the following: *dokimasia, ephebe, euthunai, idiôtês, metoikos.*
2. What is the definition of a 'citizen' in your society? How does this compare to the Athenian concept of citizenship?
3. Find out about women's struggle to get the vote in the western world. Are there still countries today which give fewer rights to women than to men?
4. What rights are foreign residents given in your country? How do these compare to those given to the metics at Athens?
5. How does your country mark the moment when a person becomes a citizen? What improvements would you make to the process?
6. Do you think it is a good idea for a society to have a form of national service for its youngest adult citizens? What benefits might such a system bring?
7. Is there anything like the system of *dokimasia* and *euthunai* for politicians today? What qualifications are needed to hold political office?
8. Would the Athenian system of having ordinary citizens run an area of public life for one year work better than the system in your society today?

---

3. The council (boulê)

The council of 500, known as the **boulê**, was the main administrative arm of government and also acted as an advisory committee to the assembly (*boulê* originally meant 'advice'). Every year, 50 councillors were selected by lot from each of the ten tribes. Even within the tribes, the lot was organised so that every deme provided a fixed number of councillors on an annual basis. Any citizen over the age of 30 was eligible to serve but no one could serve more than twice in his lifetime. This meant that a large proportion of Athenian citizens served on the council at some stage in their lives.

The council met in the Bouleuterion (Council House) in the agora on every day except public holidays; any citizen could observe its meetings. Its most important functions were as follows:

- To act as a **steering committee** for the assembly; councillors discussed matters of importance and prepared motions (known as *probouleumata*) for the assembly; these were then published several days before the next assembly meeting.
- To **oversee** the implementation of the assembly's decisions: ensuring that decrees were carried out, managing public property, supervising the collection and expenditure of public money and managing public building works.
- To supervise **elections** to elected posts and to process the *dokimasiai* and *euthunai* of all officials.
- To meet **foreign visitors** (ambassadors, embassies, etc.) on behalf of the city.

205

A drawing of the inside of the tholos, where the *prytaneis* lived during their presidency.

The prytany system

At the heart of the council was the prytany system. The Athenian year was naturally divided into ten lunar months, each of 35 or 36 days. Every tribe held the presidency of the council for one month; during this period, that tribe's 50 councillors were called *prytaneis* (singular: *prytanis*), or 'presidents', and a month was therefore called a prytany, or 'presidency'. At the end of a prytany, a new tribe was chosen by lot for the next prytany, with all the tribes serving once in the calendar year. This system was designed to prevent corruption, as nobody could plan to introduce business when a certain tribe held the presidency, nor did a councillor know in advance when he would serve as a *prytanis*.

During each prytany, the *prytaneis* lived at the public expense in the tholos, a circular building on the west side of the agora. They dealt with the mundane matters of state, reported to the council on a daily basis and prepared the agenda for council meetings. Every morning, one of the *prytaneis* was chosen by lot to be the chairman of the council for that day. He was called the **epistatês** ('superintendent') and could serve as such only once during a prytany. This meant that at least 70% of the *prytaneis* acted as the *epistatês* during a prytany. The *epistatês* also acted as the chairman of the assembly for the day.

In the following excerpt from a speech, the 4th century orator Demosthenes describes how the *prytaneis* and councillors prepared for an emergency meeting of the assembly in 339:

'It was evening when a messenger came to the *prytaneis* and told them about the capture of Elateia. They were in the middle of supper but rose at once and cleared the stalls in the agora ... while others sent for the generals. The whole city was soon in uproar.

At dawn the next day the *prytaneis* summoned the rest of the council to the *bouleutêrion*, while you all [i.e. citizens] made your way to the Pnyx. Actually the whole body of citizens had taken their places before the council could proceed to business or propose a motion. Subsequently, when the council had arrived and the *prytaneis* had reported the news they had received, the messenger was introduced and told his tale; the herald then put the question: 'Who wishes to speak?'

Demosthenes, *On the Crown* 169ff.

4. The assembly (ecclêsia)

The Greek word for 'assembly', *ecclêsia*, meant 'something called out' and when the assembly was summoned, any citizen could attend. It gathered at dawn on the Pnyx hill four times in each prytany (therefore it met 40 times a year). In addition, the assembly could be called for an emergency session if the need arose.

Before a meeting, 300 Scythian Archers, public slaves employed as a police force, herded citizens towards the Pnyx if they were chatting in the agora or wasting time elsewhere. They used a rope dyed with a red pigment and any loiterers whose clothes were marked by the rope were liable to pay a fine for tardiness. The Scythian Archers also maintained

The Pnyx.

order during the meeting. The magistrates and generals were allowed to sit at the front of the assembly, but that aside there was no seating plan. Although Aristophanes' comedies do not necessarily represent historical fact, his *Acharnians* begins with the farmer Dikaiopolis arriving at the Pnyx before an assembly meeting and so perhaps offers an insight into the start of such meetings:

> 'There's a sovereign assembly this morning and the Pnyx here is deserted. They're chattering in the agora, edging this way and that to avoid the red rope. Even the *prytaneis* aren't here yet either. They'll be late and then they'll come jostling each other for the front row like nobody's business, flooding down in throngs. But as for peace, they don't care a damn for that. Oh my city, my city! And I'm always the first to come to the assembly and take my place; and then when I'm alone, I groan and yawn and stretch, fart and don't know what to do, longing for peace, looking out at my deme. So now I have come quite prepared to shout and interrupt and slang the speakers if any of them says a single word other than on the subject of peace. But here are the *prytaneis* arriving – now that it's noon.'
>
> Aristophanes, *Acharnians* 17ff.

Before the meeting could begin, a priest had to sacrifice a pig and all traitors were cursed. The assembly then began, under the chairmanship of the *epistatês*, with a herald announcing the agenda drawn up by the council; the citizens voted on whether to proceed with this agenda. Certain business was always reserved for a certain meeting of the prytany. For example, at the first meeting of a prytany, known as a sovereign assembly (which Dikaiopolis attends), a vote of confidence in the magistrates was always held. If the agenda was approved, a herald opened the debate with the words: 'Who wishes to speak?'

The right to speak one's mind

The right to speak in the assembly was fundamental to citizenship and was governed by two important principles. *Isêgoria*, which meant 'equal speaking rights', referred to the idea that each citizen had an equal right to put forward his views in the assembly. Equally, *parrhêsia*, which meant 'speaking frankly', expressed the right of citizens to speak openly and honestly. Both these principles are now combined in our phrase 'freedom of speech'.

If a man wanted to speak, he put up his hand and waited to be summoned by the herald. Once called, he climbed up onto the speaker's platform, put a sacred wreath on his head and made his point; the passage from *Acharnians* suggests that he may have had to contend with hecklers. The orator Aeschines, writing in about 340, outlines the following rules for speakers in the assembly:

5. Athenian Democracy

'Anyone addressing the council or the assembly must keep to the matter in hand, must not deal with two separate matters together, and must not speak twice on any one matter at the same meeting. He must not engage in slanders or scurrility, or interrupt others. He must speak only from the platform and must not assault the *epistatês* ...'

Aeschines, *Against Timarchus* 1.35

Although there were no political parties as such, it seems that there were some regular speakers with a following of supporters. These were known as *rhêtôres* ('orators') and were as close as Athens came to having career politicians. Like Pericles, the *rhêtôres* were often also generals. Despite the absence of political parties, distinct viewpoints must have emerged; for example, there must have been factions of farmers or potters. We hear of one aristocratic leader, Thucydides, son of Milesias, trying to gather his supporters into one part of the Pnyx so that they could have more influence.

The assembly could discuss all matters relating to the city, including laws, the corn supply, ostracism, matters of war, peace and foreign policy, tax, finance, and the upkeep of public buildings, such as temples. A secretary kept records of the meeting. Once everyone who wished to had spoken on an issue, a vote was taken. Voting was normally by a show of hands, although for the most important topics, such as treason, secret ballots were held with black and white voting pebbles.

Turnout

It is hard to assess how many Athenians attended a typical meeting of the assembly. For important matters, a quorum of 6,000 citizens was required. In the 5th century, there was no payment for attending the assembly, although this was introduced in the 4th century – in 392, a citizen was paid three obols for attendance. Many citizens might have found the content of more mundane meetings boring and so may not have bothered to turn up. Moreover, a good number would often have been unable to attend, particularly if they were soldiers away on campaign or farmers from the rural parts of Attica (Marathon, for example, was about 42 km from Athens).

Voter turnout is an area of concern for many modern democracies too. In the UK, turnout in general elections fell from 77.72% of the electorate in 1992 to 61.36% in 2005; in the USA, 55.3% voted in the 2004 Presidential elections, a figure slightly higher than those of 1996 and 2000. By contrast, in Australia, where voting is compulsory and citizens who don't vote are fined, turnout in the 2007 general election was 94.76%.

An interesting parallel can be drawn between the direct democracy of Athens and that of the cantons in modern Switzerland. These are the country's regional governments, and two of them still practise direct democracy. Evidence from the cantons suggests that it is quite possible for 6,000 people, all with the right to speak, to discuss and vote (by show of hands) on twelve matters in less than four hours.

Review 6

1. Define the following: *boulê, ecclêsia, epistatês, isêgoria, parrhêsia, prytaneis, rhêtôres.*
2. Create a table of similarities and differences between the rules governing the Athenian assembly and those governing parliaments today.
3. What do you admire and what do you find to criticise about: (i) the council; (ii) the prytany system; (iii) the assembly.
4. How much freedom of speech do modern politicians have? Are there some things which they are not allowed to say publicly?
5. Find out how often your own politicians attend parliamentary debates. Should they be made to attend all the debates?
6. What percentage of citizens turn out to vote in (i) local elections; (ii) national elections in your society? Do you think that voting should be compulsory?
R. Read the account of the assembly's trial of the eight generals after the battle of Arginusae in Xenophon (*Hellenika* 1.7.7-35). What can we learn here about the procedures of the assembly?

---

5. Military service

Military service was a key component of citizenship. Athens had no full-time army and every citizen was liable for military service until the age of 59. As we have seen, the military role of citizens was defined by their class; those in the top two classes could afford a horse and therefore formed the Athenian cavalry. The *zeugitai*, who could afford their own armour, served as hoplites. The *thêtes* usually served in roles requiring little weaponry, such as rowing in the navy.

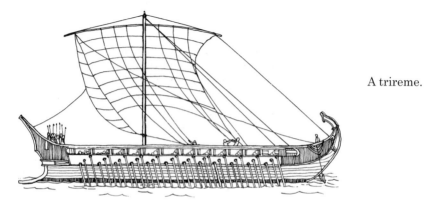

A trireme.

5. Athenian Democracy

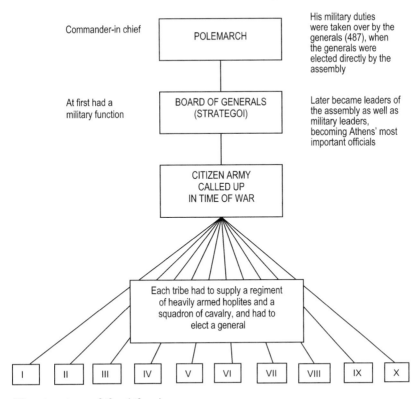

The structure of the Athenian army.

The hoplites were the heart of the Athenian army. A hoplite was a heavily armed soldier who wore a helmet, breastplate and greaves and carried a shield, spear and short sword. When drafted for military service, hoplites were expected to report for duty with at least three days' rations. Each tribe supplied one division of the army, which allowed team spirit to develop in much the same way as it does in the regimental system of modern armies. As today, a special place was found for the memory of dead soldiers – their orphaned sons were educated by the state and provided with a full set of armour upon reaching manhood (see pp. 107-8).

In the middle of the 5th century the Athenian navy had more than 300 triremes. A trireme was a long thin ship, with a ram at its head extending out from its keel. It was rowed by 170 men, who sat in three rows, one above the other, on either side of the ship. In addition to the rowers, on the deck could be found hoplites who served as marines and officers such as the trierarch and the *kubernêtês* (see below). Each trireme therefore had at least 200 men on board. In addition to the *thêtes*, Athens also employed mercenaries and metics as rowers (they were paid three obols per day) if the public funds could afford it.

Voting for war

A fascinating aspect of this 'citizen-army' was that the men who voted in the assembly to go to war were the same men who would fight in it. Discussions of war and peace must have been animated and personal, since a decision to declare war would have an immediate impact on the voter and his family.

This is of course in great contrast to modern democratic politics. For example, when American and British politicians voted to invade Iraq in 2003, not a single one of them was facing active service; moreover, only a tiny proportion would have been committing close relatives to the combat zone.

Elected officials

The military was one area where the leaders were elected rather than chosen by lot. This made good sense, since it allowed continuity in military policy and produced experienced military commanders. The ten generals in charge of the Athenian military were still accountable to the assembly. If the assembly felt that they had not conducted themselves well on campaign, they could be fined, exiled or even executed.

There are many examples of such punishments. Miltiades was fined 50 talents after his unsuccessful siege of Paros in 489 (one talent was equivalent to 6,000 drachmas); the historian Thucydides was exiled after Sparta's capture of Amphipolis in 424/3; most revealingly, there are eleven recorded executions of generals in classical Athens (six of them carried out after the battle of Arginusae in 406). It is perhaps no wonder that Demosthenes claimed that an Athenian general was in more danger of being sentenced to death by the assembly than of dying in battle.

Interestingly, the election of officials such as the generals is where Athenian democracy most closely models modern representative democracy, whereby citizens choose candidates whom they believe to be best qualified to serve them. The Old Oligarch makes this comment about election:

> 'The mass of the people steer clear of those magistracies which are of critical importance for the welfare of the whole community and which, if they were mishandled, would lead the city to ruin ... They realise that it is in their interests to leave these posts in the hands of the most influential citizens, but the people as a whole are very keen on holding the salaried magistracies which bring them a certain profit.'
>
> *Constitution of the Athenians* 1.3ff.

There were some non-military officials who were also elected to their positions, most notably the *hellênotamiai*, treasurers overseeing the finances of the whole Athenian Empire. These elected posts were all unpaid, so they tended to remain in the hands of the wealthy. Therefore, if any of the *hellênotamiai* embezzled money, it could be recovered from their estates.

6. State finance and liturgies

Athens raised revenue from various sources: the tribute paid by members of the Delian League, the fines and fees exacted in the courts, the tax on metics, taxes on all goods brought through Piraeus and taxes on the profits made in the silver mines at Laureion. However, in the absence of a general income tax, there was a further way in which the city raised significant funds. This was the **liturgy** (literally: 'service for the public') a kind of supertax on the *pentacosiomedimnoi* and wealthy metics.

There were two main types of liturgy: the **triêrarchia**, which involved paying for the upkeep of a trireme for one year; and the **chorêgia**, which required a man to pay for a chorus competing in the dramatic and musical contests at one of Athens' festivals (you can read more about the *chorêgia* on p. 105). It is likely that there were over 300 liturgies to be paid for each year – at least 200 *triêrarchiai* and perhaps more than 100 *chorêgiai*. The system seems to have worked well, not least because wealthy citizens chosen to pay a liturgy generally looked at it as an opportunity to show off their wealth and win favour with their fellow citizens.

For a trierarchy, the state provided the hull, mast and sails of the trireme, but the trierarch had to pay for all the rest of the equipment as well as the training of the crew; in all, it may have cost as much as 6,000 drachmas. Although the trierarch was also technically in command on the ship, in reality he was unlikely to be an experienced sailor and would have left the important decisions to the ship's captain, the *kubernêtês* (literally: 'helmsman'). Nonetheless, trierarchs would usually take great pride in the condition of their ship.

Review 7

1. Define the following: *chorêgia, kubernêtês, triêrarchia.*
2. Do you think that a system of public liturgies would work in your society today? If so, what liturgies would you introduce?
3. Do you think it is always better to elect representatives rather than to choose people for public service by lot?
4. To what extent does wealth and upbringing still determine the seniority of soldiers in the modern armed services?
5. Do you think that all citizens should vote in a referendum on matters of war in a modern democracy? What would be the advantages and disadvantages of such a practice?

---

7. The legal system

The Athenians took great pride in their legal system, believing that it guaranteed justice and equality for all citizens. The following lines spoken by Theseus in Euripides' *Suppliants* suggest this pride:

> 'Take it from me, a tyrant or king is the worst evil which can befall a city. Under a tyrant the law is not the law of the people but the decision of one man and so there is no equality. Now if the laws are written, instead of being the commands of a tyrant, then both rich and poor are protected by them.'
>   Euripides, *Suppliants* 426ff.

Laying a charge

When a crime had been committed, there was no state prosecution service to bring the matter to courts (in contrast to the Crown Prosecution Service in the UK or the District Attorney in the USA, for example), nor were the Scythian Archers, the police force, responsible for gathering evidence. It was up to a private citizen to bring a charge against a suspect. There were two different categories of charge. The first was called a *dikê*, which concerned a private matter, such as a dispute between two citizens about the repayment of a loan. Even a crime such as murder fell under the charge of *dikê*.

The second type of charge was called a *graphê*, an accusation of a crime against the state of Athens. Examples of a *graphê* might be the misuse of public funds by a magistrate or questionable tactics by a general on a military campaign. When a magistrate submitted his *euthunai* at the end of his year in office, any citizen could bring a *graphê* against him if he felt unhappy with his performance. The law courts could therefore hold to account the organs of the democracy – the assembly, council and magistracies.

When making a charge, the accuser had to give a summons to the accused in front of witnesses. This summons required both men to meet with an archon on a specified day. If the accused failed to appear, then he automatically lost the case. If both sides did appear, then the archon would arrange for negotiation to try to settle the matter out of court. Failing this, the archon took written witness statements and any other documentary evidence. These documents were then sealed; no new evidence could be submitted by either side after this point and the archon then set a date for the trial.

In court

The procedure of an Athenian court was very different from our courts. There was no judge to preside, nor any barristers to prosecute or defend the charge. A magistrate would act as the court chairman, but his role

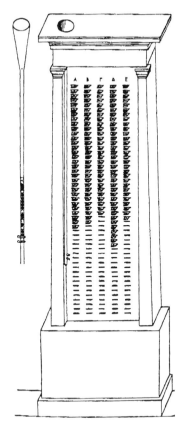

Part of an allotting machine found in the agora.

A reconstruction of an allotting machine, with the trumpet-shaped tube for the black and white marbles shown separately.

A reconstruction of a 5th century water-clock found in the agora. It ran for about six minutes.

was simply administrative and he gave no advice to the jury before they voted on the charge. Accusers and defendants spoke for themselves, although speechwriters were often hired by those wealthy enough to afford them. The speeches were timed by a water-clock (*klepsydra*) to ensure that both men spoke for the same length of time. The whole case had to be heard and judged on a single day.

There were other differences from modern court cases. When witnesses were called, they were not allowed to be cross-examined; moreover, witness statements from slaves were accepted only if the slaves had been questioned under torture, since this was seen as the only way guaranteed to make them more frightened of the law than of their master. A further quirk of the system was that a person's character could be questioned by fact or slander – the jury could be told of any previous convictions, while speakers would often try to damage an opponent by giving lurid details of his private life. No proof was needed – it was up to the jurors to decide if they believed the stories or not. Often, defendants played for the jurors' sympathy vote by getting tearful relatives to come to court dressed in mourning clothes. At the end of Plato's account of Socrates' defence-speech, Socrates shows disdain for tactics so obviously employed to garner sympathy:

> 'I hope that nobody will hold it against me, because he remembers how he himself, perhaps, was once before a jury and spent a lot of time crying to the judges and produced his children to win sympathy for himself, not to mention a lot of friends and relations to vouch for him, that I have not adopted any of these methods to win you over ... instead I rest my defence on the truth of my words.'   Plato, *Apology* 34Cff.

The dikasts

At the heart of the legal system were the jurors, known as dikasts. In fact, 'juror' is not strictly an accurate description as there was no presiding judge – the dikasts were in effect judge and jury of the case. As with the magistracies, any citizen of good character and over the age of 30 could serve as a dikast. At the beginning of each year, volunteers had to present themselves to their tribal council and each tribe chose 600 dikasts by lot. There were therefore 6,000 registered dikasts for a civil year, meaning that at least one citizen in eight was registered in any year.

The daily wage for dikasts was set at two obols by Pericles in 451, rising to 3 obols in the 420s. Although not a large amount, this must have seemed attractive to the elderly, poor or unemployed. In fact, this was probably one of the weaknesses of the system: since the dikasts tended to be poor or elderly, they were often unrepresentative of the wider citizen body. At the beginning of the year, each new dikast received a ticket (*pinakion*) bearing his name and the stamp of the owl of Athena. He then had to take the 'heliastic oath', which went as follows:

> 'I shall vote according to the laws and decrees passed by the assembly and the council, but concerning things about which there are no laws I shall decide to the best of my judgement, without favour or enmity. I shall vote only on the matters raised in the charge, and I shall listen impartially to accusers and defenders alike.'

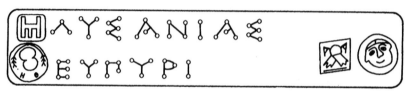

A *pinakion.*

Trials took place every day except on festival days and days when the assembly sat, which amounted to between 150 and 200 days in the year. At dawn on a court day, an order of proceedings was published and those dikasts who wanted to sit that day started to arrive (it was left to each dikast to choose on what day he wanted to sit). There followed a complex process of selecting the dikasts using an allotment machine (*klêrotêrion*). First the machine determined whether a dikast would sit on a case that day or not, and there was a good chance that he would be sent home. If he was selected, a further lottery was held to determine which of the ten courts he would sit in.

Aristophanes' *Wasps*

In 422 Aristophanes wrote a comedy called *Wasps*, which poked fun at the Athenian jury system. The Wasps of the play are the jurors who swarm around in groups, stinging people with their fines. The main character, Philocleon, is an old man who is so obsessed about serving as a dikast that he lies awake at night in his eagerness for a day at the court; when he arrives, he is more interested in securing a conviction than in seeing justice done. As ever with Aristophanes, it is hard to know exactly how accurate a view of Athenian society is presented, but the play is a rich source of information about the proceedings of the Athenian law courts.

The size of juries varied – minor cases might involve a jury of 201 dikasts, while more serious cases could see numbers of 401, 501, going up to 1501 for the most serious (the odd number ensured that there would not be a tie). That such a large number of dikasts were appointed only on the morning of the case was intended to guard against bribery, although this was not unknown, as the following passage from *Wasps* suggests. Philocleon describes turning up for court on an average day:

'We get up early, but nonetheless there's already some great brute hanging about the place where the jury is going to sit; he sidles up greasily to us with the odd spot of cash, nicked from the state funds, as a sort of present to us ... I let him soften me up a bit with the odd coin or two, but of course I don't bother about any promise I may have made to the fellow.'

Aristophanes, *Wasps* 550ff.

The dikasts would then proceed to their court and the trial began. They listened and perhaps chatted quietly with nearby colleagues. Some probably shouted abuse or support for the litigants. After both sides had completed their speeches, the case went straight to a vote. There was no formal discussion between dikasts; each one was left to make up his mind in private. As each dikast left the court, he dropped a voting token into a ballot box. If he dropped a token with a hollow axle, he had found the defendant guilty; conversely, a token with a solid axle indicated a

A ballot box found in a law court in the agora and two bronze ballots marked *psêphos dêmosia* (public ballot). The ballot with the solid axle was for 'innocent', while that with the hollow one was for 'guilty'.

not-guilty vote. A majority vote of all the dikasts was all that was required for a decision.

If a defendant was found guilty, he awaited his punishment. Some crimes had fixed penalties; in contrast to today, the Greeks did not rely on prison to punish criminals – this was considered too expensive a burden on the state. The most usual penalty was a fine, sometimes so large as to be financially ruinous (as in the case of Miltiades mentioned on p. 212). Other common punishments included loss of citizenship, confiscation of property, a spell in the stocks, exile or death.

If the defendant was found guilty of a crime for which there was no fixed penalty, then each side had to submit its plea for a punishment – the defendant would obviously ask for a more lenient sentence. Once the pleas had been heard, each dikast had to scratch a line on his wax tablet – a long line favoured the heavier penalty, a short line the lighter one. Once again, a majority vote was all that was needed. Dikasts were not allowed to suggest their own alternative penalty.

Review 8

1. Define the following: *dikê, graphê, klepsydra, klêrotêrion, pinakion.*
2. Draw up a table outlining the similarities and differences between ancient and modern court cases.
3. How important is equality before the law in your society? Are there countries today which do not give equal legal rights to all their inhabitants?
4. How are juries selected in your country? Do you think that trial before a jury is the fairest form of justice for a defendant in a court case?
R. Read *Wasps* 85-115. What might we be able to learn about the Athenian legal system from this passage?
E. What do you admire and what do you find to criticise in the Athenian legal system? How does it compare to the system in your country today?

---

8. Criticisms of democracy

Today, according to popular western thought, the argument for democracy has been won. Whatever criticisms are made of western culture, no serious case is made against democracy as a system. However, this was not so in classical Athens; some of its very greatest writers – Plato, Aristotle, Xenophon and Aristophanes among them – presented passionate arguments against democracy. Moreover, similar arguments were still being used well into the 20th century. Any critique of Athenian democracy must also examine its critics.

The demagogues

The written sources for the late 5th century claim that the quality of Athenian democracy declined after the death of Pericles in 429. According to writers such as Thucydides (who, as we have seen, was a great supporter of Pericles), into the power vacuum in the city's politics came men who were less concerned with the good of the city than with furthering their own cause. They labelled such men 'demagogues', in Greek *dêmagogoi*, which literally meant 'leaders of the people', but by which they actually meant something like 'mis-leaders of the people'. The following criticisms are typical:

> 'When Pericles died ... there was a whole series of people in popular favour who were notable for their outrageous behaviour and for their desire simply to please the people, caring only about their own popularity and success.'   *Constitution of Athens* 28.1ff.

Perhaps the most famous man to be labelled a 'demagogue' was Cleon, who was prominent in Athens during the 420s; he was viciously satirised in the plays of Aristophanes as a war-monger from a less than aristocratic background (his father had made money owning a leather-tanning factory).

However, it is difficult to know what to make of this portrayal of Cleon and the other so-called demagogues. The contemporary writers generally held aristocratic, even anti-democratic views and may have resented the success of such self-made men. It can be pointed out in Cleon's defence that he was stunningly successful in a military action at Pylos in 425, while he later died fighting in a war which Athens had been led into by Pericles himself. Modern politics make it clear how dangerous it would be to base an opinion about a politician solely on what his political opponents have written about him.

In fact, the Athenian democratic system had always produced demagogues, in the sense that from 508/7 there were always important men who could influence the assembly: Cleisthenes was arguably the first and he was later followed by men such as Themistocles and Pericles; all of them were capable of persuading fellow citizens with clever arguments. Indeed, the Athenians were discovering that in a democracy, as the orator Antiphon put it, 'victory goes to him who speaks best'. Whatever the truth about the demagogues and their critics, it is obvious that influence in democratic Athens was won by the best and shrewdest communicators – men who were arguably ancient versions of modern 'spin-doctors'.

Socrates and democracy

Both Xenophon and Plato present Socrates making two important arguments against democracy. The first was that the democratic system of Athens relied on people who were not skilled enough to fulfil their roles. According to Xenophon, one way in which Socrates developed this argument was as follows:

> 'Nobody would employ a candidate chosen by lot as a ship's captain, or a carpenter or a musician, although if these posts are badly filled, they cause far less harm than bad political appointments.'
>
> Xenophon, *Memorabilia* 1.2.9

Another strand of this argument is that the constant changeover of officials allowed no time for citizens to develop such expertise; a magistrate just had time to get used to his job when his year's term was over and it was time for another novice to learn the role from scratch.

Socrates' second argument essentially stated that the mass of people are not intelligent or educated enough to vote for what is really good for them. This meant that politicians were by necessity forced to follow the whims of the people rather than standing on principle for truth and justice. In the *Republic*, Plato has Socrates put forward the view that some people should be trained as 'philosopher-kings' to rule over the rest with wisdom and honesty; he outlines in detail the sort of education such rulers would have to undergo. Interestingly, he was happy for women to be trained as 'philosopher-kings' in his ideal state.

The freedom to criticise

However, by a remarkable paradox, the impassioned arguments made against the democracy may have been one of its greatest triumphs. For the citizens of classical Athens had more freedom to criticise their system of government than any other in the ancient world. When democracy fell in Athens in 322, this freedom of speech seems to have passed. A look at the development of comic drama at Athens bears out the point.

During the years of democracy, Athens nurtured one of the greatest political satirists in history, Aristophanes, while we also hear of other comic playwrights who were equally brutal in their opinions about public life. However, when the democratic system fell after the Macedonian conquest of 322, political satire disappeared completely from the Athenian theatre. In its place came 'New Comedy', which tended to poke fun at family relationships and domestic life – in fact, anything but political issues.

9. The legacy of Athens

When democracy died in classical Athens, it would take more than two millennia before it came back into favour. In particular, the American and French revolutions at the end of the 18th century brought about new constitutions giving the vote to a significant number of citizens. The US Constitution, written in 1788, gave the vote to free white men. It would be nearly a century before black men were given the vote. In England, although a parliament of sorts has existed since 1265, it was very limited: in 1780, less than 3% of the population were allowed to vote; it was only the Reform Act of 1867 which gave all male householders the vote.

Democracy places a wreath on the head of Demos, a personification of the people of Athens.

The western world's acceptance of democracy as the undisputed system of government is a very recent phenomenon; during the 18th and 19th centuries, democracy was considered a dirty word in many intellectual circles; in 1794, in the aftermath of the French revolution, the poet William Wordsworth wrote to a friend, 'I am of that odious class of men called "democrats" '; democracy was seen as the rule of an uneducated and baying mob. In the 20th century, even Winston Churchill, one of the iconic figures of modern democracy, quipped that 'the best argument against democracy is a five minute conversation with the average voter'.

Yet, despite its limitations, democracy has managed to emerge as the fairest way to give equality to all citizens. Perhaps the final word belongs again to Churchill:

'No one pretends that democracy is perfect or all-wise. Indeed, it has been said that democracy is the worst form of government except for all those other forms that have been tried from time to time.'

House of Commons, 11 November 1947

Review 9

1. To what extent do you think that the role of 'demagogue' is played today by the following groups: (i) politicians; (ii) spin doctors; (iii) the media?
2. Do you agree with the main criticisms of Athenian democracy? Could the same criticisms be made of modern democratic systems?
3. Do you agree with Antiphon that in a democracy 'victory goes to him who speaks best?'
4. How important is the freedom to criticise politicians in modern democracies? Is such criticism ever censored?
5. What do you think Churchill meant when he described democracy as the worst form of government except for all the others ever tried?
E. What do you think were the strengths of the Athenian democratic system? Are there ways in which you think it was better than its equivalents today?

6

Sparta

Sparta was the unique society of classical Greece. At some point during or after the 7th century BCE, the city chose a different path from all others, isolating itself from the outside world and turning itself into a military state. In this society, citizen boys were subjected to a brutal education in a military boarding school. If they graduated, they entered adulthood as professional soldiers equipped to survive extreme hardship. Today, their reputation survives in the adjective 'Spartan'.

Behind this reputation, however, lies a chilling truth. For the Spartan system survived on the mass enslavement and brutalisation of a much larger surrounding population. This was tribal terrorism on a massive scale. Sparta was once described by an ancient writer as the city where free men were the freest and slaves the most enslaved.

Thus the study of Sparta is a complex one which deals in paradoxes. How did a city with a brutal education system inspire such loyalty in its citizens? Why did such conservative people allow their womenfolk freedom and economic power unparalleled in the ancient Greek world? Why were such warlike people known throughout Greece for their love of music and dance? All these questions, and many more, make up the mystery which is Sparta.

Totalitarianism

During the early 20th century, the word 'totalitarianism' was coined to describe a new type of political system which was emerging at that time. This was a system where the government had 'total' control over its citizens in private as well as in public. One political party ruled without opposition, controlling every aspect of the state: educational, economic and social. Such societies were satirised by George Orwell in his novel *Nineteen Eighty-Four*, which gave us phrases such as 'Big Brother' and 'Thought Police'.

Some have argued that Sparta was the first totalitarian state. Read on and see if you agree with them.

I. GEOGRAPHY

The geography of Sparta allowed its people to isolate themselves from the rest of the world. The city was located in the mountainous region of Laconia, in the south-east of the Peloponnese (see maps 3 and 4). It had

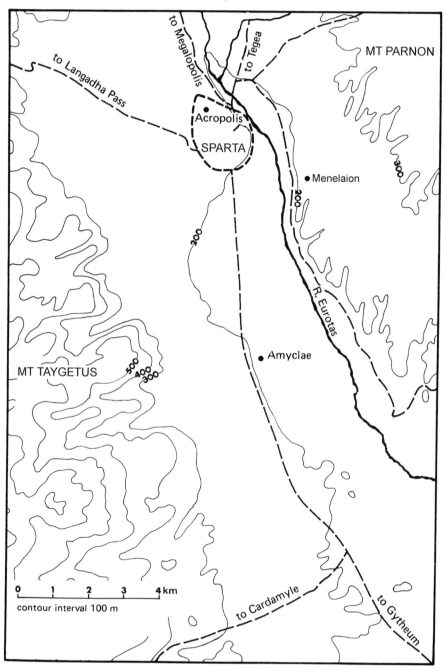

The vale of Sparta.

The fertile valley of the river Eurotas with the Taygetus range of mountains behind.

developed out of five villages along the river Eurotas, which flowed through a valley bounded by mountains on either side. To the west the Taygetus Range rose to 2,404 metres; to the east the Parnon Range peaked at 1,935 metres. Both ranges could be crossed only by a series of narrow passes, while the coastline to the south was rugged and marshy. With such natural defences, the Spartans felt they had no need of city walls.

Another benefit of the region was its rich resources. The river Eurotas ensured fertile farmland so that goods such as olives and fish were in plentiful supply; moreover, the mountainous forests were so full of wild animals that hunting became central to the Spartan way of life.

II. THE HISTORY OF THE SPARTAN SYSTEM

Mycenaean Sparta

The first mention of Sparta belongs to the mythological age of the Trojan War. For 'Helen of Troy' was originally 'Helen of Sparta', wife of king Menelaus of Sparta. Menelaus' brother, Agamemnon, king of nearby Mycenae, was leader of the Greek forces at Troy. Whether or not there was a real Helen of Sparta, a great civilisation did flourish in the Peloponnese during the middle to late second millennium BCE (*c.* 1600-1100). This is known as the Mycenaean civilisation.

The Dorian invasions

However, the prehistoric Mycenaeans had little to do with the historical Spartans who later lived in the region. Sometime in the 12th century,

Swans, cockerels and guinea-fowl decorate this ornate vase made in pre-isolation Sparta.

the Mycenaean civilisation suddenly collapsed and Greece entered a Dark Age which lasted for about 300 years. During this period invaders from the lands north of Greece invaded and colonised regions of Greece, particularly in the Peloponnese. These people were called the **Dorians**. By contrast, the peoples who had lived in and around Greece before the Dorians were called the **Achaeans**.

Dorian invaders settled in Laconia at some point after 1100. Among these invaders were people who arrived in the Eurotas valley and established four villages in Sparta (later incorporating a fifth). For a long time, these new Spartans kept to themselves. However, at the beginning of the 8th century they started to expand their territorial control; by the middle of the century they controlled the whole of Laconia. The Spartans allowed other Dorian settlers in Laconia a degree of self-government, as long as they accepted Spartan rule. These people were called **perioeci**, which meant 'those who live around'. Achaean Greeks still living in Laconia were not so lucky. They were reduced to the status of serfs, slaves who were forced to work the land for their Spartan masters. These slaves were called **helots**, which meant 'captives'.

At around the same time, other Greek cities were looking to claim new land for their growing populations. Many founded new colonies around the Mediterranean, spreading Greek culture far and wide. However, Sparta concentrated on the fertile region of Messenia across the mountains to the west of Laconia (see map 3); when it was conquered by Sparta in the last quarter of the 8th century, the majority of its population was enslaved. The amount of land now controlled by Sparta, about 3,000 square miles, was far larger than that of any other Greek city (the next largest was the 1,000 square miles controlled by Athens). Furthermore, the helot population ruled by Sparta now outnumbered the citizen population by at least ten to one.

For a time, Sparta remained an outward-looking state with trade contacts all over the Mediterranean. The city was particularly prosperous at the beginning of the 7th century, when it was famous for its ceramics, sculpture, music and poetry. Within a few decades, however, things started to change.

Tyrtaeus

Sparta's national poet, Tyrtaeus, was writing during the years of the Second Messenian War. He was a war poet, but a very different one from those of the First World War, such as Wilfred Owen, who wrote about the horrors of the battlefield. Tyrtaeus' poems urged Spartan soldiers to live up to their city's warrior ideal. His songs became part of Spartan culture and were sung by later generations at the common messes and round the campfire. The following lines illustrate the brutal vision of his poetry:

'A man is not good in war unless he has the courage to look on blood and slaughter and stand face to face with his foe and strike ... he who falls in the front rank and loses his dear life brings glory to his country, his people and his father; wounded many times in front through shield and breastplate, he is mourned by old and young alike and the whole city grieves with bitter longing.'

The Second Messenian War

Around 670 the enslaved Messenians rose up against their Spartan masters in what was known as the Second Messenian War (the first had been the war of conquest). The war was marked by a new military tactic, the phalanx, which relied upon all Spartans fighting together in massed ranks (see p. 253). This was a far remove from the traditional aristocratic warfare typified in Homer's poems; the concept of fighting for individual glory disappeared, to be replaced by the ideal of sacrificing one's life for the common good. The Spartans won the war only after 17 years of gruelling fighting; this was the defining moment in Spartan history. The facts were simple: the Spartans were vastly outnumbered by their helots and could hope to control them only by brutal and sustained repression.

At the end of the war, an entirely new method of living seems to have emerged. This became known as the **Spartan system**; the Spartans believed that it was introduced by a great reformer called Lycurgus (see below). At its heart was the idea that every Spartan citizen should be a highly trained, professional soldier. This was a new and strange idea in Greece, where professional armies had never previously existed.

One consequence of this new system was that the Spartans now began to isolate themselves from the outside world. This way, they could concentrate on controlling the enemy within: the helots. Foreign imports slowly ceased, while the quality of Spartan arts and crafts declined dramatically.

Spartan athletes

The growing isolation of Sparta can be seen in its performance at the Olympic Games. In the 8th and 7th centuries, the city was an athletic powerhouse. Between 720 and 576, 46 of the 81 known Olympic victors were Spartan, including 21 of the 36 known victors in the most important event, the stadion (see pp. 67-8). However, after this date, Spartan winners disappeared in all but the equestrian events.

The 6th and 5th centuries

During the early part of the 6th century, Sparta consolidated her strength by forming alliances with other Peloponnesian states. When Sparta won a frontier war with Tegea in 555, many other Peloponnesian states joined the new **Peloponnesian League**, each one swearing to a separate defensive and offensive alliance with Sparta. Spartan control of the Peloponnese was complete when it conquered its great rival Argos in c. 545. Laconia was now well protected from invasion by the buffer zone provided by the surrounding allies. With her borders safe, Sparta could continue to concentrate on matters at home.

6. Sparta

The early years of the 5th century were dominated by the conflict between the Greek city-states and the Persian Empire to the east. At first, Sparta was reluctant to acknowledge the threat and played no part in the famous victory of the Athenians and her allies at Marathon in 490. Yet when the Persians invaded again in 480, the Spartans won immortality for themselves by their heroic, though unsuccessful, defence at the pass of Thermopylae. At the decisive Battle of Plataea the following year the Spartans played the key role in the Greeks' victory over the Persians.

However, in the aftermath of the Persian Wars, Sparta soon became fearful and jealous of the growing Athenian Empire. The second half of the 5th century was defined by the Peloponnesian War between Athens and Sparta, which divided the Greek world. For many years it was a tactical stalemate, with Athens more powerful by sea but Sparta superior on land. The conflict saw terrible atrocities committed by Greek against fellow Greek. Eventually, the Spartans emerged triumphant in 404, but not without the crucial financial help of their former enemies, the Persians.

1600-1100	Mycenaean civilisation
c. 1000	Dorians settle Sparta and Laconia
c. 800	Town of Sparta expands to include a fifth village
c. 735	Spartans invade Messenia (First Messenian War)
c. 670	Messenian helots revolt (Second Messenian War)
after 650	Lycurgan reforms bring 'Spartan system'
555	Peloponnesian League formed
490-479	Persian Wars
431-404	Peloponnesian War
371	Defeat at Leuctra; end of the Spartan system

Decline and fall

After their victory in the war, the Spartans controlled a large Greek empire, a role to which they were totally unsuited. Their society had developed in isolation from the rest of Greece, but Spartan officers now had to manage affairs outside Sparta. They were introduced to the luxuries of the wider Greek world and were soon tempted away from their austere way of life.

Worse was to follow. The Thebans, long-time allies of Sparta, began to resent Spartan power and this led to further warfare. The number of Spartan citizens fell perhaps as low as 1,000, and Sparta had to rely on its perioeci and helots for military effectiveness. Back home in Sparta, land ownership had once again become very unequal. When Thebes defeated Sparta at the Battle of Leuctra in 371, the Spartan Empire collapsed. Messenia was freed soon after, Sparta never recovered and the Spartan system was at an end.

229

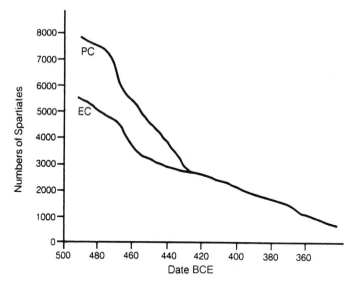

The decline in Spartan citizen manpower from the start of the 5th century. This graph gives two possible reconstructions, those of Eugene Cavaignac (EC) in 1912 and Paul Cartledge (PC) in 1987.

Review 1

1. Outline three advantages of Sparta's geographical location.
2. Define the following: *Achaean, Dorian, helot, perioeci.*
3. Why did Sparta want to conquer Messenia?
4. Explain the role in the Second Messenian War of: (i) the phalanx; (ii) Tyrtaeus.
5. What evidence is there for the growing isolation of the Spartans after the war?
6. Outline Sparta's role in: (i) the Peloponnesian League; (ii) the Persian Wars; (iii) the Peloponnesian War.
7. Why did the Spartan system eventually collapse?

III. LYCURGUS

The Spartans believed that a great reformer, Lycurgus, had instituted an entirely new way of living in Sparta. However, Lycurgus is a figure of mystery; it is not known for certain if he existed and, even if he did, it is almost impossible to date when he lived. Even the historian Plutarch, our main source of information on his life, begins his biography as follows:

6. Sparta

'Generally speaking it is impossible to make any undisputed statement about Lycurgus the lawgiver, since conflicting accounts have been given of his ancestry, his travels, and above all his activity in respect to his laws and government; but there is least agreement about the period in which the man lived.'

Plutarch, *Lycurgus* 1.1

The 5th century historian Herodotus even reports that the Delphic oracle (see p. 35ff.) suspected that Lycurgus was divine rather than human. What is certain is that the Spartans revered him and it is therefore very important to know what they believed about him. Perhaps he was a figure similar to king Arthur, a leader who may have lived and instituted a radical style of government, but whose achievements were magnified by myth and legend.

Whether or not there was a real Lycurgus, it is clear that Spartan society underwent radical reform at some point during or after the 7th century, adopting a way of living which aimed to breed equality and fairness between its citizens. The legend of Lycurgus' reforms almost certainly reflects this period of change. The following two paragraphs outline Plutarch's account of these 'Lycurgan' reforms.

The story goes that Lycurgus travelled to the Delphic oracle to receive instructions about how to reform Spartan society when it was in a state of disarray. These instructions, known as *rhêtrai* (literally: 'verbal agreements' or 'decrees'), were never to be written down; thus they were simple enough for any Spartan to learn by heart. The Spartans were admired for their obedience to their laws and some Greeks even gave this obedience a name: *eunomia* ('good order'). The *rhêtrai* covered many areas of Spartan life, including education, government, economics and morality.

In Plutarch's account, Lycurgus saw that there was great inequality of wealth among the Spartans and wanted to create a society in which all Spartan citizens enjoyed far more equality with one another. Some of the key individual reforms are listed below:

- **Land**. There was extreme inequality of land ownership in Sparta, and so all the land was redistributed so that each citizen had an allotted farm to be worked by helots.
- **Money**. Gold and silver was banned; the only legal money was made of spits of iron dipped in vinegar (to make it brittle). Money thus became valueless and trade dwindled, preventing people from gathering wealth and possessions.
- **Mess-halls**. All Spartan citizens had to eat meals together in common mess-halls (see p. 246). Rich and poor now ate the same food, curbing expensive tastes and ending lavish dinner parties.
- **Houses**. Ceilings could be fashioned only with axes, gates and doors only with saws. Houses would therefore be simple and ornate furniture would look so out of place that it would not be worth having.

231

Together with these and other reforms, Lycurgus is said to have given Spartan citizens a new name, **homoioi**, which meant 'similars'. By removing or lessening inequality and jealousy between the *homoioi*, Plutarch says that Lycurgus believed that they would then concentrate on suppressing the common foe, the helots.

IV. THE EVIDENCE

The study of Sparta is severely hampered by the lack of archaeological or literary evidence. Put simply, the Spartans built little and wrote less; consequently, Spartan society is always likely to be something of a mystery. It is very important to be aware of the limitations of our knowledge when forming opinions about classical Sparta.

1. Written sources

Spartans distrusted literature and wrote only for functional reasons. As a result, Spartan literature has survived only in the works of three poets of the 7th century: Tyrtaeus, Alcman and Terpander. The Spartans have left us little idea of how they experienced life in their society and this is a major problem for us in trying to form an accurate view of what life was like in Sparta.

Other cities of Greece (in particular, Athens) have by contrast produced great writers (historians, philosophers, playwrights and poets) who have given us a real sense of life in their cities. These writers also wrote about Sparta, but care has to be taken over their objectivity. Sparta was often in conflict with Athens and her allies, and did not encourage visitors. As a result, the accounts of outsiders are likely to be second-hand at best. However, four Greek historians do offer important insights into how Sparta was perceived outside its borders:

- **Herodotus** of Halicarnassus (*c.* 490-420) is a valuable source of information about Sparta's important role in the defence of Greece during the Persian wars of the early 5th century. In addition, although he does not tell us much about the workings of Spartan society, what he does record is very informative, particularly in relation to the kingship, women and burial rites.
- **Thucydides** (*c.* 460-400) was an Athenian who wrote about the Peloponnesian War of 431-404, about which he gives detailed information. However, as he was writing from an Athenian perspective, he cannot be relied upon for complete objectivity.
- **Xenophon** (*c.* 430-352) was an interesting exception to the rule – an Athenian who liked Sparta. His opposition to democracy in Athens eventually led to his exile from the city. When he ended up campaigning abroad with the Spartans, he was very impressed by their society. They received him into their state, giving him a home near Olympia. As an admirer of the Spartan system, Xenophon tried to

write positively about it in reaction to all the criticism it received from other writers. It is therefore unclear how balanced a view of Sparta he provides.

- **Plutarch** (*c.* 50-120 CE) was a Greek from Boeotia in central Greece (see map 3), during the period of the Roman Empire. He wrote biographies of various famous Spartans, most importantly Lycurgus. He also collected a book of famous sayings of Spartan kings, commanders and women. Although he was careful to read all the written sources available, he was writing many centuries after the fall of the Spartan system and so it is hard to assess the accuracy of his accounts.

In addition to these four, there are other voices on Sparta. Two Athenian playwrights, **Aristophanes** and **Euripides**, were writing during the period of the Peloponnesian War (you can read more about them on pp. 112 and 121). However, their characters probably tell us more about the opinions held by Athenians about the Spartans than about the Spartans themselves.

The two pre-eminent Greek philosophers of the 4th century, **Plato** and **Aristotle**, both wrote at length about political systems in the Greek world. They are therefore important sources of information about the political structure in Sparta. Plato was clearly impressed by elements of the Spartan system, since there are echoes of it in his own ideal state, which he outlined in his *Republic*.

2. Archaeology

Unlike other Greeks, Spartans didn't value grand buildings or works of art. Most of their buildings were made of wood and so no trace of them has remained. In addition, the city had no surrounding walls; Spartans liked to claim that the true walls of the city were its warriors who would protect it. Thucydides made this interesting observation about the buildings of Sparta:

> 'Suppose ... that the city of Sparta were to become deserted and that only the temples and foundations of buildings remained, I think that future generations would, as time passed, find it very difficult to believe that the place had really been as powerful as it was represented to be.'
>
> Thucydides, *History of the Peloponnesian War* 1.10

A few important archaeological sites have been uncovered. For example, the Menelaion was a shrine built on a hill about 5 kilometres south-east of Sparta. It was dedicated to Menelaos and Helen (who were worshipped as divinities), suggesting that the Dorian Greeks wanted to associate themselves with the region's Mycenaean past. Along the west bank of the Eurotas was the sanctuary of Artemis Orthia, where dances and religious ceremonies took place; it was also the scene of a brutal initiation ceremony for Spartan youths (see p. 241).

These remains of the temple of Artemis Orthia illustrate how little survives of ancient Sparta.

We can learn a good deal about the pre-isolation Spartans from their sculpture and crafts in bronze, ivory and terracotta. In the 7th and 6th centuries Spartan sculptors were active not only at home but also in cultural centres such as Olympia and Delphi: at least nine are known by name. Their bronze products were valued as diplomatic gifts and carried to the far corners of the known world. However, when Spartan trade was reduced to a bare minimum during the 6th century, the quality of its crafts declined rapidly, only adding to the mystery about life in post-isolation Sparta.

Review 2

1. Define the following: *homoioi, eunomia, rhêtrai.*
2. Which modern societies claim to have a founding father (or fathers)? How historical are these founders and what importance do they retain today?
3. Have any modern countries tried to impose reforms similar to those of Lycurgus? How successful have they been?
4. Do you approve of Lycurgus' reforms? How successful do you think they would be if they were applied today?
R. Read Herodotus' account of Lycurgus' visit to the Delphic oracle (*Histories* 1.65-6). What do we learn about his reforms from this passage?
E. Why is our knowledge of Spartan society so limited? In your opinion, how accurate is the evidence that does exist?

V. SOCIAL STRUCTURE

The success of the Spartan system relied on the rigorous enforcement of its three-tiered social structure: the **Spartiates** (or **homoioi**) at the top, the **perioeci** in the middle, and at the bottom the **helots**, the serf population who vastly outnumbered their Spartiate masters.

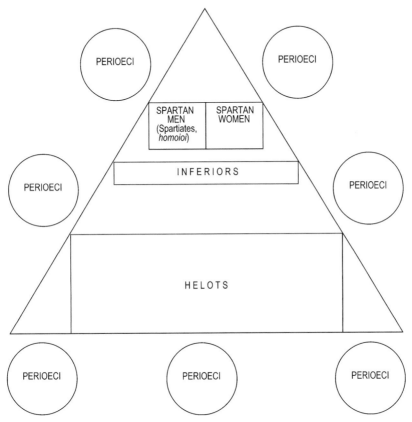

A diagram showing the structure of Spartan society.

1. The perioeci

Like the Spartiates, the perioeci were Dorian in origin. However, we know little about them since they do not feature prominently in historical records. It is estimated that there were between 80 and 100 communities of perioeci in Spartan territory, most of which were found in the less fertile parts of Laconia, either on the mountain slopes or near the coast. Within their own communities the perioeci were allowed local citizenship and a limited form of self-government; however, they had to obey Spartan orders and could not form their own policy on war and foreign relations. Whenever the Spartiates went to war, the perioeci were called up as an auxiliary force.

The chief contribution of the perioeci to the Spartan way of life was economic. They were the traders and craftsmen of Sparta who made everyday items such as clothing, shoes, furniture, storage jars and various types of metalwork. Some of them would have been fishermen or shipbuilders. Others would have been allowed to farm the less fertile regions of Laconia. As Sparta became more isolated it seems that its craftsmen were producing less ornate work and replacing it with the austere and functional goods required by the Spartiates in their day-to-day lives. For example, the advent of sober communal dining amongst the Spartiates would have ended the production of elaborate drinking bowls and dining equipment.

Members of the perioeci rarely tried to rebel during the centuries of Spartiate control, probably because they had a reasonable quality of life compared to many citizens in other parts of Greece. The Greek peoples were often at war and so most citizens spent a good deal of their lives fighting. By contrast, the Spartiates did not go to war too frequently since their main concern was the suppression of the helots. Therefore a typical member of the perioeci would have spent less time at war than a typical citizen of a city such as Athens or Thebes. As a result, it is likely that the perioeci were happy to preserve the status quo in Sparta. Thus it was in the interests of the perioeci to help Spartiates police the helots, and their villages acted as a buffer zone which prevented the helots from escaping.

2. The helots

Paul Cartledge, a modern authority on Sparta, has claimed that 'the existence of the helots is the single most important human fact about Sparta'. Without doubt, the ratio of helots to Spartiates – between 10:1 and 20:1 – defined Spartan society.

The helots, who as we have seen consisted of conquered Messenians and the original Achaean inhabitants of Laconia, were state-owned slaves who had no political or legal rights. Their main duties were as follows:

- **Farmers** on the Spartan estates (*klêroi*), which produced enough food for the whole population. Each estate had to provide a fixed amount of produce each year for its Spartiate master. Helots were allowed to keep or profit from any surplus produced in addition to this.
- **Household slaves** in the houses of the Spartiates. Helot women were particularly famous for their nursing skills (see p. 240).
- Helot men were also used as **baggage-handlers** and **skirmishers** in times of war. However, the Spartiates had to keep a careful watch over them in case they tried to rebel or desert.

The treatment of the helots by the Spartiates was often extremely brutal. They were forbidden to leave a defined area without government permission and were always under suspicion. At the beginning of each year, the newly elected magistrates, the ephors (see p. 262), would immediately declare war on the helots. This meant that helots could be attacked or killed with impunity, while they were routinely humiliated. In the following passage, Plutarch describes how alcohol was used to make helots look ridiculous:

'They would compel them to drink a lot of unmixed wine and then bring them into the common messes to show the young men what drunkenness was like. They would also order them to sing songs and perform dances that were ignoble and ridiculous but to refrain from those appropriate to free men.'   Plutarch, *Lycurgus* 28.4

Myron of Priene, a later historian whose work only survives in fragments, describes a ritual in which the helots were treated like animals:

'They assign to the helots every shameful task leading to disgrace. For they ordained that each one of them must wear a dogskin cap and wrap himself in skins and receive a stipulated number of beatings every year regardless of any wrongdoing, so that they would never forget they were slaves.'
Myron of Priene, 106 fr. 2

The Spartiates were always spreading a sense of terror among the helots to prevent rebellion. They seem to have been successful, since there is little evidence for any large-scale helot revolt between the Second Messenian War and a major revolt in 464. However, the latter rebellion had a major impact on Greek politics and perhaps pointed to the eventual fall of the Spartan Empire a century later.

It occurred after a devastating earthquake had struck the region of Laconia; in the ensuing chaos, many Messenian helots (and two perioecic villages) took the opportunity to rebel. They barricaded themselves up on Mt Ithome in Messenia (see map 4) and prepared for a long siege. The Spartans decided to call in help from their Peloponnesian allies and also from the Athenians, who were experts in siegecraft. Yet the Athenian soldiers made little impact; moreover, the Spartans began to suspect them of sympathising with the rebels, as Thucydides explains:

'The Spartans ... reflected, too, that they (the Athenians) were of a different nationality and feared that, if they stayed on in the Peloponnese, they might listen to the people in Ithome and become sponsors of some revolutionary policy.'   Thucydides, *History of the Peloponnesian War* 1.102

The Spartans therefore dismissed the Athenian forces, an act which contributed to the growing tension between the two cities. Back on Mt Ithome, the siege lasted for some years as the helots held out successfully. Faced with a stalemate, the Spartans eventually gave in and came to an agreement with the rebels: they allowed them and their families safe passage out of the Peloponnese. Athens promptly helped these newly liberated helots to resettle at Naupactos on the northern shore of the Gulf of Corinth, thus raising tensions further.

The whole episode illustrates why the Spartans were so keen to prevent the helots from coming into contact with other Greeks. Outsiders, particularly those from democratic cities such as Athens, must have been troubled by the sight of Greeks enslaved by fellow Greeks (the normal Greek practice was to enslave foreigners). Moreover, helot contact with these peoples would only have encouraged them to believe that they could and should expect to live in freedom and independence.

Nazism and Sparta

One of the most telling and disturbing legacies of the Spartan system has been the admiration it drew from Hitler and the Nazi party. Hitler sought to justify the racial superiority of the German people by citing the example of Sparta; writing in 1928, he described Sparta as 'the first racialist state', claiming that 'the subjugation of the helots by the Spartiates was only possible because of the racial superiority of the Spartans'. When Germany invaded Russia in 1941, a Nazi officer specified that 'the Germans would have to assume the position of the Spartiates, while ... the Russians were the helots'.

Hitler also admired other aspects of Spartan society, most notably its education system and the practice of eugenics, whereby deformed or disabled babies were put to death.

A silver lining?

There were perhaps small crumbs of comfort in the life of a helot. Since they were owned by the state, their treatment was not dependent on the whims of individual masters, in contrast to most slaves in the Greek world. The state distributed them to individuals, who had only limited power over them; only the state could authorise the killing of a helot. Moreover, the helots were allowed to live independently of their masters and together with their families, which was generally not the case for other slaves in the Greek world. As part of this independence the helots had freedom of religion (in contrast to slaves in other Greek cities) and could worship the gods just as the Spartiates and perioeci could.

3. Inferiors

The 'inferiors', neither slaves nor citizens, were a small group in Spartan society. They were made up of four categories. **Partheniai** were illegitimate children of Spartiate fathers and helot mothers. **Mothaces** were sons of helots often adopted as playmates for Spartan boys, who also took part in the education system.

A further category was the **neodamôdeis**, helots who had won freedom by their courage in battle. However, such courage could also be a short-cut to extermination. For the Spartiates, ever paranoid about a revolt, frequently culled the strongest helots. A famous example, which occurred after a Spartan military victory in 424, is related by Thucydides (4.80). The ephors suggested to the helots that those who had fought most bravely should come forward. The helots chose 2,000 of their number, who rejoiced in the belief that they had been freed. Putting garlands on their heads, they went round the temples and offered thanks to the gods. Thucydides darkly explains what followed: 'Soon afterwards, however, the Spartans did away with them, and no one ever knew exactly how each one of them was killed.'

The final category of inferior consisted of the **tresantes** (meaning 'tremblers'), Spartiates who had been deprived of their citizenship for acts of cowardice. Particular contempt was reserved for them, as Xenophon explains:

'In other cities the coward suffers nothing more than the stigma of cowardice – he goes to the same market-place as the brave man, sits with him and attends the same gymnasium if he wishes. In Sparta anyone would think it a disgrace to take a coward into his mess or be matched against him in a wrestling bout ... (a coward) must give way to others in the street, and rise even for younger men when seated ... he must not go about the city looking cheerful, nor must he imitate those who are without reproach; if he does, he must submit to a beating from his betters. When such disabilities are attached to cowardice, I am not surprised that Spartans prefer death to such a deprived and disgraceful existence.'

Xenophon, *The Politeia of the Spartans* 9.4ff.

Review 3

1. Draw up a table recording the rights and responsibilities of: (i) the helots; (ii) the perioeci.
2. What do you think were the advantages and disadvantages of living as a member of the perioeci? Would you have liked to have lived as one?
3. What contribution did the helots make to Spartan society?
4. What do the inferiors tell us about Spartan attitudes to cowards and helots?
5. Have any modern societies developed a social structure comparable to that of Sparta? If so, how successful have they been?
6. Why do you think Hitler so admired Spartan society?
E. Imagine you are a helot. Write an account of how you live.

VI. SPARTAN EDUCATION

The Spartans were the first people in recorded history to introduce a state education system. Yet the nature of this system was radically different from any equivalent of the modern age (even if British public schools of the Victorian era were rather too admiring of Sparta for comfort). Lycurgus, so the Spartans believed, had introduced a system which would produce outstanding and loyal soldiers: killing machines of the state, obedient to every order. Courage and conformity were moulded, individuality and creativity crushed. Death was an ever-present threat to boys at every stage of their upbringing. The system eliminated the weak.

The early years
The process started at birth. As soon as a baby had been delivered, it was taken by its father to a committee of elders for inspection. If they believed that it was deformed or too weak, the baby was left to die of exposure beside a steep slope on Mt Taygetus. This spot was called the **apothetae**, which meant 'the place of rejection'. Abandoning infants (usually for economic reasons) was common throughout the Greek world (see p. 136), but Sparta was the only city to formalise the process and base the decision on the health of the infant alone.

If a baby survived this inspection, a tough infancy awaited. Its strength was tested by bathing in wine rather than water. Spartans believed that weak or epileptic babies would be killed by the wine, while healthy children were hardened by the process. Babies were denied swaddling clothes and often left on their own in the dark, where their crying was ignored. As they grew, young children were not allowed to be fussy about their food, and they were taught 'not to be prone to ill-bred fits of temper or crying'.

> **Spartan nurses**
> Spartan nurses were widely admired for their no-nonsense approach to their duties, and many Greeks hired them to nurse their own children. The Athenian general Alcibiades was said to have been nursed by a Spartan woman called Amycla. She may perhaps have had a lasting effect on Greek politics – Alcibiades sensationally defected from Athens to Sparta in 415 during the course of the conflict between two cities.

Aged 7-12
At the age of 7, a Spartan boy came directly under the control of the city and remained so until the time of his death. Boys now left home to live in barracks. This was boarding school, but hardly of the Harry Potter

variety. It was called the **agôgê**, which meant 'rearing' – tellingly, a word normally used to describe the rearing of cattle. The *agôgê* was run by the **paidonomos**, the first headmaster in history, invariably a warrior of fearsome repute.

Most of the staff in this extraordinary school were aged around 20, young Spartans who had been the outstanding graduates of their class in the *agôgê*. Known as **eirens**, they led the boys in platoons and controlled their every move. As Xenophon dryly observed:

> 'The paidonomos ... was also given a group of young men provided with whips for floggings where necessary; the result is considerable respect and obedience there.'   Xenophon, *The Politeia of the Spartans* 2.2

During these years, the aim of the education system was to develop physical strength and obedience. The boys were closely observed by their elders, who constantly spurred them on to fight against one another. This way, they could find out how tough each boy was and which ones would be most likely to stand their ground in battle.

Boys received little by way of conventional education. They were taught only the most basic skills in reading and writing – just enough for them to communicate. While boys in the rest of Greece learnt to recite Homer by heart (see p. 139ff.), literature was not taught in Sparta, nor was philosophy. These disciplines would have encouraged young men to think for themselves and form their own opinions; this was thought very dangerous in a state which aimed to indoctrinate its young with a single world view. Plutarch explained their educational philosophy as follows:

> 'The boys learned to read and write no more than was necessary. Otherwise their whole education was aimed at developing smart obedience, perseverance under stress, and victory in battle.'
>   Plutarch, *Lycurgus* 16.6

Competition and initiation

A central feature of Spartan education was its use of competition to develop certain qualities. Boys competed in choral contests and in various sporting and combat events, including a fight staged on an island in which the aim was to drive one's opponent into the water.

Perhaps the most brutal competition was the initiation ceremony for boys in early adolescence at the sanctuary of the goddess Artemis Orthia. The boys had to snatch as many cheeses as possible from the altar, which was guarded by *eirêns* with whips which they were instructed to use as violently as possible.

Aged 14-18

When boys reached the second stage of the *agôgê* at the age of 14, their training became much more intensive. From this age they were made to go barefoot at all times so that they could run faster, scale heights more easily and clamber down cliffs. Each of the boys was given one cloak to last the whole year, whatever the weather. They had to cut their hair short and usually played naked to toughen their bodies. They were allowed baths and lotions only on a few special days each year.

Plutarch tells us that Spartan youths were also required to build their own beds from the reeds of the river Eurotas. They had to break these off with their bare hands, without the use of knives. This made the beds rougher and less comfortable. Food was deliberately rationed to enable them to survive without it on campaign if necessary. As a result the boys were forced to steal food: if they got caught, they were whipped severely – not for the moral wrong of stealing, but for the military sin of being caught.

At this age, a youth was expected to take an older male lover (bisexuality was the norm for men in the Greek world). The purpose of this relationship went beyond the sexual; for the older man played the role of a mentor and educator to his younger partner. Indeed, according to Plutarch, if a youth cried out in pain during a fight, it was his older lover who was fined by the magistrates.

Sparta and the Victorian public school

The classical world has had a profound influence on the history of education in Great Britain. Perhaps most strikingly, it is likely that the British public schools of the Victorian era tried to imitate elements of the Spartan education system. As in Sparta, upper-class Victorians sent their 7-year-old sons off to boarding school, where they would be removed from any 'soft' feminine influence and trained to rule. Both systems emphasised the importance of toughening boys by exposing them to harsh conditions. The cruelty and bullying in public schools was immortalised by Thomas Hughes in his novel *Tom Brown's Schooldays*, set at Rugby School during the headmastership of Dr Arnold. The real Dr Arnold, a great pioneer of Victorian education, had talked of wanting to 'sophronise' his pupils; this rare English word is derived from the Greek *sôphrosunê* ('self-control'), the very quality which the Spartans aimed to instil in their charges in the *agôgê*.

Aged 18-19

According to Plutarch, Lycurgus was particularly wary of youths in late adolescence, an age where he thought they were most likely to become rebellious or insolent. To prevent this, he decreed that they should be worked even harder and kept as busy as possible. Respect for elders was emphasised and, when walking in the streets, youths had to keep their hands in their cloaks, stay silent and keep their eyes fixed on the ground ahead of them.

The krypteia

Another element of the later stages of the education system was the *krypteia*, which means 'period of hiding'. Its exact nature is not clear, but it seems to have been a form of secret police. The strongest pupils in the *agôgê* were selected to serve for a period of time in the *krypteia*. Plutarch describes the process as follows:

> 'Periodically the overseers of the young men would dispatch into the countryside in different directions the ones who appeared to be particularly intelligent; they were equipped with daggers and basic rations, but nothing else. By day they would disperse to obscure spots to hide and rest. By night they made their way to roads and murdered any helot whom they caught. Frequently, too, they made their way through the fields, killing the helots who stood out for their physique and strength.' Plutarch, *Lycurgus* 28.2-3

The *krypteia* toughened up the young men further and accustomed them to killing fellow human beings – a vital ingredient of a successful soldier. It had the further advantage of keeping the helot population in a state of terror.

Review 4

1. Define the following terms: *apothetae, agôgê, paidonomos, krypteia.*
2. How does the treatment of Spartan children in their early years compare to the treatment of infants today?
3. How does the education of boys aged (i) 7-14, and (ii) 14-18, compare to the education of children of the same age in your society?
4. Which elements, if any, of Spartan education would you like to introduce into your school system?
5. Today there is great concern about the number of young men being radicalised by terrorist groups. Why do you think that young men are often seen as the best recruits for organisations such as the *krypteia*?
6. Do you think there is any place for a secret service in a society? If so, what rules do you think it should abide by?

VII. THE LIFE OF A SPARTAN CITIZEN

The decree, attributed to Lycurgus, that all Spartan citizens should be full-time professional soldiers, was a radical one. No Greek city had ever had a professional army before then. Rather, all citizens were army reservists who had to fight for their city in its hour of need.

Lycurgus' decree turned the custom inside out. Not only would Spartiates dedicate themselves to soldiering, they were even to be banned from any other type of work. The Spartan economy was placed in the hands of other groups: helots toiled on the estates; women managed the finances, while trade and craft was the province of the perioeci. The Spartiate life was spent training for war.

Aged 20-30

Spartiates were termed **eirens** until the age of 30. During these years, they were compelled to live in soldiers' barracks, even after they were married. Furthermore, they were banned from the market-place and could not do their own shopping. At this age, it seems that the men were still not trusted to conform without close supervision.

In order to foster more competitiveness between the young men, an elite troop of 300 soldiers was selected from their number (once again, Lycurgus was credited with the innovation). These 300 young Spartiates had the honour of serving as the king's bodyguard on campaign; it seems that they constantly had to justify their selection and could be replaced at any time. Moreover, those not selected were spurred on to improve themselves and watch for any faults in the elite.

Spartiates usually married towards the end of this stage of their lives. Marriage (described on pp. 248-9) was a vital rite of passage – the duty to produce offspring was just as important as the duty to fight for the state. Indeed, according to Aristotle, special privileges were given to men who fathered three or more sons:

'For they have a law by which the father of three sons is exempt from military service, and the father of four from all taxes.'   Aristotle, *Politics* 1270b

---

Music

The Spartans loved music, which was at the heart of their society. One ancient writer even compared them to cicadas (insects which chirp loudly and rhythmically) since they were always looking for a chorus! Yet this was music on Spartan terms. There were probably no solos sung in Sparta, nor any songs expressing personal feelings or emotions. Music, like everything else, was moulded to fit the Spartan system. Choral contests, in which choruses sang and danced for a prize, were very popular. Here, Spartans learnt to work well in a team and sharpened their competitive instincts. As we shall see, women were also fully included in this process; indeed, they learnt to sing and dance just as competitively as the men.

Music was also central to the military life, where it was used to instil discipline (much as a modern army trains its soldiers to march on parade). The most famous musical competition was held at the Festival of the Gymnopaediae, when whole battalions sang of Spartan courage and military glory. The songs of Tyrtaeus were sung in the messes and around the campfire on campaign, while in battle music was a key component – trumpets and pipes were used to give orders and rhythm to the phalanx.

Men who remained bachelors were publicly punished. Married women sang humiliating songs about them; they were banned from festivals, while in winter they had to parade naked in the market-place, singing that their disobedience deserved such a punishment.

Full citizens

When discussing the life of Spartiates, Plutarch says that their training 'extended into adulthood, for no one was permitted to live as he pleased'. Even in peacetime, Sparta was in essence a fortress and permanently armed camp. In fact, Plutarch says that the life of a Spartan at home was tougher than when on campaign because the harshest elements of the young men's training were relaxed in times of war. His idealised description of the rejection of the private life in favour of communal living could have come right out of Orwell's *Nineteen Eighty-Four*:

> 'Altogether he accustomed citizens to have no desire for a private life, nor knowledge of one, but rather to be like bees, always attached to the community, swarming together around their leader, and almost ecstatic with fervent ambition to devote themselves entirely to their country.'
>
> Plutarch, *Lycurgus* 25.3

Plutarch also says that, except when they went on campaign, all the Spartiates' time was taken up by choral dances, festivals, feasts, hunting expeditions, physical exercise and conversation; these activities were heavily controlled and used to train the Spartiates for war. Music, conversation, feasting and festivals all bred comradeship; physical exercise improved physique and encouraged competitiveness; hunting trained men to catch food when they were on campaign (Spartans loved hunting and their local breed of hound was famous among Greeks for its keen scent). Aside from these pursuits, Spartiates were discouraged from frequenting the market and never discussed moneymaking or commercial transactions.

Laconically speaking

Lycurgus encouraged Spartans to be men of few words, wanting them to be able to express 'a wide range of ideas in a few, spare words'. From this we get the English adjective 'laconic' (from an adjective meaning 'Spartan'), which describes an idea expressed concisely.

There were many famous laconicisms from Sparta. A wise man was once criticised for saying so little. A friend defended him with the line: 'An expert at speaking also knows when to do so.' Perhaps the most laconic comment of all came when Philip of Macedon was threatening to invade Sparta. He sent the Spartans the message: 'If I enter Laconia, I shall raze Sparta to the ground.' The Spartans sent back a one-word reply: 'If ...'!

This *kylix* (wine-goblet) showing a hunt scene was painted in the mid-6th century by a perioecic craftsman. Hunting was central to the Spartiate life and Xenophon gives a gory description of how a wild boar was hunted with nets and spears by Spartiates on foot.

The syssition

Dining was a key element of daily life for a Spartiate. He ate his meals in a mess-hall called a **syssition** ('communal eating-place'), just as Lycurgus had decreed. Each *syssition* had about 15 members and they spent considerable time with one another. On campaign the members of a *syssition* shared a tent.

Election to a mess was a requirement of Spartan citizenship. When a Spartan reached the age of 20, he applied for membership of a *syssition*. Its members held a ballot, in which each one dropped a ball of bread into an urn. If a single member squeezed his ball flat, the candidate was rejected. Failure to win election to a *syssition* meant becoming a social outcast. Any Spartan who failed to provide his monthly quota to the mess was similarly downgraded.

The *syssition* was fundamental to Spartiate society. It bred comradeship and guaranteed equality between all citizens, just as Lycurgus had intended. Furthermore, Spartans of different ages automatically socialised with one another. In other parts of Greece, most notably Athens, the generation gap was often a major source of strife.

Black broth

The diet of a Spartan was plain and healthy, including a type of black broth, which was well-known outside Sparta for its nasty taste. According to Plutarch, the broth consisted of pork cooked in its own blood and seasoned with salt and vinegar. One visitor to Sparta was so disgusted by its taste that he commented: 'Now I know why the Spartans have no fear of death.'

Each member of the *syssition* had to provide a monthly ration of goods from his plot of land (*klêros*): barley-meal, wine, cheese, figs and a little money for fish or meat. Men were allowed to miss a meal only if they were away making a sacrifice or hunting. Even then, they were encouraged to bring back the leftovers of sacrificial offerings or proceeds of a successful hunt.

At meals, the men would talk, sing and laugh together. On occasions, Spartan boys were brought into a mess to give them a sense of a man's world. They would observe the men talking politics and sharing jokes – it was particularly important for Spartans to take jokes well. Everything discussed was confidential. At each meal, the oldest member would point to the door and remind his comrades: 'Not a word goes out through this.'

Review 5

1. Define the following terms: *eiren, klêros, laconic, syssition.*
2. Explain what benefits the system of the 300 had for Spartan society.
3. In your own words describe (i) the system of election to a *syssition*; (ii) its rules of membership; (iii) the advantages of the *syssition* system.
4. Which other societies have a national dish? What does it say about them?
5. To what extent should citizens be allowed to monitor the behaviour of their fellow citizens, as happened in Sparta?
E. Write an imaginary account of the daily life of a Spartiate: (i) aged 20-30; (ii) aged 30+.

VIII. SPARTAN WOMEN

The women of Sparta lived radically different lives from women in the rest of Greece (see p. 150ff. for the lives of Athenian women). They too were seen as machines of the state – machines for the production of healthy offspring. Although Sparta allowed its women more freedom and power than any other city, this was no early example of feminism. In common with the rest of the Spartan system, the treatment of women was driven by eugenics – the desire to breed the healthiest children.

The education of girls

Sparta was unique in the ancient world (and rare in most pre-industrial societies) in providing an education system for its womenfolk. The education systems for boys and girls had the same aims – to encourage physical strength and team spirit. Unsurprisingly, Spartans believed that it was Lycurgus who devised the female education system.

From birth, girls in Sparta were treated differently from those in the rest of Greece. Spartan law required that they be given the same amount of care and food as their brothers. This was unheard of elsewhere, where girls were routinely fed less. As they grew, some of their education took place at home. Mothers or helot women probably taught them basic reading and writing skills. Once these were mastered, the girls learnt how to manage estates, which would be one of their key responsibilities in adulthood.

Girls probably received some form of public education too. Physical exercise would have been a core component of this; in the following passage, Plutarch outlines why:

'First, [Lycurgus] toughened the girls physically by making them run and wrestle and throw the discus and javelin. Thereby their children in embryo would make a strong start in strong bodies and would develop better, while the women themselves would also bear their pregnancies with vigour and would meet the challenge of childbirth in a successful, relaxed way.'

Plutarch, *Lycurgus* 14.2

In Sparta, female education was designed to promote the bearing of healthy children.

Throughout the Greek world, it was the custom for men to exercise naked in public. Indeed the very place where such exercise took place was the gymnasium, a word which literally meant 'the place to go naked' (see p. 67). Greek men were brought up to have fit bodies and to be proud of them. According to Plutarch, in Sparta this philosophy was extended to include women:

'He (Lycurgus) made young girls no less than young men grow used to walking nude in processions, as well as to dancing and singing at certain festivals with the young men present and looking on ... there was nothing disreputable about the girls' nudity. It was altogether modest and there was no hint of immorality. Instead it encouraged simple habits and an enthusiasm for physical fitness.'   Plutarch, *Lycurgus* 14.2ff.

It is interesting that the historian finds it necessary here to defend the practice of female nudity. For it cannot be overemphasised how radical such a concept was outside Sparta, where women were routinely discouraged from leaving the home; if they did so, they were compelled to cover themselves up.

Marriage
When girls reached adolescence they were not rushed into marriage, unlike other Greek women (see p. 153). This was probably to ensure that they had reached full physical development and could cope better with pregnancy. The marriage ceremony itself was quite extraordinary. The bride had her hair cut short and was dressed in a man's cloak and sandals, perhaps to make the love-making more familiar for the groom. She then waited in her groom's house until after dark. The groom would

This figurine depicts a young Spartan woman either dancing or running. Her off-the-shoulder tunic and short skirt perhaps illustrate why other, more conservative Greeks nicknamed Spartan women 'thigh-flashers'.

arrive after having dinner in his mess. He would make love to his bride and then hurry back to sleep in his mess.

The practice of living apart continued through the early years of marriage. Men were made to feel ashamed if they were caught in the company of their wives and so secretive liaisons in the dark were the norm. The purpose of this strange practice was to maintain the attraction between husband and wife. Plutarch explains the rationale:

'It was not just an exercise in moderation and self-control, but also meant that partners were fertile physically, always fresh for love, and ready for intercourse rather than being sated and pale from unrestricted sexual activity.'   Plutarch, *Lycurgus* 15.5

Once again, it was the desire to maximise the production of healthy children which defined sexual behaviour in Sparta.

This eugenicist policy gave rise to an even more extraordinary custom. For, according to Plutarch, adultery was actively encouraged in Sparta. This way, Spartiates could sleep with the wives of their comrades (if permission was granted) in order to increase the number of healthy Spartan citizens available to the state.

Economic power
Uniquely in the Greek world, Spartan women did not do any housework. Chores such as weaving, cooking or cleaning were considered beneath

the dignity of a woman who would produce Spartan warriors. It was left to domestic helots to carry out all the household duties.

The Spartan wife had a far grander economic role – she was the manager of the farming estate (*klêros*) allotted to her husband. The estate needed to produce enough food to cover her husband's contributions to the *syssition*, as well as feeding the rest of the family. The wife had economic control over the whole estate (including the helots), and took decisions about crops, equipment and the sale of any surplus.

Sparta's inheritance laws gave women further economic power. Unlike any other Greek women, a Spartan was allowed to inherit property from her father if she had no brothers. Some Spartan woman therefore became wealthy heiresses. Spartan bachelors were very keen to marry such women (unsurprisingly!) – so much so that it was left to the kings to choose husbands for them.

Upholding the ethos

As women represented half the Spartan population (as, of course, they do in any population), it was vital that they too grew up believing in their extraordinary society. They were expected to give their sons to the state at the age of 7 and to drum into their male relatives that it was glorious for them to die for Sparta. This reportedly started at an early age; for girls performing at public festivals sometimes

> '... would make fun of each of the young men, helpfully criticising their mistakes. On other occasions they would rehearse in song the praises which they had composed about those meriting them, so that they filled the youngsters with a great sense of ambition and rivalry.'
>
> Plutarch, *Lycurgus* 14.3

Practices like this caused the girls to grow up developing a fervent loyalty to the state. Indeed, Spartan women seem to have been among the system's most fanatical supporters. They may not have had any voting rights in the constitution, but there is little doubt of their influence on the men. Spartan mothers were said to send their sons off to war with the phrase: 'Either with your shield or on it!' – meaning that they should come back victorious or dead.

Indeed, Spartan women seem to have been no less laconic than their menfolk. Plutarch even put together a handbook entitled *Sayings of Spartan Women*, a truly remarkable collection considering the usual attitude to women in the Greek world. In Athens, the leading politician Pericles reportedly claimed that the best type of woman was the one who was 'least talked about by men, whether in praise or blame'.

Yet in Sparta, the female voice was a valuable propaganda weapon for scaring and impressing other Greeks. Gorgo, the wife of king Leonidas, was once asked why Spartan women were the only women in Greece who could 'rule' their husbands. She replied, 'Because we are the only women who give birth to men.' In her view, only men with the self-confidence to tolerate powerful women were real men at all. The attitude of Spartan women is well illustrated by the following epigram, in which a mother laments her son's desertion from the battlefield:

> 'Away to the darkness, cowardly offspring, where out of hatred
> Eurotas does not flow even for fearful deer.
> Useless pup, worthless portion, away to Hell.
> Away! This son of Sparta was not mine at all.'
>
> Plutarch, *Sayings of Spartan Women* 241

The Greek view of Spartan women

Spartan women were a source of intrigue and scandal outside Sparta. Other Greek men would have been very disturbed by their freedom and prominence in Spartan society. It was shocking that women socialised and exercised in public (sometimes even with men), unescorted by male relatives. There would also have been horror at the degree of economic power given to Spartan women.

A persistent criticism of Spartan women was that they were sexually promiscuous. Other Greeks were shocked to hear of women in revealing clothes who even took part in ceremonies naked; and so they mockingly nicknamed them 'thigh-flashers'. The following criticism by a female character in a play by Euripides may have been typical:

> 'However much she tried, no Spartan girl could keep her chastity. They go
> out from their homes with the young men. Their dress is disordered and
> their thighs are bare. They race and wrestle with the men. No wonder then
> that there is no virtue in your Spartan womenfolk.'
>
> Euripides, *Andromache* 595-601

Many non-Spartans were appalled by the wildly different sexual customs in Sparta and could not understand how adultery was seen as a virtue. Athenian men, obsessed with protecting their paternity, would shut their wives away from other men whenever possible.

Other criticisms of Spartan women followed on from this. Some Greeks thought that their obsession with exercise made them muscular and unattractive. Others believed that they were negligent mothers because they sent their sons off to the *agôgê* at the age of 7. They were also criticised for being over-opinionated. Aristotle claimed that Spartan men were 'ruled by their wives'. He abhorred the freedom given to them, arguing that it was a central flaw in the Spartan system.

Such views were put forward by men from cities hostile to Sparta.

Aristophanes' *Lysistrata*

Aristophanes wrote a comedy in 411 about an Athenian woman, Lysistrata, who wants to put an end to the war with Sparta. She organises a convention with a delegation of Spartan women, led by Lampito, and women from other cities. The women decide that their husbands will end the war soon enough if the women of both cities agree to hold a sex strike!

The play gives an interesting insight into how Spartan women may have been viewed at Athens. In the following lines (78ff.), Lysistrata sees Lampito for the first time and compliments her on her remarkable physique:

Lysistrata: Welcome, Lampito, my dear. How are things in Sparta? Darling, you look simply beautiful. Such colour, such resilience! Why, I bet you could throttle a bull?
Lampito: So could you, my dear, if you were in training. Don't you know I practise rump-jumps every day?
Lysistrata: And such marvellous breasts too!

Some writers, such as Aristophanes, enjoyed portraying a stereotype of Spartan women. Others, such as Aristotle, simply believed that women were inferior to men and would cause trouble if given too much power. Significantly, many who criticised them had probably never visited Sparta and were basing their opinions on hearsay and legend.

In spite of all this, it would be wrong to say that the women never received favourable opinion. Other Greeks probably admired the healthiness, strength and natural beauty of Spartan women. Lycurgus, so Spartans believed, had forbidden women to wear jewellery, cosmetics and perfume and so they relied on natural beauty to attract men. In addition, it was a Spartan princess, Kyniska, who became the first woman to achieve a victory at the male-only Olympic Games (see pp. 69-70).

Review 6

1. What do the customs of Spartan marriage suggest about the nature of male/female relationships in Sparta?
2. What economic powers did Spartan women have? How did this differ from women in the rest of the Greek world?
3. What evidence is there that women played a powerful political role? Do you think that this strengthened the Spartan system?
4. Construct a debate between an Athenian and a Spartan about the role and importance of women in society.
E. (i) Imagine you are a Spartan mother about to send off your 7-year-old son to the *agôgê*. What advice and instructions would you give him?
E. (ii) Imagine you are a Spartan girl. Describe your education and upbringing. What do you believe about the world you are growing up in?

IX. THE SPARTAN ARMY

The Spartans remained undefeated in war for almost three centuries, and their skill and bravery in battle were awesome. In the 480s, the Spartan king Demaratus, who had been exiled by his people, defected to the Persians. He acted as an adviser to the Persian king, Xerxes, on matters concerning the Greeks. According to Herodotus, Demaratus described Spartan soldiers to Xerxes in these words:

> 'Fighting singly, they are as good as any, but fighting together they are the best soldiers in the world. They are free – yes – but not entirely free; for they have a master, and that master is the Law, which they fear much more than your subjects fear you.'   Herodotus, *Histories* 7.104

When Xerxes heard this, he burst out laughing. However, Demaratus was soon proved right when a tiny number of Spartans managed to kill thousands of Persian troops at the pass of Thermopylae.

The Spartans were masters of the **phalanx**, a technique of fighting which had emerged in the 7th century. This was a rectangular formation of soldiers which was normally eight rows deep. In battle, opposing phalanxes approached each other at a deliberate pace. When they met, the two sides would thrust at each other with their spears, attempting

An artist's impression of two phalanxes meeting in battle.

A statuette of a
Spartan warrior.

to hit an unprotected area on an opponent. If a soldier in the front row
was felled, the men in the rows behind would step up one place to
maintain the defensive wall. The best soldiers would fight in the front
row to set an example.

Each hoplite held his shield in his left hand and therefore depended on
his neighbour's shield to protect his exposed right side. Any disruption to
the front line could rip a hole in the phalanx. Therefore, in battle the
soldiers needed to maintain tight discipline and react quickly to new orders
and changes in tactics. This is where the Spartans came into their own.
They trained so hard that they were the most disciplined exponents of the
phalanx in the world. They were also brilliant at reacting to a change of
orders, which would be communicated by trumpeters and pipers.

Religion was also central to military procedure. To ensure that the
gods were in favour of the mission, the king would sacrifice when setting
out from Sparta and again when he reached the border. Before a battle
he would always sacrifice to the Muses, reminding his soldiers that their
efforts could be remembered in song. If the sacrifice was favourable, the
king commanded the pipers to play the song to Castor, one of the twin
gods of Sparta, and the hoplites advanced.

Aside from their intense training, there were other reasons why the
Spartans were so successful in warfare:

- **Command structure**. The Spartan army was divided into regiments,
  each commanded by a regimental commander who was directly responsible
  to the campaigning king. Below the commanders there were other divisions

and officers so that information was relayed easily. There was no equivalent chain of command in any other Greek army.

- **Fear factor**. Spartans pursued a fleeing enemy only until they were sure of victory, believing that it was beneath their dignity to kill fugitives. Many opponents therefore chose to flee rather than face the fearsome Spartan hoplites, knowing that they would not be chased down and killed.
- **Mystique**. According to Plutarch, Lycurgus decreed that the Spartans should not come up against the same enemy too often so that their tactics would remain a mystery.

Perioeci and helots were also used on campaign. For example, at the battle of Plataea in 479, 5,000 Spartiates were joined by the same number of perioeci and 35,000 helots. Perioeci were used both as combatants and as craftsmen to repair weaponry and equipment. By the 4th century, Spartiates and perioeci were fighting alongside one another in six mixed regiments. Helots were used as baggage-handlers, slaves and runners for the Spartiates. In the later years of the Spartan system, they even fought in the front line. In order to prevent helots from rebelling while on campaign, Spartiates always carried their spears with them in camp and kept a close guard on the weapon store.

Death

The Spartans' attitude to death set them apart from other Greek societies. Spartans believed that death was worthy and desirable if it served a higher cause – the good of the city. Elsewhere in Greece, all burials took place outside the city. However, Lycurgus decreed that the dead of Sparta should be buried within the city and even near temples. This way, citizens would become more used to the reality of death. Furthermore, a Spartan could not be buried with any treasures; he was just wrapped in his red cloak. Finally, there were two categories of Spartan who were given the honour of having their names inscribed on a gravestone: men who had died in battle and women who had died in childbirth. In both cases, the ultimate sacrifice had been made for the city.

At funerals, the behaviour of Spartan women was radically different from that of other Greek women. At a conventional Greek funeral, the women led the lamenting beside the body by wailing loudly, beating their breasts and tearing their hair (see p. 169). In contrast, Spartan women were taught to show no emotion except pride for a fallen relative. A story told by Xenophon admirably illustrates this. In 371, after the news of the defeat at the battle of Leuctra was reported back to Sparta, he says that:

> 'On the following day you could see those women whose relatives had been killed going about looking bright and cheerful, whereas those whose relatives had been reported as still alive were not much in evidence, and those few who were out and about were looking gloomy and sorry for themselves.'
>
> Xenophon, *Hellenika* 6.4.16

The inside of this Laconian cup shows two young warriors carrying a dead comrade from the battlefield.

Uniform and weapons

The basic item of a hoplite's uniform was a tunic, over which a corselet of bronze (later of leather) protected the torso. On top of this was the famous cloak, dyed red to hide any blood. To protect his legs a hoplite wore greaves, while leather boots were also used in battle. The uniform was completed by a plumed helmet; although it gave great protection to the head, it did not make vision or hearing very easy. Hoplites were also allowed to wear their hair long in battle as it was believed that this made them larger in stature and more frightening. A hoplite carried three important weapons:

- **Shield**. The round shield (*hoplon*) was always inscribed with a capital L, signifying 'Lacedaemonia' (another term for 'Sparta').
- **Spear**. The spear, about three metres in length, was the main weapon for phalanx-fighting.
- **Sword**. If the hoplite lost his spear or fought his enemy at close quarters, he could resort to using the short sword, which hung on the right side of a belt around his waist.

This vase seems to depict a Spartan hoplite (long hair, shaved top lip)
confronting a mounted spearman.

A bronze spear-head discovered near Sparta.

No example of the Spartan short sword has survived. This bronze model, just
over 30 cm long, is probably slightly larger than life size.

257

Right: This spectacular marble sculpture was excavated from the Acropolis area of Sparta in 1925 and immediately named 'Leonidas', although it more probably depicts a god or a hero. However, it undeniably presents a Spartan image of a warrior, with the top lip characteristically shaven.

Left: This Spartan warrior wears his red cloak wrapped around his chest. The left-right axis of his crest indicates that he is a general, or perhaps even a king.

An Athenian once joked that sword-swallowers used Spartan swords because they were so short, to which a Spartan replied: 'We find them long enough to reach the hearts of our enemies.' Spartans were particularly contemptuous of armies (such as the Persians) who relied on arrows in battle. To a Spartan, real courage could be shown only in hand-to-hand fighting, whereas arrows were used at a distance and were thought 'womanish' because they resembled spindles.

The Battle of Thermopylae

The Battle of Thermopylae in 480 was the epitome of Spartan heroism in battle – but it was in fact a military defeat! At least 100,000 Persians (and possibly more than twice that number) led by king Xerxes had conquered the northern half of Greece and were heading south. The route into southern Greece required them to march through the narrow pass at Thermopylae, where the mountains dropped down to within a few metres of the sea.

The Greek allies sent a mixed force of about 7,000 to defend the pass for as long as possible while the rest of the Greek forces regrouped and planned the defence of southern Greece. At the head of this force were Sparta's king Leonidas and a hand-picked selection of 300 Spartan soldiers, all of them fathers of living sons. When the Persians arrived at Thermopylae the Greeks were already in place to defend a wall which they had rebuilt in the middle of the pass.

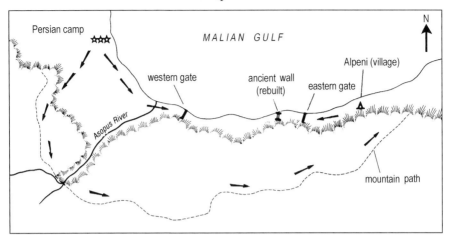

A plan of the battle of Thermopylae. The Greek allies took up a position near the rebuilt ancient wall and used the village of Alpeni as their supply base until they were trapped by the Persian soldiers who arrived to the east via the mountain path.

There was a tense stand-off for four days, while Xerxes tried to coax the Greeks into surrender without a fight. During this time he sent a spy on horseback to survey the Greek camp. He was astonished to hear that the Spartans were preening themselves for battle by combing their hair. Demaratus explained to Xerxes that the men were preparing themselves for a glorious death in battle.

When the fighting finally started, it was carnage. The Persians, unable to match the superior fighting skills of the Greeks, were easily beaten off for two days. Thousands of them were killed, set against the loss of just a few Greeks. However, on the evening of the second day the Greeks were betrayed. A local man, Ephialtes, sold out to the Persians, informing them of a path over the mountains which came out at the other side of the pass of Thermopylae.

As dawn broke on the third day, the Greek forces learnt from scouts that they were about to be caught in a pincer grip. Leonidas dismissed most of the Greek forces, keeping about 1,500 in the pass in what was effectively a suicide mission. Led by the 300 Spartans, the allies fought with every last breath – Herodotus says that if they lost their weapons they even fought with their hands and their teeth.

Almost every Spartan was killed. Although it was technically a defeat, the courage shown by the Spartans was an inspiration to the rest of the Greek world. In the course of the following months, they were able to beat off the Persian threat for good. Herodotus records that, soon after the battle, an inscription was set up at the spot:

'Go tell the Spartans, Stranger passing by,
that here, obedient to their laws, we lie.'

Herodotus, *Histories* 7.228

Leonidas (*c.* 535-480)

The Spartans were led at Thermopylae by king Leonidas, who has gone down as the most famous Spartan in history. If Lycurgus had wanted to create an icon for his warrior state, he couldn't have come up with anything better than Leonidas. Before the Persians invaded, the Delphic oracle informed the Spartans that their city would either be conquered or 'the whole land of Lacedaemon will mourn the death of a king of the house of Heracles'. In short, when he set out to defend the pass, Leonidas believed that his death would be the necessary price for Sparta's survival.

Leonidas' extraordinary courage in battle was almost matched by his inspiring laconicisms. As he left Sparta for Thermopylae, his wife Gorgo is said to have asked him if he had any instructions for her. He replied simply: 'Marry a good man and bear good children.' When the two armies were preparing to do battle, Xerxes gave Leonidas a final chance to surrender honourably, sending a runner with the message: 'Deliver up your arms', to which he replied: 'Come and get them!'

At dawn on the third day of the battle, when the Greeks learnt that they would be trapped in the pass, Leonidas advised his men: 'Eat a good breakfast, for tonight we dine in the Underworld.' In the final heroic fighting that day, Leonidas was indeed killed and there followed a momentous struggle for his body, which the Persians eventually captured. Persians normally showed respect to the dead of their enemies, but the enraged Xerxes ordered the body of Leonidas to be decapitated. His head, driven onto a stake, rotted publicly for all to see. But his example lived on and a year later the Persians were driven from Greece for good.

Review 7

1. Explain how the Spartan approach to death differed from that of other Greek peoples.
2. What made the Spartan army so successful?
3. How were the uniform and weapons of a Spartan hoplite designed to aid fighting in the phalanx?
4. Read Herodotus' account of the Battle of Thermopylae (*Histories* 7.208-28). Which details illustrate the typical character of the Spartans?
E. Imagine you are a Spartan preparing to fight at Thermopylae. Write an account of your build-up to the battle.

X. SPARTAN GOVERNMENT

The most important instructions given to Lycurgus by the oracle at Delphi concerned the reform of Spartan government. These instructions were known as the Great Rhêtra. The government consisted of four different bodies: two **kings**, five **ephors** (the leading magistrates), the **gerousia** (a council of elders) and the **ecclêsia** (the assembly of all male citizens). Individual power was closely checked by this structure and change was very difficult to achieve without wide consensus.

1. The kings

Sparta had two kings at a time and two royal families, the Agiads and the Eurypontids; Spartans claimed that both royal families were directly descended from the mythological hero Heracles. In reality, the dual kingship probably emerged when the early villages of Sparta joined together as a larger political unit, a process known as *synoecism*, or 'living together' (see p. 178); it was also an effective way of preventing one individual from gaining too much power. The two kings ruled in partnership and had equal power under the constitution. Each king's heir was the first-born son after his father had become king. Their main responsibilities were as follows:

- **Commanders** of the Spartan army. After 505, only one king was allowed to command the army on campaign; he had overall command on the battlefield. However, his performance was scrutinised by two of the ephors, who were required to accompany him and report back to the *ecclêsia* on his efforts.
- They also wielded important influence through their role as **religious leaders**. They were effectively the chief priests of Sparta and their people believed that they were intermediaries with the gods.
- Politically, the Spartan constitution tried to limit the power of the kings. Their **judicial powers** consisted of arbitration in only three areas: the marriage of heiresses, the adoption of children and the maintenance of public highways. Yet they were also afforded political power by their automatic membership of the *gerousia*.

Moreover, it is likely that the kings wielded significant political and social influence through their symbolic importance for the Spartan people. Spartans believed that their kings had divine ancestry and approval. Not only were they descended from Heracles, the hero who became an immortal, their office had also been divinely sanctioned by the oracle of Apollo at Delphi. Thus the kings were powerful symbols of Spartan history and society, and they must have been treated with reverence by their people.

> **The death of a king**
> The importance of the kingship is illustrated by the Spartan reaction to a king's death, which triggered a tide of public grief. Horsemen carried the news throughout the country and many thousands of people (Spartiates, perioeci and helots) were obliged by law to attend the funeral. The whole community observed ten days' mourning, beating their foreheads as a sign of grief, lamentation and moaning, and cried out that the dead king was the best that they had ever had. As we have seen, these customs were almost the polar opposite of any other Spartan funeral, where death was met with a firmly stiff upper lip and absence of emotion.

Both kings were given certain privileges:

- Their heirs did not have to go through the *agôgê*, perhaps because they alone did not need to be trained to obey orders.
- The kings were wealthy landowners, owning land among the territory of the perioeci as well as their hereditary estates in Spartan land.
- They were served their food first at their *syssition* and were also given double portions.
- They had seats of honour at public festivals, while the members of the *ecclêsia* stood up when the kings entered.

However, if the people were unhappy with the performance of the kings, then they could be deposed after due trial before the *gerousia* and ephors; in fact, no fewer than six kings or regents seem to have been tried or deposed during the 5th century.

2. The ephors

The board of five ephors, which was elected each year by the *ecclêsia*, developed into the most powerful element of the government. One indication of this is that the senior ephor gave his name to the civil year. The ephors served a term of one year; any Spartiate over the age of 30 could stand for election but no one could serve more than once.

Originally, the ephors were probably officials elected to keep a check on the kings (a role suggested by the name 'ephor', which meant 'overseer') and this remained one of their key responsibilities. Each month, the kings and ephors exchanged oaths, as Xenophon recorded:

> 'The ephors swear on behalf of the city, the king for himself. The king swears that he will rule according to the established laws of the city, the city swears to do no damage to the royal authority provided the king keeps his oath.' Xenophon, *Constitution of the Spartans* 15.7

It is interesting to note here that the ephors are portrayed as the Spartiates who represent the interests of the whole city.

The ephors took on special responsibilities when Sparta went to war. They decided the number of Spartiates, perioeci and helots to be called up and how many wagons and pack animals would be needed to carry medical supplies and spare equipment. As we have seen, two ephors also went on campaign to accompany the king and report back on his performance. The ephors had various other important duties:

- **Foreign affairs**. They could allow foreign representatives to enter Spartan territory and even to address the *ecclêsia*.
- **Education**. They were responsible for the education system and the appointment of the *paidonomos*.
- **Security**. Internal state security was in their hands. They appointed the captains of the 300 and chose the members of the *krypteia*.
- **Legal affairs**. They judged civil cases on their own and sat with the *gerousia* to form the Supreme Court of Justice.
- **Government**. They presided over the *ecclêsia* and scrutinised the performance of lesser magistrates.

The ephors took up office on the first full moon after the autumnal equinox. Their first act was to issue a decree that all citizens should 'shave their top lips and obey the law'. After this, they declared war on the helots.

3. The gerousia

The *gerousia*, which meant 'council of elders', consisted of 30 men – the two kings and 28 other elected Spartiates over the age of 60. The *gerousia* wielded considerable power in Sparta. Its main function was to prepare and debate bills for the *ecclêsia* to vote on. However, if they were not happy with the way the *ecclêsia* had voted, they could withdraw the proposal. In effect, the *gerousia* could veto any decision taken by the *ecclêsia*. The *gerousia* also acted as judges in criminal law cases.

The *gerousia* is perhaps the embodiment of the Spartan respect for one's elders. The lyric poet Pindar said of the city that 'the councils of old men are pre-eminent there', while Xenophon made the following observation about the contest of election to the body:

'Athletic contests are honourable too, but they are merely trials of physique, whereas the competition for the *gerousia* involves a test of the noble qualities of the spirit. Thus just as the spirit is superior to the body, to the same degree contests of spirit merit greater rivalry than those of physique.'   Xenophon, *The Politeia of the Spartans* 10.3

As Xenophon intimates here, election to the *gerousia* was probably the highest honour a Spartiate could achieve.

When a vacancy came up on the *gerousia*, the election ceremony itself was strange (Aristotle even described it as childish). Candidates were brought into the *ecclêsia* one by one, their order of appearance being decided by lot. The Spartiates in the *ecclêsia* shouted if they approved of a candidate. In an adjoining room other Spartans, unaware of the order of the candidates, listened to the loudness of the shouting. The candidate who was greeted with the loudest shouting was elected to the *gerousia* and he served in this role for the rest of his life.

4. The ecclêsia*

The *ecclêsia* was the assembly for all adult Spartiates. It was thus the most democratic element of the constitution, although the vast majority of the population – women, perioeci and helots – were not represented. The *ecclêsia* met outside the city every month at new moon and the bills prepared by the *gerousia* were put to the vote. The members of the *ecclêsia* could not discuss or amend proposals; they had to listen to the views of the ephors and kings and then vote for or against them. They voted by acclamation (i.e. clapping/shouting); if this did not provide a clear winner, then the Spartiates were divided into groups 'for' and 'against'. This voting procedure survives in the British House of Commons today.

Thucydides (1.79-88) gives an account of the *ecclêsia* in action. When the Spartans debated whether to go to war with Athens in 432, two representatives of allied cities spoke, followed by two Spartans. One of the kings, Archidamus, recommended to the *ecclêsia* that they reject the proposal. In contrast, an ephor called Sthenelaidas argued in favour of going to war. In the end, the vote of the *ecclêsia* decided the matter: they chose to go to war.

How effective was the constitution?

Other Greeks were often unsure how to describe the Spartan system of government, since it included elements of various political systems. This confusion is best expressed by Plato, who says of the Spartan constitution:

> 'I do not know what name to give it. The board of ephors is tyrannical, but Sparta sometimes seems the nearest thing to a pure democracy of all states. It would be absurd to deny that it is an aristocracy, and it includes a monarchy – the oldest in the world.'   Plato, *Laws* 4.712

Much of the criticism of the constitution focused on the *gerousia*. This elderly group of citizens probably ensured that Sparta remained such a

*The Spartan assembly is sometimes referred to as the *apella*, although this is almost certainly a mistake. The term comes from a confusion between the fact that the assembly met on the feast day of Apollo, and so the Greek verb *apellasdein*, which meant 'to celebrate the festival of Apollo', came to be misinterpreted as 'to hold an assembly', with *apella* being misunderstood to mean 'assembly'. I therefore use the conventional Greek name for an assembly, *ecclêsia*.

conservative society. Aristotle also commented that it was dangerous to leave so much power in the hands of men who might go senile. He also claimed that they were often prone to bribery and favouritism.

	Rights and duties
Kings (2)	Military and religious leaders. They also oversaw: • marriage of heiresses • adoption of children • public highways
Ephors (5)	The most powerful members of the constitution, responsible for: • overseeing the kings • civil and criminal judgements • foreign affairs • internal security and education • state finances and magistrates
Gerousia (28 + 2)	Prepared bills for the *ecclêsia* on: • foreign policy • changes in the law • matters of war and peace Judged criminal cases and could administer: • death penalty • banishment • fines
Ecclêsia	Could vote on: • election of ephors and *gerousia* • appointment of generals • questions of war and peace • foreign policy and signing of treaties • the king to lead the army on a campaign They could also suggest a change to the law to the *gerousia*, who would consider putting it to a vote.

Review 8

1. What powers and privileges did the Spartan kings have? How important do you think they were to Spartan society?
2. In your own words, describe the powers and duties of the ephors.
3. Why do you think Xenophon believed that election to the *gerousia* was so highly prized? Do you agree that it was a childish system of election?
4. How much power do you think ordinary Spartiates held as members of the *ecclêsia*?
E. What do you think were the strengths and weaknesses of the Spartan constitution? How does it compare to the governmental system in your country?

In Search of the Greeks

XI. SPARTA AND THE WIDER GREEK WORLD

The Spartans were the most controversial of the Greek peoples. Their society was so distinct that they attracted rage and admiration from other Greeks in equal measure. As has already been seen, Spartan women engendered particularly strong feelings.

Sparta was especially hated in Athens, its greatest rival in the Greek world. From the time the Spartan king Cleomenes meddled in Athenian politics in 510, the two cities endured a tense relationship throughout the 5th century and beyond, despite their alliance during the Persian Wars. During the harsh years of the 431-404 war, the Spartans were generally loathed in Athens.

We can learn a good deal about Athenian views of Sparta from the famous funeral speech of 430 attributed to the Athenian general Pericles by Thucydides (2.34-46). Indeed, this is the best starting point for examining Athenian attitudes to Sparta. The speech commemorated the Athenian war dead after the first year of fighting and represented a defence of the Athenian way of life. The following excerpt illustrates how the two societies are contrasted:

'And, just as our political life is free and open, so is our day-to-day life in our relations with each other. We do not get into a state with our next-door neighbour if he enjoys himself in his own way, nor do we give him the kind of black looks which, though they do no real harm, still do hurt people's feelings. We are free and tolerant in our private lives.'

Thucydides, *History of the Peloponnesian War* 2.37

Of the other common criticisms of Sparta, the following are perhaps the most typical:

- **Foreign policy**. The Spartans were keen to ensure that their Greek allies preserved governments sympathetic to the Spartan cause. As such, they often supported oligarchic governments and suppressed the rise of democracy and tyranny in other Greek states. This did not always make them popular with other Greek peoples.
- **The agôgê** seems to have been regarded with disdain; it was felt to be cruel to send sons away from home at the age of 7, depriving them of warm clothing and adequate amounts of food. Many (particularly educated Athenians) were also appalled by the lack of literature and poetry in Spartan education. A typical sneer is recorded in Plato's *Laws* (689CD), where an Athenian refers to Greeks (almost certainly Spartans) who 'can neither read nor swim'.
- **The helots**. As is suggested by the helot revolt of 464, the suppression of the helots could cause unease in other cities. All Greeks believed that it was acceptable to enslave foreigners, whom they regarded as barbarians, but they felt very uneasy about the enslavement of fellow Greeks.

266

- **Conservatism**. Spartans were famous for their conservatism and dislike of change. Some thought that Sparta declined as a military power because she was unprepared to learn the new military tactics which were emerging in the 4th century.

The depth of the hatred of Sparta felt by many Athenians in the late 5th century is perhaps suggested in the following lines, spoken by a character in a tragic play by Euripides:

> 'Most hateful of all mankind, dwellers in Sparta, plotters of treachery, lords of the lie, schemers of evil, your success in Greece is a crime. What wickedness is not found among you? Murder rampant; greed and dishonesty; treacherous thoughts and treacherous deeds; to hell with you!'
>
> Euripides, *Andromache* 445ff.

Spartan xenophobia

In their turn, Spartans were deeply suspicious of the outside world. Spartans believed that when Lycurgus instituted his reforms he was quick to purge Laconia of any outside influences by ordering the expulsion of foreigners – the Spartan system could not allow its citizens to be tempted by the luxuries or ideas of the outside world. In this respect, Sparta was an eerie forerunner to many communist states of the 20th century.

Lycurgus reportedly banned foreigners from entering Laconia in case they developed into teachers of 'evil practices'. Plutarch says that he was concerned because 'by definition foreigners must bring in foreign ideas with them, and novel ideas lead to novel attitudes'. While cities like Athens welcomed such an influx of new ideas, in Sparta they were seen as subversive intruders with the power to undermine the city.

The travel ban worked both ways. Lycurgus apparently banned Spartans from travelling outside Laconia in case they acquired 'foreign habits' and copied 'lifestyles based upon no training'. In addition, he was concerned that Spartans should have no exposure to types of government different from that of Sparta. Spartans were particularly suspicious of democracy, believing that it gave too much power to the common citizen and did not allow for swift and clear decision-making.

Although we cannot be sure about what the Spartans believed about other Greeks, it is fair to make some assumptions. Their propaganda would have told them that other Greeks were spoiled by a lavish and luxurious lifestyle, with too much eating and drinking and too many flashy buildings. Militarily, Spartans would surely have looked down on other Greek armies, which did not contain professional, highly trained soldiers.

Review 9

1. In your own words, outline the typical criticisms other Greeks made of Sparta.
2. Find out about societies of the modern world who have prevented their citizens from leaving their country. Do you think a government ever has the right to introduce such an embargo?
3. How is Lycurgus' reported suspicion of immigrants reflected by attitudes in your society? Do you think this policy was beneficial for Sparta?
E. (i) Imagine that you are either (a) an Athenian, or (b) a Spartan living in the 5th century. Compose a speech either criticising or defending the Spartan system.
E. (ii) Do you think that Sparta was a totalitarian state?

XII. THE LEGACY OF SPARTA

The 21st century interpretation of ancient Sparta has moved markedly away from the rose-tinted view held by many in the 19th century – in particular by educationalists in Victorian Britain and by those fighting for the freedom of Greece from Ottoman rule. Such people concentrated almost exclusively on the positive aspects of the Spartan legacy – notions such as supreme courage. Yet, as we have seen, the Spartan system has also inspired the genocidal Nazis. As modern history has become more focused on individual human experience, the spotlight has rightly been turned on the immense helot suffering required to sustain the Spartan system – suffering probably far greater than in other cities where slavery was taken for granted.

However, although the legacy of Sparta to western civilisation is less obviously visible than that of Athens, it should not be underestimated. From the Spartans come values such as duty, loyalty, patriotism and self-discipline. Moreover, at a crucial moment of European history, the 300 Spartans' heroic, if doomed, defence at Thermopylae inspired the Greek allies to believe that they could repel the Persian invasion. If the Persians had conquered Greece in 480, then it is highly unlikely that ideas such as democracy, drama or freedom of speech could have flourished in Athens. Thus, by a remarkable irony, it was the authoritarian and fiercely anti-democratic Spartans who led the Greek fight for freedom, so preserving the legacy of Athens which we value so highly today. That is some legacy in itself.

Chronology

Century	Events	People
800 Era of colonisation begins Greek alphabet introduced	1st Olympic Games, 776 1st Messenian War	 Homer?
700		Hesiod
Social unrest in Greece Rise of phalanx fighting Age of tyrants begins	2nd Messenian War	Lycurgus?
600 Coinage introduced		Solon
		Peisistratos
500	Persian Wars, 494-479 (documented by Herodotus)	Cleisthenes Pindar Aeschylus
Athenian Empire	Pericles' building programme at Athens Peloponnesian War, 431-404 (documented by Thucydides)	Pericles Sophocles Euripides Aristophanes Socrates
400	Battle of Leuctra, 371 Philip of Macedon conquers Greece, 338	Xenophon Plato Aristotle Demosthenes

Appendix 1

Attica and Athens

1. Attica

Attica (see map 5) was a region extending over about 1,600 square kilometres (1,000 square miles) in the south-east of Greece. Roughly triangular in shape, it was bordered on two sides by sea; to the north-west lay the regions of Boeotia and Megara. In common with many parts of Greece, Attica's landscape was a combination of mountain ranges and plains.

In one of these plains lay the city of Athens, about 8 km (5 miles) inland from its harbour. Until 493 this was located at **Phaleron**, however after this **Piraeus** became the main harbour; in fact, there were actually three harbours at Piraeus: a large one for commercial ships and two smaller ones for warships. As a major international port, Piraeus had a varied and cosmopolitan population. By the middle of the 5th century, the town was joined to Athens by two long protective walls, which ensured that supplies could reach the city if it was under attack (a further wall joined the city to Phaleron).

Although a large proportion of the people of Attica were farmers, the region did not readily support agriculture; it was the driest part of

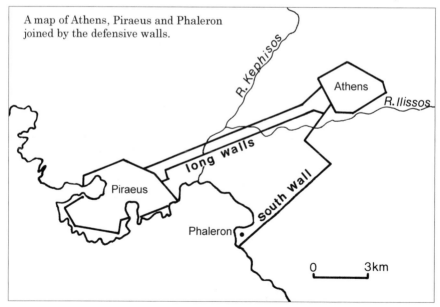

A map of Athens, Piraeus and Phaleron joined by the defensive walls.

Greece and so the soil was not particularly fertile. The hillier regions could support only the olive, Attica's most vital crop. Grapes were also produced in abundance, but most of the grain had to be imported from other parts of the Mediterranean. Attican farmers tended to identify themselves far more closely with their local deme than with the city of Athens; many would have left their own communities only infrequently. In his play *Acharnians*, Aristophanes presents a stereotype of the typical Attican farmer in his portrayal of the chorus, farming folk from **Acharnae**.

Attica was comparatively abundant in raw materials; there was plenty of clay and no shortage of building stone, including high quality marble mined from Mt Pentelikos and Mt Hymettos. The latter mountain was also an important area for bee-keeping. In the south of Attica silver had been mined at **Laureion** from the 8th century; the Athenians struck a rich seam in 483 just in time to fund a navy to counter the Persian threat.

2. Athens

The city of Athens (see map 6) was very small by modern standards; indeed, it is really more comparable to a small country town. Soon after the victory over the Persians in 479, a 6.5 km (4 mile) defensive wall was erected. This was the outer perimeter of Athens and it gave entry into the city by at least 13 separate gates.

The city's focal point was the Acropolis, a hill rising to 120 metres above the surrounding plain. To the north-west was the agora, the civic, political and commercial heart of Athens. To the west of the Acropolis lay two smaller hills – the **Areopagus** ('crag of Ares') and the **Pnyx** ('crowded place'); the former was the seat of the Council of the Areopagus, the latter the meeting place for the Athenian assembly.

The Acropolis
The Athenians had abandoned their city during the Persian invasion of 480; once this threat had been repelled, they returned to find a devastated Athens. For thirty years no attempt was made to rebuild the temples on the Acropolis, the sack of which served as a reminder of how close the Athenians had come to utter destruction. However, in the 440s Pericles instituted a great building programme to glorify the city. Under the supervision of the sculptor Pheidias, the new buildings made the Acropolis the inspirational beacon of Athens for which it remains so famous (see map 7).

At the heart of the new site was the **Parthenon**, the temple to Athena Parthenos ('the maiden'). It was completed in 432, by which time Pheidias' massive gold and ivory statue of Athena had been set up inside. Soon afterwards, a monumental new gateway, the **Propylaia**, was constructed. Later in the 5th century was built the **Erechtheion**, named after Erechtheus, a legendary king of Athens. However, this

271

temple was actually dedicated to Athena and Poseidon and was said to mark the spot where they had competed to be patron of the original city. Inside was contained the sacred olive-wood statue of Athena, to which a new *peplos* was dedicated at the Panathenaia each year.

The Acropolis had various other temples, shrines, altars, statues, officially inscribed stones and personal offerings. It was also a water source supplied by natural springs. Built into the rock face on the south side was the theatre of Dionysos, which swept down to the god's sanctuary. To the east the Odeion was built as a concert hall as part of the building programme in the 440s.

The agora
In pre-classical times the agora had hosted the Athenian assembly and the earliest dramatic performances; it had also contained a race-track which was used for athletic events (which continued to be held there at the Panathenaic Games). By the classical period, however, the agora was primarily a commercial and political space (the word 'agora' is related to words meaning 'gathering' and 'public speaking'), teeming with shops and stalls. The following fragment from the comic poet Eubolos gives a witty list of the goods on sale:

'You will find everything sold together in the same place at Athens: figs, witnesses to summonses, bunches of grapes, turnips, pears, apples, givers of evidence, roses, medlars, porridge, honeycombs, chick-peas, lawsuits, milk and curds, myrtle, allotment machines, irises, lambs, water-clocks, laws, indictments.'
Eubolos fr. 74

The agora was surrounded by boundary stones (*horoi*), which marked it out as a religious precinct; at the north end, the **altar of the twelve gods** was the agora's religious heart (see p. 274). The whole area was shaded by plane trees and surrounded on three sides by **stoas**, colonnades where men met to conduct business or friends met to catch up. The painted stoa (named after the paintings on its walls) was located on the north side of the agora; to the west was the stoa of Zeus, which contained the king archon's office; further round was the largest of the stoas, the south stoa. The Panathenaic Way passed through the east side of the agora.

Many important political buildings were located in the vicinity. The council met in the **bouleuterion** (a new version was constructed in about 400, measuring about 16 by 22 metres); the **tholos** was a round building (18.32 metres in circumference) which housed the *prytaneis* (see pp. 206-7); the official weights and measures were also kept here. To the south of the tholos was the **strategion**, the office building of the ten generals. Also located nearby was the **shrine to the eponymous heroes**, where notices were placed concerning matters such as proposed new laws, the agenda for an assembly meeting and lists of men required for military service.

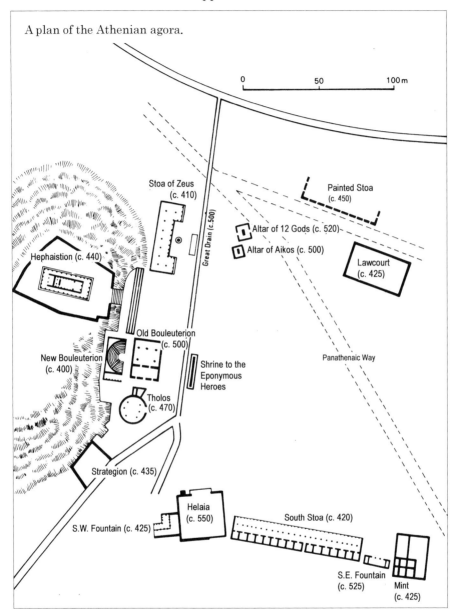

A plan of the Athenian agora.

The other key buildings in the area were the law courts. Trials were held in several parts of the agora, but the oldest and most important law court was the **helaia**.

The kerameikos

To the north-west of the agora lay the kerameikos, the potter's quarter of the city (the name *kerameikos* came from the word *keramos*, meaning 'potter's clay', from which we derive 'ceramic'). Here the vast majority of everyday items used in the city were made of fired clay, items such as baths, grills, cookers, pots and vases. Between the agora and the kerameikos was a large temple to Hephaistos, the god of blacksmiths.

The Panathenaic Way led out from the agora through the kerameikos towards two of the most prestigious gates in the city: the Dipylon Gate, through which the Panathenaic procession progressed each year, was the larger; nearby was the Sacred Gate, which marked the start of the Sacred Way to Eleusis.

The roads outside the city were lined with burial grounds, since burial was not permitted inside the city walls. The area outside the Dipylon Gate was known as the 'outer kerameikos', which contained the city's largest cemetery; it was here that, according to Thucydides, Pericles made his famous funeral speech in 430.

An artist's impression of the altar of twelve gods in the Athenian agora.

Appendix 2

Greek Currency Values

Coinage came to Greece from Lydia in Asia Minor (see map 2) in about 600. Before that, Greeks had transacted business by barter: cattle, sheep and weights of metal were all used for exchange with food and other commodities.

When the Athenians started to use coins, the name given to their smallest coin, the **obol**, reflected the practice of bartering with amounts of metal, since *obolos* in Greek originally meant 'iron spit'. Six obols made a **drachma**, which itself literally meant a 'handful' (i.e. a handful of obols). These two were the everyday values used by Athenians. However, for much larger transactions two further values were used: 100 drachmas made one **mina** (or **mna**) and 60 minae constituted one **talent**. These two values were never actually minted: they simply represented weight measures used for commodities (e.g. grain) or metals like silver or gold.

6 obols	=	1 drachma
100 drachmas	=	1 mina (or mna)
60 minae	=	1 talent

Even though it wasn't the smallest unit, the drachma was the main unit of currency (in the same way as the pound sterling or the US dollar are today, even though they can be broken down into pence and cents respectively). The most common coin in classical Athens was the *tetradrachmon*, worth four drachmas; on one side it featured an image of Athena, on the other an owl.

Athenian four-drachma coins with an owl and an olive sprig on one side, and the image of Athena on the other.

Values

It is almost impossible to give the precise value of a drachma in modern money. However, we do have some evidence for the value of a drachma at the end of the 5th century:

bare minimum for a person to live on	3 obols per day
jury service (expenses)	3 obols per day
wage for a hoplite on campaign	1 drachma per day
wage for a skilled worker	1 drachma per day
a year's wheat for one man	15 drachmas
an ox for ploughing	50-100 drachmas

Perhaps the most helpful point to remember about the drachma was that it was the typical daily wage for a skilled worker.

Owls to Athens

As Athenian coins all carried the image of an owl on one side, they were nicknamed 'owls'. The 'owl' was the strongest currency in the Greek world since people could trust these coins to contain a full weight of the best silver – the mines at Laureion provided the Athenians with so much high quality silver that there was never a reason for them to produce bad coins. The 'owl' remained the dominant currency of the Greek world until it was conquered by the Romans in the 1st century BCE.

Since the Athenians did not need to import coins from abroad, they coined the phrase 'to bring owls to Athens' to express the idea of giving someone something they do not need. Similar phrases have evolved in other languages. In English, the same concept is conveyed by the phrase 'to carry coals to Newcastle', since Newcastle-upon-Tyne is the main city in a region of England famous for its tradition of coal-mining, while the Spanish say 'to give wheat to Castile' (*dar trigo a Castilla*). Interestingly, however, German has retained the original Athenian maxim since *'Eulen nach Athen tragen'* simply means 'to bring owls to Athens'.

Appendix 3

The Greek Calendar

The Greek year followed a 12 month lunar cycle; each new year began with the new moon in *Hekatombeiôn* (the middle of June according to our calendar). The months of the Athenian civil year were as follows:

Hekatombeiôn	June-July
Metageitniôn	July-August
Boêdromiôn	August-September
Pyanepsiôn	September-October
Maimaktêriôn	October-November
Poseideiôn	November-December
Gamêliôn	December-January
Anthestêriôn	January-February
Elaphêboliôn	February-March
Mounikhiôn	March-April
Thargêliôn	April-May
Skirophoriôn	May-June

Since the Athenian year ran from mid-June, dates in this book are often given in the overlapping form of our calendar (e.g. Cleisthenes brought in his reforms during the civil year 508/7). However, where an event took place at a specific point in the year, just one year of our calendar is given (e.g. the City Dionysia took place in *Elaphêboliôn*, so Thespis is said to have won the first prize for tragedy in 534).

Appendix 4

Greek Musical Instruments

Music was central to life in ancient Greece; in the 5th century, two types of instrument were particularly important: the *kithara* and the *aulos*.

The *kithara* was a type of lyre with seven strings. It had a deep, wooden sounding box, with parallel ribs rising out of each side. The tops of the ribs were linked by a crossbar, from which the strings stretched back down to the sounding box. It was played with a plectrum held in the right hand, while the left hand could be used to pluck or damp the strings. The *kithara* usually accompanied dances, recitals of epic poetry, odes and lyric songs. However, it could also be played unaccompanied at events such as musical competitions and *symposia*.

The *aulos* was a woodwind instrument which usually had two reeds and two pipes; each pipe typically had three or four finger holes. It sounded similar to a modern oboe, and was generally played by a professional musician (known as an *aulêtês*) to accompany events as diverse as sacrifices, choral dances and the long jump in athletic contests.

An *aulos*-player.

A *kithara*-player and an *aulos*-player provide
musical entertainment for guests at a symposium.

A *kithara*-player.

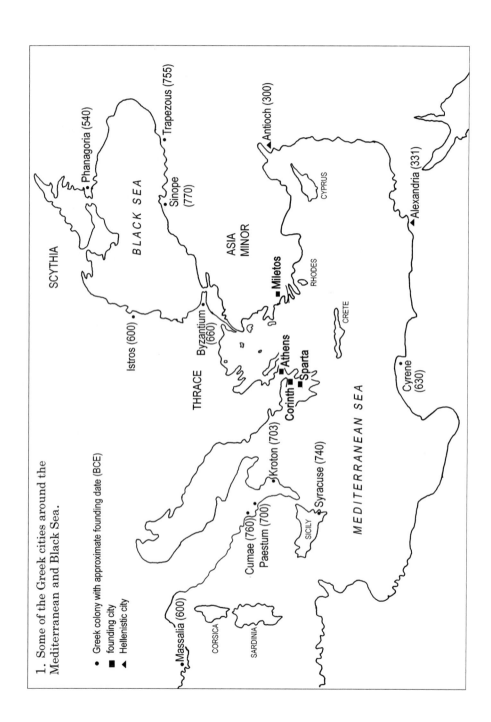

1. Some of the Greek cities around the Mediterranean and Black Sea.

- Greek colony with approximate founding date (BCE)
- ■ founding city
- ▲ Hellenistic city

SCYTHIA

Phanagoria (540)

Trapezous (755)

Antioch (300)

BLACK SEA

Sinope (770)

Alexandria (331)

CYPRUS

ASIA MINOR

Istros (600)

Byzantium (660)

Miletos

THRACE

RHODES

Athens

CRETE

Corinth

Sparta

Kroton (703)

Cyrene (630)

MEDITERRANEAN SEA

Syracuse (740)

Cumae (760)

SICILY

Paestum (700)

Massalia (600)

CORSICA

SARDINIA

2. Greece, the Aegean and Western Asia Minor.

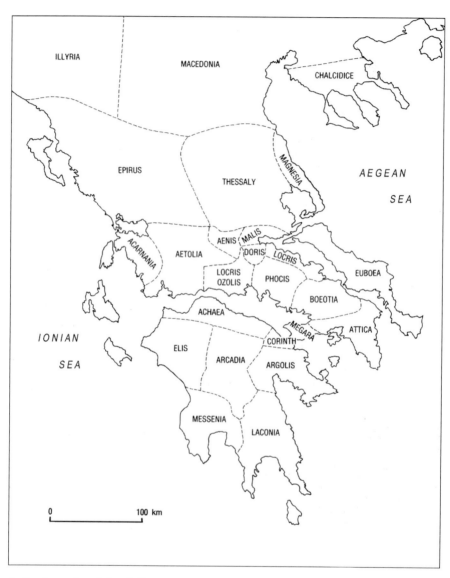

ILLYRIA

MACEDONIA

CHALCIDICE

EPIRUS

THESSALY

MAGNESIA

AEGEAN

SEA

ACARNANIA

AETOLIA

AENIS MALIS

DORIS

LOCRIS

LOCRIS
OZOLIS

PHOCIS

EUBOEA

BOEOTIA

ACHAEA

MEGARA

ATTICA

IONIAN

CORINTH

ELIS

ARCADIA

ARGOLIS

SEA

MESSENIA

LACONIA

0   100 km

3. Regions of mainland Greece.

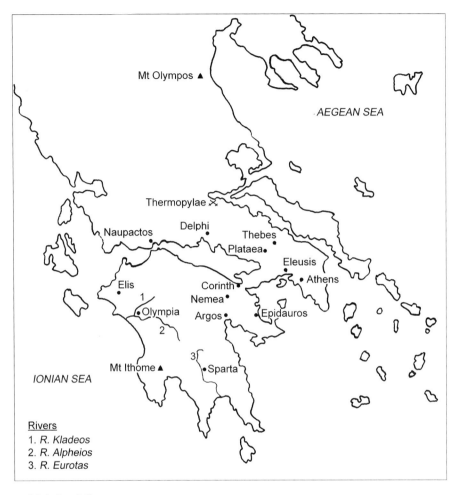

Mt Olympos ▲

AEGEAN SEA

Thermopylae ✕

Delphi

Naupactos

Thebes

Plataea

Eleusis

Elis

Corinth

Athens

Nemea

Olympia

Argos

Epidauros

Mt Ithome ▲

Sparta

IONIAN SEA

<u>Rivers</u>
1. *R. Kladeos*
2. *R. Alpheios*
3. *R. Eurotas*

4. Mainland Greece.

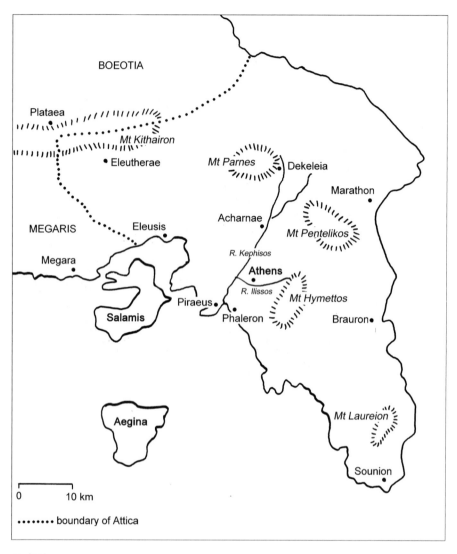

BOEOTIA

Plataea

Mt Kithairon

Eleutherae

Mt Parnes

Dekeleia

Marathon

MEGARIS

Eleusis

Acharnae

Mt Pentelikos

Megara

R. Kephisos

Athens

R. Ilissos

Mt Hymettos

Piraeus

Phaleron

Brauron

Salamis

Aegina

Mt Laureion

Sounion

0   10 km

•••••••• boundary of Attica

5. Attica.

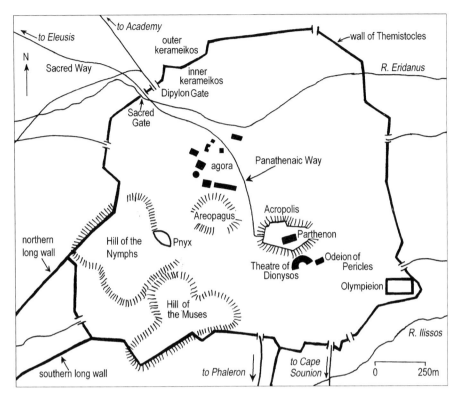

6. 5th century Athens.

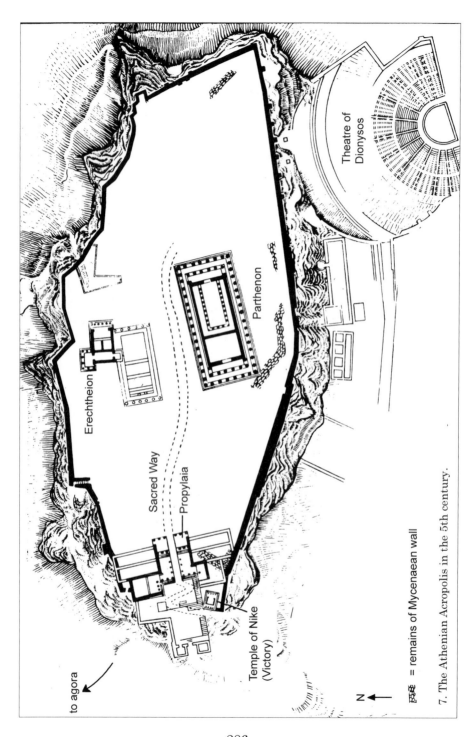

Theatre of
Dionysos

Parthenon

Erechtheion

Sacred Way

Propylaia

Temple of Nike
(Victory)

to agora

N

▓▓ = remains of Mycenaean wall

7. The Athenian Acropolis in the 5th century.

Index

Index

Acknowledgements

Quotations from the following are taken from the Penguin Classics translation (translators' names in brackets): Herodotus: *Histories* (Aubrey de Sélincourt); Thucydides (Rex Warner); Plutarch: *The Rise and Fall of Athens* (Ian Scott-Kilvert); Plutarch: *On Sparta* (Richard J.A. Talbert); Homer: *Odyssey* (E.V. Rieu); Homer: *Iliad* (Martin Hammond); Aristophanes: *Plays* (David Barrett and Alan H. Sommerstein); Plato: *Apology* (Hugh Tredennick and Harold Tarrant); Sophocles: *King Oedipus* (E.F. Watling); quotations from Euripides are from James Morwood's World's Classics translations and John Davie's Penguin translations.

Image sources and locations are as follows (numbers refer to the pages of this book): Bibliothèque Nationale, Paris, 7; Staatliche Museen zu Berlin, 8, 14, 246; British Museum, 9, 10, 22, 32, 45, 63, 69, 72, 126a, 197, 257b; World Health Organisation, 15; Deutsches Archäologisches Institut, Athens, 18, 99, 108, 134, 191, 221; M. Emerson, *Greek Sanctuaries* (Bristol Classical Press, 2007), 34, 37; akg-images, London/© Peter Connolly, 35, 47, 56, 68b, 71, 73, 74, 131, 136, 148, 154, 155, 157, 165, 174, 215, 218; After H.D. Amos & A.G.P. Lang, *These Were the Greeks* (Duckworth, 1996), 17, 38, 118, 132a, 190, 270, 273, 286; Yann Arthus-Bertrand/CORBIS, 58; After G. Greef, *Greece: A Guide for Students of Classical Civilisation* (Greef, 1997), 59; Metropolitan Museum of Art, New York: Rogers Fund, 68a; J. Swaddling, *The Ancient Olympic Games* (British Museum Publications, 1980), 65, 75; Antikensammlung, Munich, 81; Vatican Museums, Rome, 86; Martin von Wagner Museum, Würzburg, 95; Sonia Halliday Photographs, 97; After David Taylor, *Acting and the Stage* (Allen & Unwin, 1978), 101, 110, 115; Cleveland Museum of Art, 103; National Archaeological Museum, Athens, 116, 172, 254; J. Paul Getty Museum, Malibu, 125; Mansell Collection, 126b; R. Garland, *Religion and the Greeks* (Bristol Classical Press, 1994) 24, 25, 26, 27, 138, 171; Archaeological Museum of Dion, 151; S. Karouzou, *The Amasis Painter* (Clarendon Press, 1956), 158; Louvre, Paris, 170; R. Barrow, *Athenian Democracy* (Macmillan, 1973), 132, 182; After P. Bradley, *Ancient Greece: Using Evidence* (Edward Arnold, 1992), 187, 211, 235, 259; After J. Thorley, *Athenian Democracy* (Routledge, 1996), 189; JACT, *The World of Athens* (Cambridge University Press, 1984), 206; T. Webster, *Life in Classical Athens* (Batsford, 1978), 207; L. Fitzhardinge, *The Spartans* (Thames & Hudson, 1980), 224; Susan Bird, 226, 279; Paul Cartledge, 234; Richard Hook (Osprey Publishing), 253; Davis Museum and Cultural Center, Wellesley College, 257a; Wadsworth Museum, Hertford, CT, 258l; Archaeological Museum, Sparta, 258r; National Archaeological Museum, Taranto, 278; E. Curtius and F. Adler, *Olympia* vol. 2 (Berlin, 1896), 60; Eva Wilson, 93; Antikenmuseum, Basel, 119; M. Balme and G. Lawall, *Athenaze* (Oxford University Press, 1995), 195; S. Goldhill, *Love, Sex and Tragedy* (John Murray, 2004), 218.

Every effort has been made to trace copyright holders of material reproduced in this book, but if any have been overlooked, the publisher will be pleased to make the necessary arrangements at the first opportunity.